Monetary and Fiscal Policy
in a Growing Economy

Macmillan Series in Economics
Lawrence R. Klein, Consulting Editor

Duncan K. Foley / Miguel Sidrauski

MASSACHUSETTS INSTITUTE OF TECHNOLOGY

The Macmillan Company
Collier-Macmillan Limited, London

Monetary
and
Fiscal Policy
in a
Growing Economy

Copyright © 1971, The Macmillan Company

PRINTED IN THE UNITED STATES OF AMERICA

The Macmillan Company
866 Third Avenue, New York, New York 10022

COLLIER-MACMILLAN CANADA, LTD., TORONTO, ONTARIO

This work was supported by the National Science Foundation (grants number
GS 1585 and number GS 1876). The views expressed here are the authors' sole
responsibility, and do not reflect those of the National Science Foundation, the
Department of Economics, nor of the Massachusetts Institute of Technology.

Library of Congress catalog card number: 70–99113

PRINTING   3456789   YEAR   23456789

 To Carmela

Preface

This book represents a revision and reconstruction of macroeconomic theory. The main feature of our model is that it can be used interchangeably as a static model of instantaneous equilibrium and as a monetary growth model. In particular, investment is explicitly treated both as part of the claims on resources and as an addition to productive capacity.

The key to this analysis is our thorough separation of stock and flow variables and decisions. Money, bonds, and capital are stock variables, while consumption goods and investment are flows. The rate of investment and the price level are determined simultaneously by the interaction of stock and flow markets. The model assumes price flexibility and full employment, but can be used to study a wide variety of issues including the relative roles of monetary and fiscal policy, the burden of the government debt, inflation, and policies to enforce optimal saving.

Our treatment is self-contained, but some familiarity with Keynesian static models and Solow-type growth models will be very helpful to the student. We offer a complete exposition of two-sector production theory, which is the basis of our model. Throughout we try to present propositions and arguments in three parallel lines: graphically, algebraically, and verbally. We hope that the graphic presentation will make our ideas available to a wide spectrum of students.

Part I of the book builds up our model sector by sector and presents its general static equilibrium. Part II analyzes a sequence of simple growth versions of the model and culminates in a detailed discussion of the burden of the government debt. Part III, which is somewhat more advanced, treats problems of inflation and growth, expectations, optimal growth, and international finance. Individual chapters from Parts II and III can be studied on the basis of Part I to make up teaching units of varying lengths. A chapter-by-chapter bibliography suggests source and background readings.

Karen Hagstrom Johnson and Stanley Fischer were our research assistants during the drafting of the manuscript and made invaluable contributions to the substance and style of this book. Joseph Stiglitz performed a monumental labor in reading the manuscript before publication. Without his effort the book might never have reached the printer.

We would like to thank Mary Bartsch, Louise Woodland, Ellyce Anapolsky, Risa Goldberg, Linda Price, and Noël Rebello, who typed various drafts of the manuscript, and Beatrice Rogers for proofreading our manuscript.

We held conversations with several economists during the writing of this book, among whom were Robert M. Solow, James Tobin, Don Patinkin, Christian von Weizsäcker, James Mirrlees, Frank Hahn, Peter Diamond, Michael Rothschild, and many M.I.T. graduate students. Karl Shell was our collaborator on the work reported in Chapter 15 and contributed ideas and suggestions for other parts as well.

Both authors were supported by National Science Foundation grants while writing this book.

Miguel Sidrauski died suddenly September 1, 1968, just after the manuscript of this book reached essentially its present state, except for final editing and polishing. It is customary for authors, after acknowledging the help of other scholars, to accept responsibility for remaining errors. These errors, more numerous than they would otherwise have been, must in this case rest on me alone.

Duncan K. Foley

Contents

3 THE ASSETS MARKETS 27

4 THE CONSUMPTION GOODS MARKET 53

5 THE COMPLETE MODEL: STATICS 67

6 THE COMPLETE MODEL: DYNAMICS 87

II Dynamic Exercises 101

Monetary and Fiscal Policy
in a Growing Economy

1 Introduction

To avoid as much as possible disappointments and misapprehensions, we begin with some comments about this book that will serve as disclaimer and apology.

1–1 Scope and Subject

We are not concerned with the relative effectiveness of fiscal and monetary policy in combating unemployment and inflation. In our model both the government's control over its expenditures and taxes and its ability to make open market operations in its own debt are powerful instruments. The focus of the analysis, in fact, is how the tools interact to influence the share of output that society invests. This is sometimes called the question of fiscal-monetary mix.

The primary issue we study is one of resource allocation, not resource utilization. In our model flexible prices eliminate the possibility of unemployment. The importance of the mix of fiscal and monetary policy is that it influences the share of full employment output going into investment. One way of looking at this influence is that the mix helps determine the relative price of investment and consumption goods.

1

In view of the substantial difficulties modern economies experience in maintaining full employment, it would be pointless for us to ignore the problem of unemployment altogether. As a substitute for a full employment goal for the government we introduce a price stabilization goal throughout most of the book. The idea is that any policy that in our model produces deflation would imply unemployment in a world of wage and price rigidities. It is probably possible to introduce wage-price inflexibility into our model explicitly and thereby force the level of employment to become an endogenous variable, although we do not study this variation in this book. If unemployment were introduced, the close relation of our model to conventional Keynesian models would be quite apparent. The reader should interpret the word *stabilization* throughout the book to mean *price stabilization*, but it will not hurt to remember that in a world with price rigidity, stabilization of prices and employment are closely connected.

The model we use in this book permits the government to choose both the level of prices and the share of investment in output by manipulating its fiscal and monetary tools. We generally require the government to hit a certain target price level and study the residual freedom it has to determine the consumption-investment mix. We hope that this is not too far removed from the situation of actual governments, which can reach full employment using many different combinations of fiscal and monetary policy and must choose among them.

The price stabilization goal that we assign to the government not only includes a commitment to avoid deflation (or in the rigid price case, unemployment) but also requires the government to prevent inflation. The theoretical argument for the undesirability of inflation is much weaker than the argument against unemployment, but in public life the political pressures to stop inflation seem to be almost as strong as the pressures to prevent unemployment. We implicitly assume that the political and real costs of an uncontrolled price level are severe enough so that price stabilization can be taken as an end in itself. In a model where the consequences of inflation and deflation are explicit, our price stabilization goal would be an oversimplification.

1–2 Methodology

We quite shamelessly assume that the economy is always in equilibrium, that the prices observed at any instant clear all the markets we study. In particular, inflation and deflation never occur because the economy is in disequilibrium and is searching for the right price level. In this model, inflation or deflation indicates a continuously changing equilibrium price level.

This feature of our model will be disturbing to readers who believe resolutely that the economy is always in disequilibrium, that rising prices are a sign of excess demand and so on. We hope that the analysis will not be prejudged on this basis. The difference is one that can be settled only empirically. We assume that the observed configuration of prices in an economy remains very close to the configuration that would clear all markets and that most of the changes we observe reflect movements of an equilibrium rather than movements toward an equilibrium.

What defense can we give of a procedure that may seem patently absurd to many economists? First, we believe our model gains substantial clarity and richness because we have so single-mindedly followed the logic of equilibrium. This is a claim that only a reading of the book and an aesthetic judgment can settle. Second, our model includes most of the stylized features of reality that others have appealed to disequilibrium concepts to explain. Leading cases are the phenomena of investment and inflation. The analysis goes further than this and suggests fairly narrow specifications for econometric models to explain and describe these phenomena. We argue that the present approach and the specifications it suggests cannot be rejected without some serious econometric attempt to measure their significance. Presumably some part of the variance in econometric series represents movements toward an equilibrium and some part movements of an equilibrium. We feel the first hypothesis has received a great deal of attention, perhaps at the expense of the second. Of course, this particular model is not the only way to include equilibrium ideas in economic dynamics.

Finally, the reader is welcome to think of our short-run results as long-run results and to believe that the phenomena we describe, such as the relation between the price of capital and rate of investment, are true only in a gross or average sense over long periods of time.

We emphasize that *short run* does *not* mean disequilibrium in this book; it means instantaneous equilibrium. *Long run* in this book is an elegant variation for *steady state*; that is, it describes the asymptotic tendency of the economy when certain parameters or policies are held constant. We regret any confusion this vocabulary may cause. The expressions *long run* and *short run* are too deeply ingrained for us to give them up voluntarily, and their meaning is too fuzzy for us to feel guilty about bending them to our purpose.

1–3 Specifications

There are several features of the model that may seem arbitrary, restrictive, or unconvincing.

To us the most disturbing problem is our inability to provide a convincing microeconomic derivation of the consumption function and assets demands. The difficulty here seems to be profound. From an ideal theoretical point of view the choice of a consumption path and assets holdings should be studied simultaneously. To our knowledge there is only one case in which this analysis is possible and convincing, the case of full intertemporal competitive equilibrium with markets for contingent commodities. In this situation each individual knows all future prices in all contingencies, and these future prices actually occur. Each firm or household can choose a path for investment or consumption, and the choice of path simultaneously implies a portfolio of assets at each instant. Under these strong hypotheses there is no need to distinguish, as we do, between stock decisions and flow decisions, because they are always mutually consistent. This is an interesting theoretical study, but it is peculiarly unsuited to studying the effects of government policy because there is no room in the intertemporal equilibrium model for discretionary policy or for a desire for liquidity by consumers.

We have taken a rough-and ready approach to this problem by assuming functions with convenient properties for our purposes. We use the proportional consumption function and include expected capital gains as part of disposable income in many parts of the book. In other places we introduce total wealth in the consumption function but without removing property income from disposable income, a procedure that suggests a kind of double counting. In our assets demand functions we include national output measured in consumption good units as a measure of transactions. This is also open to criticism, since choosing investment goods or money as numéraire would alter the functions. In these cases we can only make a plea that many will find doubly damning: we knew it was not exactly right, but we went ahead and did it anyway.

The bond we use in the model is a fixed-price, variable interest rate asset like a savings account. Some people would prefer to use a consol with a fixed interest payment and a variable price. We experimented with consols and decided that they complicated the exposition without adding an enormous number of insights.

Finally, we should remark on our use of the two-sector production model rather than the usual one-sector model. This is a case where the complication did seem to be justified by an increase of insight and logical clarity.

The one-sector model is a special case of the two-sector model, so that all the arguments we give hold, with suitable restrictions on the shapes of certain functions, in the one-sector case. A good practice in reading this book is to work out our exercises and propositions for the one-sector production model. There are two difficulties, as far as we can see, with the one-sector model. First is the strong implication of a fixed relative price of capital, which discourages conceptual experiments involving movements in the relative price of capital even in partial equilibrium analysis. Second is the confusion about causality that arises in many minds when a function is replaced by a correspondence (as is true in the one-sector model where the supply of investment becomes perfectly elastic). It is possible to avoid these confusions by careful argument, but it seems easier to begin with a model where they simply cannot arise.

1–4   Organization

We have divided the book into three parts.

Part I, " The Model," consists of Chapters 2 through 6, which describe in great detail the various sectors of the model and the logic of their inter-action. A thorough grasp of the ideas of Part I is a necessary and sufficient condition for reading any other chapter.

Part II, " Dynamic Exercises," is a group of somewhat abstract and scholastic exercises. The purpose of Part II is to show in simple cases how to analyze dynamic properties of the model and to study simple exercises that are favored by textbook writers, such as " the effects of an open market purchase." We urge the reader to use Part II only as long as he needs practice or is really interested in some particular exercise.

Part III, " Issues in Theory and Policy," consists of short papers that use the basic model or a variant to study specific problems. Any of these chapters can be read separately, except that Chapter 14 assumes knowledge of the adaptive expectations model introduced in Chapter 13. These chapters are more difficult than the rest of the book.

We have deferred all references to the literature to the Bibliography, which is organized chapter by chapter. One difficulty with a book of this kind is that almost none of the individual ideas and concepts of the model are original. In fact, since the model purports to study so many sectors of the economy, almost every economic thinker of the last two hundred years has had something to say about the issues we discuss. The Bibliography is not intended to be exhaustive; it emphasizes writers whom we have read and who we think will provide useful guides for the interested student.

Omissions are the result of our ignorance or carelessness, not of any malevolent intention.

Because this book discusses basic issues in macroeconomics about which many people feel strongly, we want to avoid claiming too much either for the analysis or for ourselves. We have tried to be careful throughout to specify the model exactly and make clear the assumptions we use. We realize that certain features of our argument go counter to popular ideas about macroeconomic theory and also that these features are often precisely those that have been present in other economists' work. This makes it easy for us to seem arrogant on the one hand or ungracious on the other.

We offer the book as an exposition of an eclectic tradition that strikes us as particularly coherent and logically convincing. Throughout we have tried to make the exposition clear and available, though we may sometimes have failed. The chief use of this kind of model seems to be to be as a framework within which a variety of phenomena and theories can be studied and discussed. We hope that somewhere, sometime, some student may find it possible to think a little more clearly about macroeconomics as a result of our effort.

Finally, we should apologize, since our subject concerns the rise and fall of empires and the fate of millions, for our flat and humorless prose. Somehow logic and abstraction have deposed the kings and erased the irony from our language, leaving as protagonists schedules that shift, governments that decide, and variables that converge. We hope at the least that the reader with a fanatic interest in macroeconomics will find the book readable.

The Model

2 Production and Growth

2-1 Introduction

All economies are based on the production of certain outputs from inputs. An increase in outputs can come either from an increase in the amounts of inputs or from some change in technology that allows the same inputs to produce a larger output. In this book we study only the first kind of growth, the result of increased availability of inputs.

Inputs themselves are of two kinds: those provided by nature or social processes beyond the control of economic decisions and those that are accumulations of past output. The amount of accumulation that has taken place in the past depends on the sequence of decisions made by the society as to how much of its current output to consume and how much to save and invest.

The social decision between consuming and investing can be looked at in two ways. First, consumers and government decide to spend some part of income and to save some part. This determines a demand for consumption goods. But at the same time profit-maximizing producers face a relative price between consumption and investment goods. Their production

9

possibilities can be represented as a convex frontier (see Figure 2–3) showing the consumption-investment alternatives available to the society. Producers will choose the point on this frontier where the marginal rate of transformation between investment and consumption is equal to the ratio of the price of capital to the price of consumption goods. This determines a supply of consumption goods.

These two decisions must in some way be reconciled, by changes in relative prices, by changes in employment, or by suitable government policies affecting aggregate demand.

In this model we emphasize the importance of relative prices in transmitting the social choice as to how to divide resources between consumption and investment. We need a complete model of production that will give a convex production possibility frontier. (As the reader will see, the model works just as well with a flat production possibility frontier, but in the context of the model, a flat frontier seems to be a special case because it suggests so strongly that the price of capital is fixed. Even in the flat case, the price of capital must transmit to producers the social signal of how much investment is worth compared to consumption.) The simplest model that can be worked out completely is the well-known two-sector model of production in which two factors, labor, N, and capital, K, combine to produce additions to capital, I, and consumption goods, C.

The purpose of this chapter is to study thoroughly and completely the factor market equilibrium of a two-sector economy. We derive the supply curves of consumption and investment goods as a function of relative prices and the relation between factor prices, wages and rentals, and relative output prices. These results are the fundamental productive relations to which we add assets markets and demand for consumption goods in Chapters 3 and 4 to complete the model of the economy. Anyone who is thoroughly familiar with two-sector production models can glance through this chapter to become acquainted with our notation and look carefully at Propositions 2–1 through 2–4.

Throughout this chapter we treat the relative price of capital as an exogenous variable. It is, of course, determined inside the model through the interaction of the markets for assets and for consumption goods. As we shall see, the price of capital is a conceptually useful variable because when we know it and the supply of capital per capita, we know everything about the markets for factors and productive decisions. We know what the wage rate and the rental rate will be and what outputs of consumption and investment goods producers will choose. We summarize these relationships here so that we can use them in the further development of the model.

2-2 The Two-Sector Production Model

Typically, different production techniques are used in the various sectors of an economy. To reflect this fact in a two-sector economy, we suppose that the relation of outputs to inputs in the two sectors is different. At each moment of time, the output of consumption goods is given by a function:

$$(2\text{-}1) \qquad\qquad C = F_C(K_C, N_C).$$

C is the output of consumption goods. K_C and N_C are the amounts of capital and labor employed in the production of consumption goods, and we assume that the services of capital are proportional to the stock employed. Similarly, for additions to capital, investment goods, the function is

$$(2\text{-}2) \qquad\qquad I = F_I(K_I, N_I).$$

We assume throughout that capital does not depreciate, though there is no difficulty in introducing exponential depreciation in which a given proportion of the capital stock disappears at each instant of time. We also assume in each case that the isoquants are concave to the origin and that both functions are homogeneous of first degree, that is, that doubling both inputs exactly doubles output. This means that we can write them as

$$(2\text{-}3) \qquad\qquad C = N_C F_C\left(\frac{K_C}{N_C}, 1\right) = N_C f_C(k_C)$$

$$(2\text{-}4) \qquad\qquad I = N_I F_I\left(\frac{K_I}{N_I}, 1\right) = N_I f_I(k_I),$$

where k_C and k_I are the ratios of capital to labor in the consumption and investment goods sectors and f_C and f_I will be called intensive production functions.

If firms are competitive, if there is perfect factor mobility between sectors, and if both commodities are produced, the rental rate to capital and the wage rate, that is, the prices of the services provided by capital and labor per unit time, will be equal in both sectors and equal to the value of the marginal product of the respective factors. The value of the marginal product is the marginal physical product times the price of output. We take the consumption good to be the numèraire so that its price is one, and the price of capital in terms of consumption goods we call p_k. The requirement that rentals to capital and wages be the same in both sectors and equal to the value of the marginal products can be written

$$(2-5) \quad \frac{\partial F_C}{\partial K_C}(K_C, N_C) = p_k \frac{\partial F_I}{\partial K_I}(K_I, N_I) = r = f'_C(k_C) = p_k f'_I(k_I)$$

$$(2-6) \quad \frac{\partial F_C}{\partial N_C}(K_C, N_C) = p_k \frac{\partial F_I}{\partial N_I}(K_I, N_I) = w = f_C(k_C) - k_C f'_C(k_C)$$

$$= p_k(f_I(k_I) - k_I f'_I(k_I)).$$

When the production functions are written in intensive form, a prime denotes the derivative.

In addition, if there is full employment of both factors of production, the total of the factors employed must be equal to the total available:

$$(2-7) \quad\quad\quad\quad\quad\quad\quad K_C + K_I = K$$

$$(2-8) \quad\quad\quad\quad\quad\quad\quad N_C + N_I = N.$$

Equations (2–5) through (2–8) can be used to find K_C, K_I, N_C, and N_I when K, N, and p_k are given. They therefore determine outputs in both sectors and factor prices, given the relative price of capital and availability of capital and labor.

We can study this equilibrium by using graphs. In Figure 2–1a, we plot an isoquant of the investment sector, measuring labor input horizontally and capital input vertically. Figure 2–1b shows an isoquant of the consumption goods sector, but we put the origin in the upper right-hand corner. The absolute value of the slope of the tangent to the isoquant at any point is equal to the wage–rental ratio that would lead producers to use inputs in the proportions represented by the point. This wage–rental ratio is the same on all isoquants at all points along a ray like OAB because the production functions are homogeneous of first degree. As we rotate the ray counterclockwise from OAB to $OA'B'$ or PAB to $PA'B'$, the wage–rental ratio rises because of the concavity of the isoquants. Along any ray the ratio of capital to labor is constant; as the ray moves counterclockwise, the ratio of capital to labor increases. That is, the higher the ratio of capital to labor, the higher the wage-rental ratio in each industry.

In Figures 2–2a and 2–2b, the two sectors are drawn together. The width of the box represents the available labor; its height, the available capital resources. Any point inside the box represents a division of resources

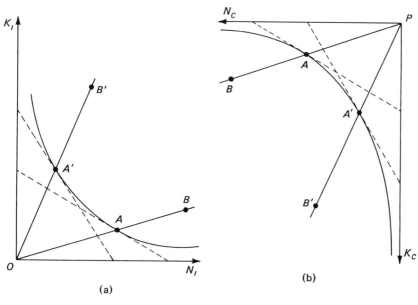

Figure 2–1

between the two sectors. The heavy line OAP in each figure is the locus of points where the isoquants are tangent, which from Equations (2–5) and (2–6) is a necessary competitive market equilibrium condition. Since wages and rents must be equal in the two sectors, the wage-rental ratio must also be equal, which implies tangency of the isoquants. Obviously, as we move along this line from O to P, the rays in both sectors must rotate in the same direction because the wage-rental ratios must be moving either up or down in both sectors. In Figure 2–2a, both rays rotate counterclockwise as we move from O to P so that the wage-rental ratio rises, as does the ratio of capital to labor in each sector. In Figure 2–2b, the movement is clockwise, and the wage-rental and capital-labor ratios are falling. It is easy to see that in Figure 2–2a, at all points below the diagonal line connecting the corners, the ratio of capital to labor in the investment sector is lower than the ratio of capital to labor in the consumption goods sector. Figure 2–2b corresponds to the case in which production of investment goods is more capital-intensive than the production of consumption goods at all possible equilibrium prices.

After this chapter we shall consider in general only the case in which the consumption goods sector is more capital-intensive, and we call it, without prejudice, the usual capital intensity case.

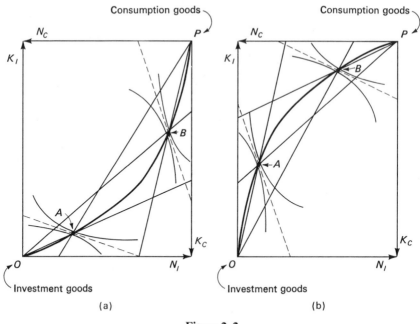

Figure 2–2

2–3   Effects of a Change in Relative Prices

The locus of points of tangency in Figures 2–2a and 2–2b corresponds to a production possibilities frontier, shown in Figure 2–3. The point labeled A in Figure 2–3 represents the allocation of resources between the investment and consumption goods sectors that corresponds to the points labeled A in Figures 2–2a and 2–2b.

That the production possibility frontier is convex to the origin can be shown by the use of the box diagram in Figure 2–4. We have shown already that the OP curve lies everywhere above or below the diagonal. We arbitrarily choose to draw the case where the OP curve lies above the diagonal, but the argument holds in the other case as well. Consider the point A_1, on the OP curve and draw two lines at equal distances from A_1, parallel to the factor price line at A_1. Since the production functions are homogeneous of first degree, the increase in the output of investment goods from I_0 to I_1 is the same as it is from I_1 to I_2, and the decrease in the output of consumption goods from C_0 to C_1 is the same as the decrease from C_1 to C_2. Let A_0 be the point where the I_0 isoquant intersects the contract curve and A_2 the point of intersection of the I_2 isoquant and the contract

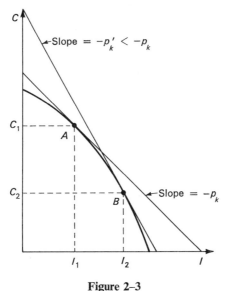

Figure 2–3

curve. As we move from A_0 to A_1 and from A_1 to A_2, the increases in the output of I are the same. The decreases in the output of C, however, become larger as we move from A_0 to A_1 and from A_1 to A_2. The decrease in the output of consumption goods between A_0 and A_1 is smaller than the difference between C_0 and C_1, while the decrease in the output of consumption goods between A_1 and A_2 is greater than the difference between C_1 and C_2. Since $C_2 - C_1 = C_1 - C_0$, it follows that to obtain equal increases in the production of one commodity, we have to give up larger and larger quantities of the other. This is exactly what is meant by the convexity of the production possibility curve.

Market equilibrium requires that the marginal rate of transformation be equal to the relative price of capital, that is, requires that production take place where the tangent line to the production frontier has a slope equal to $-p_k$. As p_k increases to p_k', it is clear from Figure 2–3 that the output of investment goods will increase and the output of consumption goods decrease. Such an increase in p_k is shown by the movement from A to B in Figure 2–3, with the resultant increase of I from I_1 to I_2 and decrease in C from C_1 to C_2. We have, therefore, proved:

PROPOSITION 2–1   *Given a convex production frontier, an increase in the price of capital increases the rate of production in the investment goods sector and decreases the output of the consumption goods sector.*

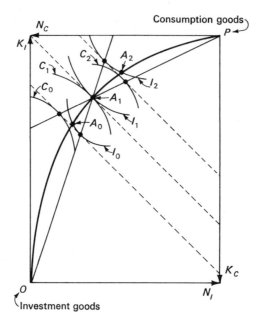

Figure 2–4

At this point we should note that this very general proposition depends only on the convexity of the production frontier, *not on its strict convexity.* The one-sector production model, which has a straight-line production frontier, is a special case of the two-sector model and meets all our assumptions, though it implies particular shapes for some schedules that we develop later.

An increase in the rate of production of investment goods implies that the economy moves along the contract curve away from the origin for investment goods, *O*, in the box diagrams. This means that the capital intensity of production in each sector will rise as the economy moves from *A* to *B* because in Figure 2–2a there will have to be counterclockwise rotation of the capital intensity rays for both sectors. We know that the wage-rental ratio rises as the capital intensity rises, so that we have proved:

PROPOSITION 2–2   *If the consumption goods sector is more capital-intensive than the investment sector, an increase in the price of capital results in a rise in capital intensities in both sectors and a rise in the wage-rental ratio. If capital intensity is higher in the investment sector, an increase in the price of capital lowers capital intensities and the wage-rental ratio.*

We leave it to the reader to carry out this exercise for Figure 2–2b (the reverse factor intensities case) and confirm the second part of the proposition.

2–4   Effects of a Change in Factor Supplies

What happens if the total amount of capital available increases while the price of capital is held constant? The first thing to notice is that the marginal products in equations (2–5) and (2–6) depend only on the ratio of capital to labor in each sector, not on the absolute amounts of capital and labor employed. This is an implication of the homogeneity of the production functions. Given p_k, these two equations determine the capital intensities, which will not be changed by a shift in the overall ratio of capital to labor as long as p_k remains constant. It may seem paradoxical that the total proportions of capital to labor can increase without changing the proportions in each sector, until we consider that if we shift *both* labor and capital from the less capital-intensive sector to the more capital-intensive sector, the only way to maintain a constant proportion of capital to labor in the expanding sector is to add new capital to the system. When there is an increase in the supply of capital in the system with the price of capital held constant, *both* labor and capital will be moved to the capital-intensive sector. Where we assume that the production of consumption goods is more capital-intensive, an increase in the capital stock will lead to the employment of less of both factors in the investment goods industry and a fall in output of investment goods. The output of consumption goods rises. This can be seen in Figure 2–5a, where we show the effects of an increase in capital, with p_k held constant, for the usual capital intensity case. Since capital intensities in both sectors will remain the same after the change in k, because these depend only on p_k, the new equilibrium will be at the intersection of the old OA ray and the new $P'A'$ ray, which is parallel to the old PA ray in the consumption goods sector. Neither capital intensities nor the wage-rental ratio will change, but as is clear from Figure 2–5a, output of consumption goods must increase while output in the investment sector must fall absolutely, despite the increase in total resources. The point A' is clearly closer to O than the point A, which implies a lower output of investment goods. The shift of the production frontier is shown in Figure 2–5b, where output shifts from A to A' with no change in p_k. We leave it up to the reader to work out the case in which the investment sector is more capital-intensive.

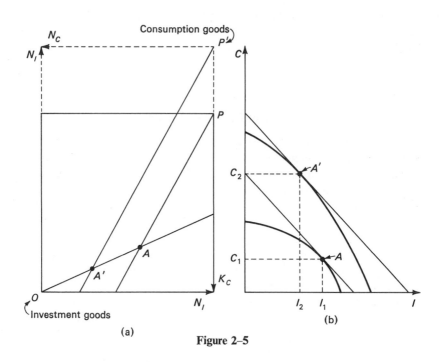

Figure 2–5

Propositions 2–3 and 2–4 on this argument hold for any p_k at which both investment and consumption goods are actually produced.

PROPOSITION 2–3 *Neither capital intensities nor wages and rentals are affected by a change in the overall ratio of capital to labor when the price of capital is held constant.*

PROPOSITION 2–4 *If the consumption goods sector is more capital-intensive than the investment sector, an increase in the overall ratio of capital to labor with the price of capital constant will increase output in the consumption goods sector and decrease output in the investment sector. If capital intensity is higher in the investment sector, an increase in the overall ratio of capital to labor will decrease output in the consumption goods sector and increase output in the investment sector.*

We emphasize that we are here considering only the *partial* effects of a change in factor supplies; a change in factor supplies will generally affect other variables in the economy so that p_k, and, therefore, factor intensities will also shift.

We can sum up the results of the discussion so far by writing the total equilibrium outputs of consumption goods and investment as a function of the price of capital and the total availabilities of capital and labor. This can be seen by solving Equations (2–5) through (2–8) for K_C, K_I, N_C, N_I for a given p_k, K, and N and then using equations (2–1) and (2–2) to write

$$(2\text{–}9) \qquad\qquad\qquad C = Q_C(K, N, p_k)$$

$$(2\text{–}10) \qquad\qquad\qquad I = Q_I(K, N, p_k)$$

Note that these functions are homogeneous of first degree in K and N together; doubling both inputs exactly doubles output. This follows because doubled K_C, K_I, N_C, and N_I will satisfy equations (2–7) and (2–8), and will also satisfy equations (2–5) and (2–6), because the ratios of capital to labor will be the same. Output in both sectors therefore will double because the production functions in equations (2–1) and (2–2) are homogeneous of first degree.

We can write the per-capita output of consumption and investment goods as

$$(2\text{–}11) \qquad \frac{C}{N} = Q_C\!\left(\frac{K}{N}, 1, p_k\right) = q_c(k, p_k); \quad \frac{\partial q_c}{\partial p_k} < 0, \frac{\partial q_c}{\partial k} \gtrless 0 \text{ as } k_c \gtrless k_I.$$

$$(2\text{–}12) \qquad \frac{I}{N} = Q_I\!\left(\frac{K}{N}, 1, p_k\right) = q_I(k, p_k); \quad \frac{\partial q_I}{\partial p_k} > 0, \frac{\partial q_I}{\partial k} \lessgtr 0 \text{ as } k_c \gtrless k_I.$$

2–5 Specialization

In Sections 2–3 and 2–3 we dealt with the effects of changes in factor supplies and relative prices on the output level in each of the sectors. In all of the exercises we assumed that relative prices and factor supplies were such that the economy was not specialized to the production of only one commodity. If the economy is specialized, the effects of changes in the price of capital or in the supply of capital may be different from those described above. If the price of capital rises or falls by an amount that keeps production specialized, there will obviously be no change in output because all resources are committed to one sector. Likewise, if the supply of capital changes but not by enough to end specialization, the output of the sector where production is taking place will rise or fall with the supply of capital regardless of factor intensities. When production is specialized, the economy acts as if there were only one output and as if the other sector did not exist.

2–6   Effects of Government Expenditure

In later parts of this book, we study the effects of government expenditures. Any government expenditure tends to reduce supplies of factors, outputs, or both to the private sector. In this section we concentrate on the effects of production by the government.

When the government hires factors to engage in production, it may change both the slope of the private sector production possibility frontier, by absorbing more of one factor than another, and its position, by reducing the supply of factors available to the private sector. We assume that the government hires the services of factors, paying the going market rental and wage rates, and produces a consumption good. National defense, police services, and education are examples of publicly produced consumption goods. The important point to notice about our description of government expenditures as consumption is that we assume such expenditures do not lead to increases in the capital stock.

To avoid complicating the discussion, we make the special assumption that private and public consumption goods are perfect substitutes in production.

The effect of government production on the private sector's production possibility curve is straightforward in this case. Suppose the economy is initially producing at a point A in Figure 2–6. Suppose now that the government decides to produce some amount, E.

A point on the new private sector production possibility frontier will be A', where the output of investment goods is the same as at A, the private output of consumption goods is reduced by exactly the amount of production of public consumption goods, and the slope of the frontier is the same as that at A. Given that the government intends to produce a given amount E of consumption goods, we could repeat the analysis we have applied to points A and A' for each point on the original private sector production frontier to obtain the new private sector frontier, $P'P'$. At each point on $P'P'$, the output of private consumption goods is less by E than at the point on PP where the output of investment goods is the same, and relative product prices are the same as at the point on PP where the output of investment goods is the same.

The allocation of production between investment goods and consumption goods (public and private) at any given price of capital is unaffected by the level of government expenditure. The production frontier for the society as a whole is not affected by government expenditure, though the production frontier for the private sector is. That is, government expenditures are neutral in the sense that a change in the level of government expenditures,

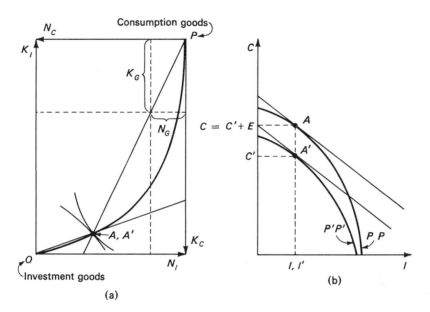

Figure 2–6

given constant relative prices, does not change the production mix between consumption and investment goods for the economy as a whole.

We can write total supplies of private consumption goods and investment as

$$(2\text{–}13) \qquad\qquad C^P = Q_C(K, N, p_k) - E$$

$$(2\text{–}14) \qquad\qquad I = Q_I(K, N, p_k),$$

where C^P is the production of private consumption goods and E is real government expenditures. In per-capita terms, we have

$$(2\text{–}15) \qquad\qquad \frac{C^P}{N} = q_c(k, p_k) - e$$

$$(2\text{–}16) \qquad\qquad \frac{I}{N} = q_I(k, p_k),$$

where $e = E/N$.

2–7   Growth

One important source of growth in output in this model is the natural growth of labor input. We assume that the supply of labor grows exponentially at a rate n, so that the total available labor, N, is given by

$$(2\text{–}17) \qquad\qquad N = N_0 \exp(nt).$$

Differentiating with respect to time yields

$$(2\text{–}18) \qquad\qquad \dot{N} = \frac{dN}{dt} = nN_0 \exp(nt) = nN.$$

What we are primarily interested in from a policy point of view is how the government can influence output and its composition. In studying this problem, it is convenient to take the growth of labor for granted and concentrate on changes in per-capita consumption and output, which the government can influence by inducing changes in the per-capita capital stock. This ignores the crucial issues of population control.

The growth in per-capita consumption that we study arises solely from changes in k, the overall ratio of capital to labor. It is clear that if k is to be kept constant, K has to be growing at the same rate as N, so that

$$(2\text{–}19) \qquad\qquad \frac{\dot{K}}{K} = \frac{I}{K} = n.$$

Dividing by N and multiplying by K, we find the amount of per-capita investment that is necessary to maintain the per-capita stock of capital despite population growth:

$$(2\text{–}20) \qquad\qquad \frac{\dot{K}}{N} = \frac{I}{N} = nk,$$

and using (2–16), we have

$$(2\text{–}21) \qquad\qquad q_I(k, p_k) = nk$$

if $\dot{k} = 0$.

In Figure 2–7, we plot the $\dot{k} = 0$ schedule, which shows the combinations of k and p_k that keep per-capita stock of capital constant; this is the locus of pairs (k, p_k) that satisfies (2–21). The p_k and $\bar{p}_k$ schedules

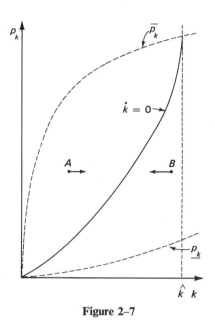

Figure 2–7

are the boundaries of the specialization regions where there is production only of consumption or investment goods, respectively.

The fact that these schedules are drawn as increasing functions of k is justified in the usual factor intensity case by the following argument. Suppose for some k_0 that all $p_k > \bar{p}_{k_0}$ resulted in specialization in investment. Then for $k_1 > k_0$, could there be a $p_{k_1} < \bar{p}_{k_0}$ that resulted in specialization? No, because when $k = k_0$ and $p_k = p_{k_1}$, the economy produces some consumption goods, and as k increases to k_1, Proposition 2–4 tells us that the output of consumption goods must increase in the usual factor intensity case if p_k stays at $\bar{p}_k$. This is illustrated by the shift in the production possibility frontier in Figure 2–8. A similar argument shows that the specialization price for consumption, $\underline{p}_k$, cannot decrease as k gets larger.

As k increases in (2–21), the right-hand side increases, but for a given p_k the output of investment actually decreases as a consequence of Proposition 2–4. This implies that a higher p_k is necessary to maintain a higher k, which justifies the upward-sloping schedule in Figure 2–7. It is clear that this schedule must lie above the $\underline{p}_k$ schedule if n is positive, since some investment is required to keep k constant. On the other hand, the capital stock can never become so large that the economy cannot maintain it by

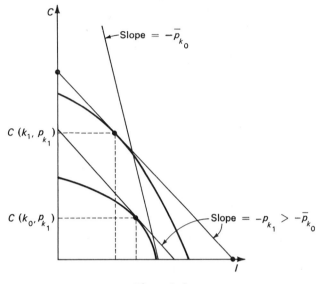

Figure 2–8

specializing in investment. Such a maximum is shown in Figure 2-7 as $\hat{k}$, where the $\dot{k} = 0$ schedule intersects the $\bar{p}_k$ specialization schedule. At such a capital stock the $\dot{k} = 0$ schedule becomes vertical.

We can also derive the slope of the $\dot{k} = 0$ locus by use of calculus; differentiating equation (2–21) totally we obtain

$$\frac{\partial q_I}{\partial p_k} dp_k + \left(\frac{\partial q_I}{\partial k} - n \right) dk = 0$$

or

$$\frac{dp_k}{dk} \bigg|_{\dot{k}=0} = -\frac{(\partial q_I/\partial k) - n}{\partial q_I/\partial p_k} > 0.$$

The numerator is negative and the denominator positive, thus confirming the positive slope of the $\dot{k} = 0$ locus for $k_C > k_I$. (When $k_I > k_C$, the slope of the $\dot{k} = 0$ schedule depends on the relative sizes of $\partial q_I/\partial k$ and n.)

What happens if we get a (k, p_k) pair not on the $\dot{k} = 0$ schedule drawn in Figure 2–7? If the price of capital is higher than necessary to maintain the capital stock, as at point A, the extra investment will tend to raise the ratio of capital to labor as indicated by the arrow. Just the opposite occurs at a point like B. In fact, we can write the rate of change in the per-capita stock of capital, k, as the per-capita investment left over after the necessary nk has been deducted:

(2–22)
$$\dot{k} = \frac{\dot{K}}{N} - \frac{\dot{N}}{N}\frac{K}{N}.$$

Using (2–16) and (2–18), we have

(2–23)
$$\dot{k} = q_I(k, p_k) - nk.$$

This relation is basic to our model, since, given a series of p_k values for each instant of time and k at time zero, this equation describes the values that k will take on through time. For example, if p_k stays constant at p_k^* (see Figure 2-9) and if $(k(0), p_k^*)$ is to the left of the $\dot{k} = 0$ schedule, the capital stock must increase until it reaches k^*, where the amount of investment induced by p_k^* is just equal to nk^*.

The government can influence the accumulation of capital by controlling p_k. In Chapters 3, 4, and 5 we show how p_k is determined by the relative supplies of capital, interest-bearing debt, money, the scale of government expenditures, and the government budget deficit. It is the government's control over its own debt and expenditures that permits it to influence growth in this model. The effects of debt management and deficit operations on the equilibrium price of capital, and hence on the stock of capital, are the chief concern of this book.

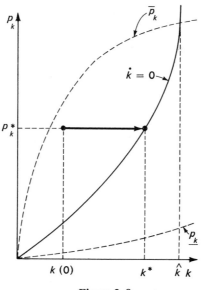

Figure 2–9

The Assets Markets

3–1 Introduction

There are three types of assets in our model: real capital, bonds, and money. The demand for assets by wealth owners is similar to the demand for consumption goods in the theory of consumer choice. Given the consumer's tastes, the quantity of each commodity demanded depends on the consumer's budget constraint and the set of relative prices. Similarly in the theory of assets choice, given the wealth owner's preferences, the quantity demanded of each of the assets at each instant depends on his total wealth, the set of assets prices, and their rates of return.

A wealth owner's preferences among assets will depend on his subjective estimates of the risk attached to holding each asset. A risk-averse wealth owner will in general diversify his portfolio, that is, hold assets that have different expected rates of return if the risks of the different assets are not perfectly correlated. We shall not give a derivation of our assets demands along these lines for three reasons. First, our purpose is to study the interaction of government policy tools in a growing economy, and a detailed discussion of the theory of risk bearing would take us too far afield. Second, the demand functions for assets that have been proposed

27

to date depend heavily on assumptions about subjective estimates of the riskiness and correlation of returns to the various assets. Third, certain important phenomena, for example, the fact that people hold demand deposits despite the fact that savings deposits have a higher return and no greater risk, have not been successfully integrated into these theories.

We choose instead to begin our analysis with the demand functions and to specify their shape directly. We do this clearly understanding the desirability of a deeper account of assets demands at some microeconomic level but confessing our inability to supply one now. Our conclusions will, of course, have to be modified when our assumptions can be corrected by a deeper theory.

The demands for assets in our model will depend on (a) total nonhuman wealth as measured by the net value of money, bonds, and capital; (b) income; and (c) the expected rates of return on the three assets. Since we are studying only the disposition of nonhuman wealth, it does not seem terribly restrictive to omit human wealth from the assets demand functions. This amounts to assuming that, given the level of income, the desired division of a given amount of nonhuman wealth among the available assets is not affected by the amount of human wealth.

Income enters the demand functions as a measure of the transactions demand for money. Cash balances yield a return in kind if payments and receipts do not exactly match for the average wealth owner or if there is uncertainty about timing of payments and a cost to switching from cash to bonds. Many measures of this return have been proposed, such as the aggregate value of transactions, or disposable income. We choose to measure it by real income measured in consumption units, $q = q_C(k, p_k) + p_k q_I(k, p_k)$. In Figure 3–1, q is represented by the intersection of the p_k price line with the vertical consumption axis. As p_k rises to p_k', the value of output also rises to q', so that real income rises with the price of capital.

We assume that an increase in the level of income increases the demand for money. At any given levels of wealth and rates of return an increase in the demand for one asset must involve a decrease in the demand for at least one other asset. In fact, we assume that neither the demand for bonds nor that for capital increases when the level of income rises.

The remaining important variables are expected rates of return. One dollar invested in real capital yields a return with two components. The first is $r(p_k)/p_k$, the rental rate per unit of value of capital, equal to the marginal product of capital in the investment goods sector, which is the real income wealth owners obtain from renting a unit of their capital to business firms. The rental rate per unit of value of capital depends only

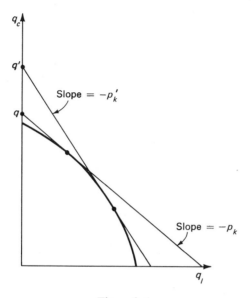

Figure 3–1

on the price of capital goods. As shown in Proposition 2–2, a rise in the
price of capital, by shifting resources to the labor-intensive sector, increases
the capital intensity in both the consumption and the investment goods
sectors, reducing the rental rate and lowering $r(p_k)/p_k$. The second component of the rate of return to capital is the expected capital gain on the
unit of capital, equal to the rate at which the consumption price of capital
is expected to increase over time, π_k. We can write the instantaneous rate
of return to capital as $\rho_k = r(p_k)/p_k + \pi_k$.

We assume that money holdings earn no interest. There is, however
the possibility of capital gains and losses on money due to changes in
the price level. Since we take consumption goods to be the numéraire,
we work with the consumption goods price of money, p_m. This is equal
to the amount of consumption goods a single unit of money will buy and
is the inverse of p, the price level. We call the expected rate of change
in p_m, π_m, and this is equal to the expected rate of deflation. An increase
in the expected rate of inflation means a *fall* in π_m; money will be losing
value faster. The rate of return to money, ρ_m, is exactly equal to π_m.

We assume that bonds have a fixed money price realizable on demand
and a variable interest rate, like a savings account or call loan. Bonds
issued by the government and by individuals are perfect substitutes. We
are concerned only with the net demand for bonds by the private sector.

We measure the per-capita quantity of government bonds, b, in money units since a bond can always be turned into one unit of money. The interest rate, i, is determined in the market so that private individuals are content to hold the net amount of bonds the government has issued. This quantity may be negative, since at low interest rates on bonds private individuals may want to borrow from the government to hold money or capital. Because the value of a bond is fixed in money terms, changes in p_m will also give rise to real capital gains or losses on bonds. The rate of return to bonds is $\rho_b = i + \pi_m$, the interest rate plus the expected real capital gain from holding the bond.

There are many other types of bonds of differing maturities and with other special features that might have been considered. In particular, many models of assets markets include consols, which pay a fixed money yield and have a variable price. For any bond with a variable price, the analysis is complicated by the possibility of capital gains due to changes in the interest rate and by the fact that the total value of outstanding government debt is affected by changes in interest rates. If we included bonds of differing maturities, we would also have to consider the determinants of the yield structure. These problems can presumably be overcome, but we choose the simpler line of attack.

At each moment of time, the real per-capita quantities of money $(m^d p_m)$, net bonds $(b^d p_m)$, and real capital $(k^d p_k)$ that wealth owners desire to hold in their portfolios depend on their real per-capita nonhuman wealth, a; the rates of return on money, bonds, and capital, ρ_m, ρ_b, and ρ_k; and the aggregate per-capita level of real income. We assume that all assets are gross substitutes, that is, that an increase in the rate of return on one of them raises the quantity demanded of this asset and lowers the quantity demanded of the other two assets. Finally, we assume that the marginal propensities to increase the holdings of money and capital out of an increase in wealth are positive but less than one, while the marginal propensity to increase net bond holdings may be positive or negative. We can write these demand functions as

$$(3\text{--}1) \qquad m^d p_m = L(a, q, \rho_m, \rho_b, \rho_k) = L\left(a, q, \pi_m, i + \pi_m, \frac{r(p_k)}{p_k} + \pi_k\right)$$

$$(3\text{--}2) \qquad b^d p_m = H(a, q, \rho_m, \rho_b, \rho_k) = H\left(a, q, \pi_m, i + \pi_m, \frac{r(p_k)}{p_k} + \pi_k\right)$$

$$(3\text{--}3) \qquad k^d p_k = J(a, q, \rho_m, \rho_b, \rho_k) = J\left(a, q, \pi_m, i + \pi_m, \frac{r(p_k)}{p_k} + \pi_k\right)$$

with the following restrictions on partial derivatives:

$$1 \geqslant \frac{\partial L}{\partial a} \geqslant 0, \frac{\partial L}{\partial q} \geqslant 0, \frac{\partial L}{\partial p_m} > 0, \frac{\partial L}{\partial p_b} < 0, \frac{\partial L}{\partial p_k} < 0,$$

$$\frac{\partial H}{\partial q} \leqslant 0, \frac{\partial H}{\partial p_m} < 0, \frac{\partial H}{\partial p_b} > 0, \frac{\partial H}{\partial p_k} < 0,$$

$$1 \geqslant \frac{\partial J}{\partial a} \geqslant 0, \frac{\partial J}{\partial q} \leqslant 0, \frac{\partial J}{\partial p_m} < 0, \frac{\partial J}{\partial p_b} < 0, \frac{\partial J}{\partial p_k} > 0$$

and

$$(3\text{-}4) \qquad a = kp_k + (b + m)p_m = kp_k + gp_m = k^d p_k + (b^d + m^d)p_m,$$

where g stands for the aggregate per-capita nominal stock of government debt including money and superscript d for demanded. Note that equation (3–4) is the wealth constraint: the total value of assets demanded must be equal to the value of actual assets holdings.

From the wealth constraint, we can see that

$$(3\text{-}5) \qquad \frac{\partial L}{\partial a} + \frac{\partial H}{\partial a} + \frac{\partial J}{\partial a} = 1$$

$$(3\text{-}6) \qquad \frac{\partial L}{\partial q} + \frac{\partial H}{\partial q} + \frac{\partial J}{\partial q} = 0$$

$$(3\text{-}7) \qquad \frac{\partial L}{\partial p_j} + \frac{\partial H}{\partial p_j} + \frac{\partial J}{\partial p_j} = 0 \qquad \text{where } j = m, b, k.$$

In writing the per-capita demand for assets this way, we are ignoring distribution effects; that is, we assume that aggregate portfolio decisions are independent of the distribution of wealth and income in the economy.

It is important to note at this point that if all returns were subjectively certain, wealth owners would hold real capital and bonds only if they yielded the same rate of return. The two assets would be perfect substitutes and market equilibrium would require $\rho_k = \rho_b$. In our model we do not assume that returns are subjectively certain, so that wealth owners, who are assumed to be risk averse, will in general diversify their portfolios. This diversification, of course, is justified only if assets are not subject to the same risk. Take, for example, the case of cash balances and suppose that money is no longer the means of payment and it still yields a zero nominal return. In this case it would be completely dominated by the fixed-price bond, and wealth owners would desire to hold zero cash balances as long as bonds paid a positive interest rate. Although the rate of return on bonds is uncertain because the price level may change, the same uncertainty applies to money, and the riskiness of a given portfolio is not diminished by holding some cash in it. If, instead of a fixed-price variable income bond, we had a fixed income variable price bond, money might still be held—even if it were not the means of payment and there were no transactions costs—because the return to bonds would have an additional uncertain element that arises from the possible variation in its money price. In any case, whether we have one type of bond or another, the risk involved in holding bonds is not the same as the risk involved in holding capital, so that wealth owners may hold both capital and bonds even if their rates of return are not the same.

Equilibrium in these markets requires that the quantities demanded and supplied of each of these assets be equal; that is, $m = m^d$, $b = b^d$, and $k = k^d$. Given these equalities, we can divide the numerator and denominator in the left-hand side of equations (3–1) and (3–2) by the total stock of debt $g p_m$, and we obtain the following assets market equilibrium conditions:

$$(3\text{–}8) \qquad (1/x)g p_m = L(a, q, \rho_m, \rho_b, \rho_k) = L\left(a, q, \pi_m, i + \pi_m, \frac{r(p_k)}{p_k} + \pi_k\right)$$

$$(3\text{–}9)$$
$$[1 - (1 \mid x)]g p_m = H(a, q, \rho_m, \rho_b, \rho_k) = H\left(a, q, \pi_m, i + \pi_m, \frac{r(p_k)}{p_k} + \pi_k\right)$$

$$(3\text{–}10) \qquad k p_k = J(a, q, \rho_m, \rho_b, \rho_k) = J\left(a, q, \pi_m, i + \pi_m, \frac{r(p_k)}{p_k} + \pi_k\right)$$

where $x = g/m$ is the debt-money ratio, the variable controlled by open market operations.

At any moment of time the private sector's stocks of capital and its holdings of nominal government debt are given. The stock of capital is the result of past savings that have materialized in real capital accumulation, and the stock of government debt is the result of past government budget deficits. While each individual, if he wants, can shift his portfolio from capital to government debt or vice versa, the private sector as a whole cannot. Given the nominal stock of debt and the aggregate stock of capital, any attempt on the part of wealth owners to shift their port-folios will result in a change in the prices of these assets and their rates of return so as to make the quantities demanded of each of these assets equal to the quantities inherited from past savings and past government deficits.

From the point of view of the private sector as a whole, it is not only the aggregate nominal stock of debt that is given but also its composition. The composition of the government debt is the result of past government open market purchases and sales, as well as of past government decisions to finance deficits by printing money and by issuing bonds. While each individual wealth owner separately can reduce his holdings of money by purchasing bonds or can increase his money holdings by selling bonds, the private sector as a whole cannot. Again, any attempt on the part of the private sector to do this will result in changes in the prices and rates of return of the assets so that the existing stocks of bonds and money find a place in the portfolios of wealth owners.

Finally, the expected capital gains or losses on each of the assets pre-sumably depend on the behavior of the price of capital and the price of money in the past, as well as on how people extrapolate past behavior into the future. In addition, expectations about future price changes may also depend on the behavior of the government itself. A change in govern-ment behavior may induce people to believe that the government has changed its policy goals and may result in a change of the private sector's expectations about future price behavior. The formation of expectations is a rather complicated subject and we shall have nothing to say about it until Chapters 13 and 14. Until then we assume that the price of capital goods is not expected to change and, therefore, that expected capital gains on the existing stock of capital are zero. This simplifying assumption is justified only when the economy is growing in such a way that the price of capital is constant. When the economy is growing in some other way, the price of capital will vary through time so that our assumption is not plausible. The simplifications derived from assuming $\pi_k = 0$ are substantial, and the price of capital usually settles down to a constant value in the steady state so that this assumption does not affect our conclusions about the steady-state equilibrium.

Although the price of capital goods will usually be stable in the steady state, the price of money may be changing. In fact, the price of money will increase or decrease depending on whether the nominal stock of government debt grows at a lower or a higher rate than the economy. Assuming that $\pi_m = 0$ without making sure that the government follows a policy aimed at making $\dot{p}_m/p_m = 0$ would not be justified because we would then be neglecting a variable, the expected rate of inflation, that affects the steady-state equilibrium of our model.

3–2 Determination of the Equilibrium Rate of Interest and the Equilibrium Price of Capital for a Given Price of Money

From the equilibrium condition in each of the assets markets, it follows, given the supply of each of the assets, the price of money and the rate at which this price is expected to change, that there are different combinations of the price of capital and the rate of interest for which the demand and supply of each of the assets are equal. We now consider separately each of these markets.

(A) THE MONEY MARKET

An increase in the money rate of interest lowers the quantity of real cash balances demanded because it raises the rate of return to bonds, one of money's competing assets. In Figure 3–2, we present the quantity of money demanded as a decreasing function of the rate of interest. The

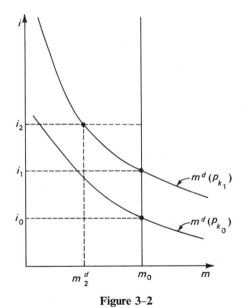

Figure 3–2

b, k, p_m, π_m, π_k are constant, p_k rises from p_{k_0} to p_{k_1}.

intersection of this demand schedule for money and its aggregate supply, m_0, determines the rate of interest that equilibrates the money market for given stocks of bonds and capital, a price of capital goods, the consumer price level, and the rate at which this price level is expected to change.

An increase in the price of capital goods raises the real quantity of money demanded on three accounts. First, it increases the consumption value of the private stock of wealth; second, it lowers the rate of return to real capital, one of the alternative assets to cash balances; and, third, it increases national income measured in consumption goods units, thus raising the quantity of real cash balances demanded for transactions purposes. In terms of Figure 3–2, this means that as p_k rises from p_{k_0} to p_{k_1}, the m^d schedule shifts to the right, increasing the interest rate that equilibrates the money market from i_0 to i_1.

It follows from Figure 3–2 that the higher the price of capital, the higher is the rate of interest for which the excess demand for money is equal to zero. The line that connects all the pairs (i, p_k) for which the money market is in equilibrium for given supplies of assets, for a given price level and expected rate of inflation, is therefore upward-sloped, as depicted by the *mm* line in Figure 3–5.

If when $p_k = p_{k_1}$ in Figure 3–2, the interest rate rises from i_1 to i_2, the demand for money falls to m_2^d, thereby creating an excess supply of money at the price of capital p_{k_1}, since the supply of money is unchanged at m_0. At any point to the right of the *mm* schedule in Figure 3–5, there is excess supply in the money market (ESM), while at any point to the left of this schedule there is excess demand for money (EDM).

(B) THE CAPITAL GOODS MARKET

The demand for capital depends, among other things, on its own price and the rates of return on its competing assets. A rise in the price of capital creates an excess supply of capital on three accounts. First, under the usual capital intensity hypothesis, it shifts resources to the labor-intensive sector, lowering the rental rate per unit value of capital. Second, it increases the value of the stock of capital and total private wealth by equal amounts, but since the propensity to hold capital out of any increase in wealth is less than one, the rise in the demand for capital is less than the increase in its value. Third, the rise in p_k increases national income, raising the demand for cash balances, which, given the total stock of wealth, according to our assumptions may be partially reflected in a decrease in the demand for capital.

The demand for capital is depicted in Figure 3–3 as a decreasing function of its own price. The intersection of the demand for capital goods

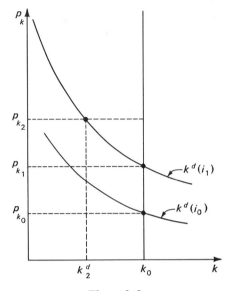

Figure 3–3

m, b, p_m, π_m, π_k are constant. i falls from i_0 to i_1.

with its aggregate supply determines the price of capital that equilibrates the capital goods market when the interest rate is equal to i_0.

A decrease in the rate of interest from i_0 to i_1 lowers the rate of return on one of the assets competing with real capital. Wealth owners will shift away from bonds and into money and capital. This means that as the rate of interest falls, the demand for real capital shifts upward. At p_{k_0} there is now excess demand for capital, which for a given k_0 can be eliminated only by an increase in p_k from p_{k_0} to p_{k_1}.

The kk schedule in Figure 3–5 depicts the pairs (i, p_k) for which the capital goods market is in equilibrium. Since, as shown in Figure 3–3, a decrease in the interest rate increases the price of capital that equilibrates the capital goods market, the kk schedule is downward-sloped. Assume now that while $i = i_1$ in Figure 3–3, the price of capital rises from p_{k_1} to p_{k_2}. While the supply of capital is unchanged, its demand has decreased to k_2^d and there is now excess supply in the capital goods market. From this it follows that at any point above the kk schedule the supply of capital goods exceeds their demand (ESK), while at any point below the kk line the price of capital is too low and there is excess demand for capital (EDK).

The kk and mm schedules divide Figure 3–5 into four quadrants: II and IV, where there is excess demand or supply in both the money and the capital goods markets, and quadrants I and III, in which one market has excess demand and the other excess supply.

(C) THE BOND MARKET

As indicated in equation (3–9), equilibrium in the bond market is also affected by changes in the interest rate and the price of capital. An increase in the rate of interest creates excess demand for bonds. The rate of interest that equilibrates the bond market is determined by the intersection of the demand schedule for bonds, b^d, which is an increasing function of the interest rate, and the outstanding stock of bonds, b_0, as indicated in Figure 3–4.

The demand schedule for bonds need not be confined to the positive quadrant. At low interest rates the private sector may want to hold a negative amount of government interest-bearing debt; that is, they may desire to borrow from the government in order to hold cash and capital.

An increase in the price of capital affects the demand for bonds in three different ways. First, it increases the value of the private stock of wealth, which may increase or decrease the demand for bonds. Second, it lowers the rate of return to capital, thereby further raising the demand for bonds. Third, the rise in p_k increases real national income, thereby increasing the demand for real cash and according to our assumptions possibly reducing

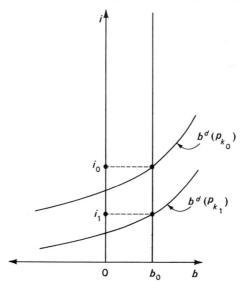

Figure 3–4
m, k, p_m, π_m, π_k are constant. p_k rises from p_{k_0} to p_{k_1}.

the demand for bonds. It follows that a rise in the price of capital may either increase or decrease the net private demand for bonds, depending on the strength and signs of the wealth and substitution effects on the one hand and the transaction effect on the other. That is, as p_k rises, the demand for bonds in Figure 3–4 may shift to the right or left, and the value of i that equilibrates the bond market may either rise or fall. Figure 3–4 shows the case in which positive wealth and substitution effects are stronger than the income effect; the bond market equilibrium rate of interest falls with an increase in p_k from p_{k_0} to p_{k_1}.

This means that the bb schedule in Figure 3–5 may have a positive slope like the $b_0 b_0$ line or a negative slope like the $b_1 b_1$ schedule, depending on whether an increase in the price of capital creates excess supply or excess demand in the bond market. In any case an increase in the rate of interest always creates excess demand in the bond market; that is, independently of the slope of the bb schedule, at any point to the left of it there is excess supply of bonds (ESB) and anywhere to its right there is excess demand in the bond market (EDB).

Given the wealth constraint

$$(3\text{–}4) \qquad k^d p_k + (b^d + m^d) p_m = k p_k + (b + m) p_m,$$

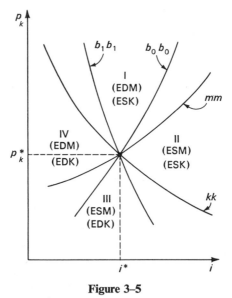

Figure 3–5

$g, k, p_m, \pi_m, \pi_k, x$ are constant.

we can see that if the money and the capital goods markets are in equilibrium at some (i^*, p_k^*), the bond market must also be in equilibrium at (i^*, p_k^*). This can be shown by rewriting the wealth constraint as

$$(3\text{–}11) \qquad (m^d - m)p_m + (k^d - k)p_k = (b - b^d)p_m.$$

Since at (i^*, p_k^*) the left-hand side of (3–11) is equal to zero, the right-hand side must also equal zero; that is, the excess supply of bonds is equal to zero. This means that the bb schedule intersects the mm and kk schedules at (i^*, p_k^*). It is not necessary, therefore, to consider the effects of any changes in exogenous variables in all three markets; any two are sufficient. In the first exercise that follows, we do consider all three markets, but thereafter we pay explicit attention only to the money and capital markets.

From the wealth constraint (3–11), it also follows that if wealth owners think that the share of capital and money in their portfolios is too high, they must also think that the share of bonds in portfolios is too low. If the demand functions (3–1) through (3–3) obey the wealth constraint (3–11), then there can be no pair (i, p_k) in Figure 3-5 for which there is excess demand or excess supply in the three markets. The bb line divides Figure 3-5 into two parts, one that contains all points with excess demand for bonds and the other with all points of excess supply of bonds. It follows that this schedule, whether it has a positive or a negative slope, has to go through quadrants I and III; if it were to go through II and IV, there would be cases of excess demand in the three markets, and we have proved that this is inconsistent with the wealth constraint.

3–3   Effects of a Change in the Composition of the Government Debt

We now have all the tools required to describe the effects of a change in the aggregate stock of debt, its composition, the stock of capital, and the expected rate of inflation on the equilibrium price of capital and the market rate of interest. Consider first the effects of an open market purchase, which increases the quantity of money and reduces the quantity of bonds by the same amount.

Given the price of money, an increase in the quantity of money resulting from an open market operation does not affect the value of the privately held stock of government debt. The open market operation will usually change private wealth indirectly by affecting the assets markets equilibrium price of capital, but there is no net change in the value of the government debt because the private sector loses bond holdings exactly equal in value to the increase in the money supply. Hence, given a positive stock of government debt, an increase in the money supply that results from an open market operation is equivalent to a decrease in x, the ratio of debt to money. If the aggregate stock of debt is negative, that is, if the government is a net lender, an open market purchase results in a still negative but algebraically larger x. In other words, an open market purchase always moves the ratio of debt to money toward zero.

A change in the composition of the government debt with unchanged assets prices and rates of return has no effect on the quantity of capital goods demanded. Hence an open market operation does not move the kk schedule. In the money market, the decrease in x creates excess supply, and for this market to remain in equilibrium, the demand for money has to rise. To raise the quantity of cash balances demanded, the interest rate has to fall or the price of capital has to rise. This means that the decrease in the ratio of debt to money shifts the mm schedule to the left, from $m_0 m_0$ to $m_1 m_1$, as indicated in Figure 3–6; and the mm schedule now intersects the kk schedule at a higher price of capital, p_{k_1}, and a lower rate of interest, i_1.

On the other hand, the decrease in the ratio of debt to money is equivalent to a reduction in the supply of government bonds and therefore creates excess demand in the market for bonds. For the bond market to remain in equilibrium, this excess demand has to be eliminated by a decrease in the rate of interest. This means that the bb schedule also shifts to the left, from $b_0 b_0$ to $b_1 b_1$. We know that if (i_1, p_{k_1}) clears the money and capital markets, it will also equilibrate the market for bonds. The bb schedule shifts until it intersects the $m_1 m_1$ and kk schedules at p_{k_1} and i_1. We conclude that:

PROPOSITION 3–1   *Given the price of money, the rate at which this price is expected to change, and the total stocks of government debt and capital, a decrease in the absolute value of the ratio of debt to money lowers the rate of interest and increases the price of capital that equilibrates the assets markets.*

In Figure 3–6, we have drawn the bb schedule with a negative slope. The same result will hold if the slope of the bb schedule is positive. In succeeding exercises we leave it to the reader to check the movements of the bb schedule.

That Proposition 3–1 is correct can also be proved by differentiating any two of equations (3–8) through (3–10) partially with respect to p_k,

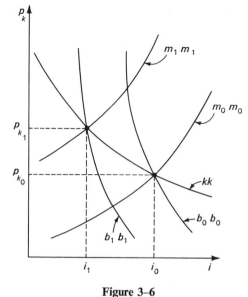

Figure 3–6

g, k, p_m, π_m, π_k are constant. x falls from x_0 to x_1.

i, and x. Using equations (3–8) and (3–10) for this purpose, we obtain the following expressions:

$$(3\text{–}12) \qquad \frac{dp_k}{dx} = \frac{g\,p_m}{x^2\Delta}\left(-\frac{\partial J}{\partial \rho_b}\right) < 0 \quad \text{if } g > 0,$$

$$> 0 \quad \text{if } g < 0;$$

$$(3\text{–}13) \qquad \frac{di}{dx} = \frac{g\,p_m}{x^2\Delta}\left(\frac{\partial J}{\partial p_k} - k\right) > 0 \quad \text{if } g > 0,$$

$$< 0 \quad \text{if } g < 0;$$

where

$$(3\text{–}14) \qquad \Delta = \frac{\partial L}{\partial p_k}\frac{\partial J}{\partial \rho_b} - \left(\frac{\partial J}{\partial p_k} - k\right)\frac{\partial L}{\partial \rho_b} < 0.$$

Recall that under the usual capital intensity hypothesis $r(p_k)/p_k$ falls as p_k rises. Since we assume $\pi_k = 0$, $\rho_k = r(p_k)/p_k$ and $\partial \rho_k/\partial p_k < 0$;

$\partial q/\partial p_k > 0$ from Figure 3–1. These facts imply that

$$(3\text{–}15) \qquad \frac{\partial L}{\partial p_k} = \frac{\partial L}{\partial a} k + \frac{\partial L}{\partial q} \frac{\partial q}{\partial p_k} + \frac{\partial L}{\partial \rho_k} \frac{\partial \rho_k}{\partial p_k} > 0$$

and

$$(3\text{–}16) \qquad \frac{\partial J}{\partial p_k} - k = \left(\frac{\partial J}{\partial a} - 1 \right) k + \frac{\partial J}{\partial q} \frac{\partial q}{\partial p_k} + \frac{\partial J}{\partial \rho_k} \frac{\partial \rho_k}{\partial p_k} < 0,$$

which justifies the signs in equations (3–12) and (3–13).

We have again proved Proposition 3–1. A decrease in the absolute value of the ratio of debt to money creates excess supply in the money market and excess demand in the market for bonds. For wealth owners to be in equilibrium with the new composition of the government debt, the interest rate on government debt has to fall. The fall in the rate of return on one of its competing assets in turn raises the demand for real capital and results in a higher equilibrium price of capital.

3–4   Effects of an Increase in the Stock of Government Debt

An increase in the stock of government debt, with an unchanged composition, increases private wealth and raises the demand for capital on the part of wealth owners. At the initial price of capital p_{k_0} and the initial interest rate i_0, in Figure 3–7, there is now excess demand for capital. This rise in demand requires a higher price of capital to equilibrate the capital goods market. For a given interest rate and a given supply of capital goods, wealth owners will hold a higher stock of government debt only if the price of capital goods is higher. As a result of the increase in g, the kk schedule shifts upward, from $k_0 k_0$ to $k_1 k_1$, as indicated in Figure 3–7.

The higher stock of government debt increases the demand for money at a given p_k by an amount equal to the increase in the aggregate stock of debt times the marginal propensity to hold cash out of any rise in wealth: that is, $dm^d = (\partial L/\partial a)dg$. On the other hand, the increase in the money supply is equal to $(1/x)dg$. Remembering that $x = g/m$, the change in excess demand can be rewritten as $m[(\partial L/\partial a)(a/m)(g/a) - 1](dg/g)$. Since the value of the capital stock is positive, g/a is less than one. Unless the wealth elasticity of the demand for cash is greater than or equal to the inverse of g/a, the increase in the aggregate stock of government debt

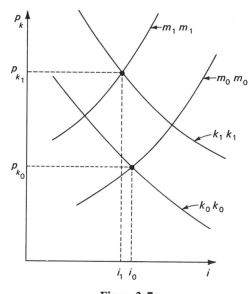

Figure 3–7

k, p_m, π_m, π_k, x are constant. g rises from g_0 to g_1.

will create excess supply in the money market. Since there is no empirical evidence to suggest that the wealth elasticity is even close to the inverse of g/a, we shall assume, with reasonable confidence, that the increase in g results in excess supply of money. (For the United States, since the ratio of wealth to income is above 3 and the ratio of total government debt to income is somewhat less than 1/2, the ratio g/a is probably somewhat below 1/6.)

To eliminate the excess supply created in the money market, either the interest rate has to fall or the price of capital has to rise. As g rises, the mm schedule shifts upward and to the left, from $m_0 m_0$ to $m_1 m_1$, as indicated in Figure 3–7. Since both the kk and the mm schedules have shifted upward, the equilibrium price of capital increases as a result of the increase in the aggregate stock of government debt.

The assets markets equilibrium rate of interest may rise or fall as a result of the increase in g, depending on whether the mm or the kk schedule shifts farther. There are three effects at work in the markets: the wealth effect of the increased g on the demand for each asset, the sensitivity of the demands for capital and money with respect to the rate of return for capital, and the sensitivity to a change in income of the demands for money, capital, and bonds. The stronger the first and second with respect to capital relative to money and, for the given income elasticity of money, the stronger the third for capital relative to bonds, the more likely it is that the rate of interest will fall when the aggregate stock of debt rises.

We can now state:

PROPOSITION 3-2   *Given the aggregate stock of capital, the price of money, the rate at which the price of money is expected to change, and the composition of the government debt, an increase in the stock of government debt may raise or lower the equilibrium price of capital and rate of interest. A sufficient condition for the price of capital to rise is that the wealth elasticity of the demand for money not be greater than the ratio of total wealth to the stock of government debt.*

From this point on we assume that this sufficient condition holds.

We can prove these results by differentiating equations (3–8) and (3–10) partially with respect to i, p_k, and g, to obtain the following:

$$(3\text{–}17) \quad \frac{\partial p_k}{\partial g} = \frac{p_m}{\Delta} \left[\frac{\partial J}{\partial a} \frac{\partial L}{\partial \rho_b} + \frac{\partial J}{\partial \rho_b} \frac{1}{x} \left(1 - \eta_{ma} \frac{g}{a} \right) \right] > 0 \quad \text{if} \left(1 - \eta_{ma} \frac{g}{a} \right) > 0,$$

$$(3\text{–}18) \quad \frac{\partial i}{\partial g} = \frac{p_m}{\Delta} \left[- \frac{\partial J}{\partial a} \frac{\partial L}{p_k} - \frac{1}{x} \left(\frac{\partial J}{\partial p_k} - k \right) \left(1 - \eta_{ma} \frac{g}{a} \right) \right],$$

where Δ is again given by (3–14), and $\eta_{ma} = (\partial L/\partial a)(a/m)$. Because the aggregate stock of debt and the price of money in terms of consumption goods appear only in a multiplicative form in equations (3–8) through (3–10), everything we have said about the effects of a change in g also applies to changes in p_m. What matters is the change in the consumption value of the stock of debt, not whether this change arises from a changed price level or a changed supply of debt. *The effect of an increase in p_m is also, under the sufficient condition of Proposition 3–2, to raise p_k.*

3–5   Effects of an Increase in the Stock of Capital

When the capital stock increases, supply in the capital market increases by the same amount. The increase in demand is equal to the marginal propensity to hold capital out of any increase in wealth times the increase in k less the decrease in the demand for capital that originates from the increase in the demand for cash to finance a higher level of transactions. Since the propensity to hold capital out of any increase in wealth is less than one, an increase in the stock of capital creates excess supply in the capital goods market. The excess supply lowers the price of capital at which this market is in equilibrium for any interest rate, so that the kk schedule shifts downward from $k_0 k_0$ to $k_1 k_1$, as indicated in Figure 3–8.

Because the increase in k raises private wealth and real income, the demand for cash increases. For the money market to remain in equilibrium with an unchanged stock of money, the rate of interest must rise or the price of capital must fall to lower the demand for cash. This means that the mm schedule shifts downward and to the right from $m_0 m_0$ to $m_1 m_1$, as shown in Figure 3–8.

For wealth owners to hold a higher stock of capital in their portfolios with an unchanged supply of other assets, the price of capital has to fall, while the equilibrium interest rate may increase or decrease. We can summarize this by stating:

PROPOSITION 3–3   *Given the stock of government debt, its composition, the price of money, and the expected rate of inflation, an increase in the stock of capital lowers the assets markets equilibrium price of capital but may result in either a higher or a lower assets markets equilibrium rate of interest.*

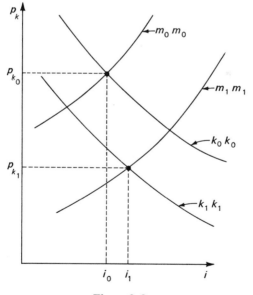

Figure 3–8
g, p_m, π_m, π_k, x are constant. k rises from k_0 to k_1.

We prove this by differentiating equations (3–8) and (3–10) partially with respect to i, p_k, and k to obtain

$$(3\text{–}19) \quad \frac{\partial p_k}{\partial k} = \frac{1}{\Delta} \left\{ \left[p_k \left(\frac{\partial J}{\partial a} - 1 \right) + \frac{\partial J}{\partial q} \frac{\partial q}{\partial k} \right] \frac{\partial L}{\partial \rho_b} - \frac{\partial J}{\partial \rho_b} \left(\frac{\partial L}{\partial a} p_k + \frac{\partial L}{\partial q} \frac{\partial q}{\partial k} \right) \right\} < 0$$

and

(3–20)

$$\frac{\partial i}{\partial k} = \frac{1}{\Delta} \left\{ -\left[p_k \left(\frac{\partial J}{\partial a} - 1 \right) + \frac{\partial J}{\partial q} \frac{\partial q}{\partial k} \right] \frac{\partial L}{\partial p_k} + \left(\frac{\partial J}{\partial p_k} - k \right) \left(\frac{\partial L}{\partial a} p_k + \frac{\partial L}{\partial q} \frac{\partial q}{\partial k} \right) \right\},$$

where once again Δ is given by equation (3–14).

3–6 Effects of an Increase in the Expected Rate of Inflation

Consider a situation, as depicted in Figure 3–9, in which the pair of values (i_0, p_{k_0}) clears the assets markets when the expected rate of capital gains on government debt is equal to π_{m_0}. What happens when the expected

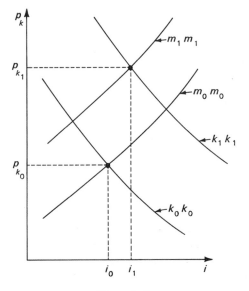

Figure 3–9
g, k, p_m, π_k, x are constant. π_m falls from π_{m_0} to π_{m_1}.

rate of deflation falls to $\pi_{m_1} < \pi_{m_0}$? If wealth owners expect smaller capital gains or larger capital losses on government debt, what is the effect on the equilibrium p_k and i?

The rise in the expected rate of inflation at any given rate of interest lowers the rate of return on both bonds and money. The decline in the rate of return on both of these competing assets induces wealth owners to shift their holdings from government debt toward real capital and creates excess demand in the capital goods market. At any moment of time, however, the aggregate stock of capital is given; it can only change through time, and it cannot increase instantaneously to satisfy the excess demand created by the higher expected rate of inflation. The result must be an increase in the price of capital at which the capital goods market clears. This means that the kk schedule shifts upward and to the right, from $k_0 k_0$ to $k_1 k_1$, in Figure 3–9, as a result of the change in wealth owners' expectations.

The increase in the expected rate of inflation lowers the demand for money because it depresses its own rate of return. On the other hand, the rate of return on bonds has also fallen, and under our assumptions this increases the demand for cash. The mm schedule may shift up or down.

The new intersection of the mm and kk schedules must be at a higher price of capital, even if the mm schedule shifts down and to the right. To see this, suppose that p_k remained constant and that i rose by enough to keep $\rho_b = i + \pi_m$ constant despite the fall in π_m. At this point there would be excess demand for capital because the rate of return on bonds and capital would be the same as before the fall in π_m, but the rate of return to money would be lower. All points on the new kk schedule corresponding to the same or lower p_k therefore require a higher ρ_b than before the fall in π_m. But the new mm schedule could not pass through a point where the rates of return to both bonds and capital were higher than before the fall in π_m because the fall in π_m is a fall in the rate of return to money. The only possibility is that the new mm schedule intersects the new kk schedule at a higher price of capital. This is illustrated by Figure 3–9, where the mm shifts from $m_0 m_0$ to $m_1 m_1$.

We can prove that the price of capital must rise by differentiating equations (3–8) and (3–10) with respect to i, p_k, and π_m, to obtain the following:

(3–21) $$\frac{\partial p_k}{\partial \pi_m} = \frac{1}{\Delta} \left(\frac{\partial J}{\partial \rho_m} \frac{\partial L}{\partial \rho_b} - \frac{\partial L}{\partial \rho_m} \frac{\partial J}{\partial \rho_b} \right) < 0,$$

where Δ is given by (3–14). An increase in the expected rate of inflation, that is, a fall in π_m, necessarily increases the assets markets equilibrium price of capital.

The effects of an increase in the rate of inflation on the assets markets equilibrium rate of interest are ambiguous. Since we can expect the higher rate of inflation to create excess supply in the bond market, the rate of interest will have to rise to equilibrate it. The increase in the rate of inflation, however, will probably also create excess supply for money, which puts downward pressure on the interest rate. Which way the interest rate will go depends on which one of the two financial markets returns to equilibrium first as the price of capital rises. This in turn depends on the size of the excess supply or excess demand created in the money market as a result of the higher rate of inflation and on the responsiveness of the demand for each of these assets to changes in the price of capital.

The expression for the change in the rate of interest due to a change in the expected rate of inflation is obtained by differentiating equations (3–8) and (3–10) partially with respect to p_k, i, and π_m:

$$(3\text{–}22) \quad \frac{\partial i}{\partial \pi_m} = \frac{1}{\Delta}\left[-\left(\frac{\partial J}{\partial \rho_m} + \frac{\partial J}{\partial \rho_b}\right)\frac{\partial L}{\partial p_k} + \left(\frac{\partial J}{\partial p_k} - k\right)\left(\frac{\partial L}{\partial \rho_m} + \frac{\partial L}{\partial \rho_b}\right)\right].$$

We can state:

PROPOSITION 3–4 *Given the price of money, the stocks of capital and real government debt, and the composition of the debt, an increase in the expected rate of inflation raises the assets markets equilibrium price of capital and may raise or lower the assets markets equilibrium rate of interest.*

3–7 Summary

It follows from the experiments that we have just conducted and from the assets markets equilibrium conditions that the price of capital and the rate of interest can be written as functions of the real stock of debt, the stock of capital, the expected rates of change in the price of money and capital and the composition of the debt, if the Jacobian of the system (3–8) through (3–10) meets the requirements of the implicit function theorem.

$$(3\text{–}23) \qquad\qquad p_k = \Phi(\gamma, k, \pi_m, \pi_k, x)$$

$$(3\text{–}24) \qquad\qquad i = \Psi(\gamma, k, \pi_m, \pi_k, x),$$

where $\gamma = g p_m$ is the real stock of government debt.

From Propositions 3–1 through 3–4 we know that (if the assumption following Proposition 3–2 with regard to the wealth elasticity of the demand for money holds) the partial derivatives of these functions are

$$(3\text{--}25) \qquad \frac{\partial p_k}{\partial \gamma} > 0; \qquad \frac{\partial p_k}{\partial k} < 0; \qquad \frac{\partial p_k}{\partial \pi_m} < 0; \qquad \frac{\partial p_k}{\partial x} < 0.$$

$$(3\text{--}26) \qquad \frac{\partial i}{\partial \gamma} \gtrless 0; \qquad \frac{\partial i}{\partial k} \gtrless 0; \qquad \frac{\partial i}{\partial \pi_m} \gtrless 0; \qquad \frac{\partial i}{\partial x} > 0.$$

We plot an aa schedule in Figure 3–10, which shows the pairs of values of the price of money and the price of capital for which the assets markets are in equilibrium. Because an increase in the price of money is equivalent to an increase in the aggregate stock of debt, the higher this price, the higher will be the price of capital at which wealth owners will hold the stock of capital. This justifies the upward-sloping aa schedule in Figure 3–10; p_k and p_m move together in the assets markets. In addition, we have drawn the aa schedule so that it does not intersect the p_k axis at a positive price of capital. This implies that a positive price of money is always required for the assets markets to clear. We can derive this by assuming that for any finite rate of return on capital, wealth owners will desire to have at least part of their wealth in the form of cash. It should

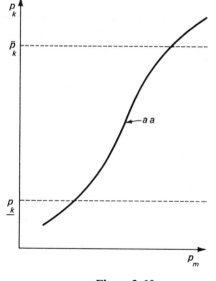

Figure 3–10

g, k, π_m, π_k, x are constant.

be clear to the reader that associated with each (p_m, p_k) point on the *aa* locus is an equilibrium rate of interest. Since the effects of a higher aggregate stock of debt on the rate of interest are ambiguous, we do not know how this rate changes as we move along the *aa* curve. There is no reason to believe that it changes monotonically with p_m.

Finally, we should note that up to this point we have dealt only with situations in which the economy's capital stock and the price of capital are such that both consumption and investment goods are produced. We have not considered cases in which the economy is specialized in the production of only one commodity. It is easy to see, however, that the slope of the *aa* schedule does not depend on whether the economy is specialized or not. Suppose the economy is specialized in the production of consumption goods and there is an increase in the price of capital. It will still be true that private wealth measured in consumption goods units rises and that the rate of return on capital falls. The rate of return on capital is equal to the ratio of the marginal product of capital in the consumption goods sector to the price of capital. An increase in p_k that is not large enough to induce firms to produce some amount of investment goods does not affect the marginal product of capital in the consumption goods sector, but since the price of capital rises, the rate of return on capital falls. Hence, when the economy is specialized in the production of consumption goods, the effects of an increase in p_k on the demand for assets are the same as when the economy is not specialized. On the other hand, when relative prices are such that firms produce only investment goods, the increase in the price of capital will raise income and wealth measured in consumption goods units, but the rate of return on capital will remain constant. The rate of return on capital is equal to the marginal product of capital in the investment goods sector. An increase in p_k without a change in the capital stock does not affect output in the investment goods sector when the economy is already specialized to the production of investment. Even if the rate of return to capital is insensitive to changes in p_k, we can see from equation (3–17) that as long as $[1 - \eta_{ma}(g/a)] > 0$, an increase in g or p_m will raise p_k. The slope of the *aa* is positive above $\bar{p}_k$ and below p_k, the specialization prices.

Since an increase in the stock of debt, in the proportion of the debt that is monetized, or in the expected rate of inflation raises the equilibrium price of capital in the assets markets for any given price of money, the *aa* schedule shifts upward from $a_0 a_0$ to $a_1 a_1$, as indicated in Figure 3–11, in response to any one of these changes. For any given p_m, the price of capital at which wealth owners are in equilibrium after these changes is higher.

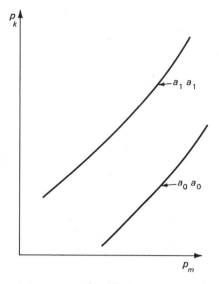

Figure 3–11
k, π_k are constant. g rises or π_m falls or x falls.

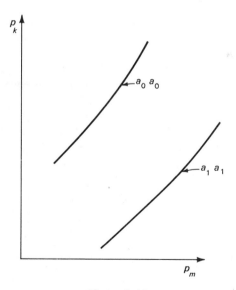

Figure 3–12
g, π_m, π_k, x are constant. k rises.

On the other hand, an increase in the stock of capital lowers the price of capital at which wealth owners desire to hold their increased stock of wealth; that is, as k increases, the aa schedule shifts downward from $a_0 a_0$ to $a_1 a_1$, as indicated in Figure 3–12. Given the price of money p_m, for the assets markets to remain in equilibrium, the price of capital has to fall after an increase in the stock of capital.

As we have shown in Chapter 2, given the economy's factor endowments, its rate of growth depends on the equilibrium price of capital. In this chapter we have analyzed how this equilibrium price is determined in the assets markets for a given price of money. We have also seen that the government, through monetary policy, can affect the equilibrium price of capital for a given price of money. But what determines p_m itself? Any change in the supply of assets, in their composition, or in the expected rate of inflation will affect not only the price of capital but also the price of money, which in this chapter we have taken as given. To understand the total effect of any of these changes, we have to analyze the joint determination of the equilibrium prices of money and capital, and for this purpose we have to consider the demand and supply conditions in the market for consumption goods. This is the subject of Chapter 4.

The Consumption Goods Market

4–1 Introduction

In Chapter 3 we derived a schedule of pairs (p_m, p_k) that were compatible with assets markets equilibrium, given the size and composition of the government debt, expectations about price level changes, and the capital stock. To complete our model we need a second schedule, called the cc, the locus of (p_m, p_k) pairs which equilibrate the market for consumption goods. The intersection of the two schedules will determine the overall equilibrium (p_m, p_k).

Just as the government can, by changing the size or composition of its own debt, influence the position of the aa schedule, it can, by adjusting the size of its expenditures or deficit, change the supply and demand for consumption, thereby influencing the position of the cc schedule.

Government policy acts by regulating aggregate supply and demand. A deficiency of demand will be met by a fall in prices or, if prices are sticky, by unemployment; excess demand, by a rise in prices. If the government wishes to enforce certain desires about the price level, it must ensure that aggregate supply and demand for consumption goods are equal at the desired price level. Taking the stock of capital and the price of capital as given, the market for consumption goods can be looked at in two ways,

53

either as determining the price level given government policy or as determining the government policy necessary to enforce a certain price level.

4-2   Supply

From Chapter 2 we know that the supply of consumption goods per capita depends explicitly on the capital stock, k, given at any moment by past accumulation; the price of capital, p_k; and government expenditures, measured by e. The privately available per-capita supply of consumption goods can be written

$$(4\text{--}1) \qquad c^s = q_C(k, p_k) - e.$$

Notice that only k, p_k, and e affect the supply of consumption goods. The price of money has no influence on the supply side of this market.

4-3   Demand

We now come to the question of the variables that affect the aggregate demand for consumption goods. A satisfactory theoretical answer to this question would describe the decision that the consumer makes to divide his income among all alternatives. He can buy consumption goods or save by purchasing capital, bonds, or money. At the present time this decision is well understood only on assumptions about subjective expectations, which we want to do without in this book. As in Chapter 3, we have to confess our inability to provide a satisfactory answer and try to offer a plausible, empirically acceptable demand function without supplying a theoretical derivation of it.

In this book we assume that consumption demand is a function of wealth and total disposable income. In doing this we neglect rates of return, which may be theoretically important in determining consumption. Substantial rate of return influences on consumption may upset some of our findings in ways that will be clear to anyone who becomes familiar with the behavior of the model. We also lump together different kinds of income, property and nonproperty income, for example, that in some theories have different effects on consumption.

We write the demand for consumption goods as

$$(4\text{--}2) \qquad c^d = c(a, y) \quad \text{with} \frac{\partial c}{\partial a} > 0, 1 > \frac{\partial c}{\partial y} > 0,$$

where y is disposable income.

This consumption function includes as a special case the popular proportional savings hypothesis, which we use in many places:

$$(4\text{–}3) \qquad\qquad c^d = (1 - s)y \quad 1 > s > 0.$$

It remains for us now to analyze the determinants of wealth and income. We have already discussed wealth and its components in Chapter 2. We shall now proceed with a consideration of disposable income.

4–4   Disposable Income

Disposable income has four components:

(a) Factor earnings from employment in the private sector and in the public sector;

(b) Government taxes and transfers, including interest on bonds;

(c) Capital gains or losses on capital from expected changes in the price of capital; and

(d) Capital gains and losses on money and bonds from expected changes in the price level.

Our definition of disposable income differs from the usual national accounting definition because we include *expected* capital gains on capital and government debt. We implicitly assume that when individuals anticipate capital gains or losses, they treat them like any other income in making decision as to how much to consume and how much to save.

(A) FACTOR EARNINGS

It follows directly from the rules of accounting that total factor earnings must always equal the value of output. Because our production functions exhibit constant returns to scale, marginal product factor payments will sum to total output. Since the government pays competitive factor prices and has the same production possibilities as the private consumption goods sector, government expenditure will not affect this equality. Therefore,

$$(4\text{-}4) \qquad\qquad w + rk = q_C(k, p_k) + p_k q_I(k, p_k).$$

(B) TRANSFERS, TAXES, AND INTEREST

Certain government operations add to and subtract from disposable income. The government collects taxes, pays out interest on its bonds, and makes transfers such as welfare and social security payments. To simplify matters we assume that the tax and transfer operations are lump sum, that is, that they change disposable income without changing any of the prices or rates of return in the system. Since labor in our model is assumed to be supplied inelastically, a wage tax or subsidy would meet these requirements, as would a head tax.

If v is per-capita transfers measured in money terms and t nominal per-capita taxes, we can write the total net contribution of these government operations to disposable income as

$$(4\text{–}5) \qquad\qquad z = ib + (v - t).$$

The government deficit or surplus which must be financed by issuing or retiring government debt is the sum of expenditures and the tax, transfer, and interest items:

$$(4\text{–}6) \qquad\qquad dp_m = e + ibp_m + (v - t)p_m.$$

The deficit is important because it represents the link between present and future stocks of national debt. The expression for the rate of change of the national debt g is

$$(4\text{–}7) \qquad\qquad d = \dot{g} + ng.$$

A deficit of ng allows the total debt to grow as fast as the population and thereby maintains g, the per-capita stock of debt, at a constant level. If d exceeds or falls short of ng, then $\dot{g}/g$ is greater or less than zero, and the per-capita debt is changing.

In everything that follows we choose to think of the fiscal branch as deciding two magnitudes: real expenditures, e, and the nominal deficit, d. This means that taxes and transfers must be continually adjusted in nominal terms to hit the target deficit, offsetting, for example, changes in interest payments on the outstanding stock of bonds whenever necessary.

This choice of government policy parameters represents a compromise between simplicity and realism. We feel that in the short run it is both possible and likely that the policy makers will formulate their goals as a level of real expenditures and a certain nominal deficit. The point to remember is that a *constant deficit* policy may involve frequent changes in taxes and transfers, which will all be behind the scenes.

(c) EXPECTED CAPITAL GAINS ON THE STOCK OF CAPITAL

Holders of capital may expect some change in the relative price of capital, and this will also affect disposable income. If π_k is the expected rate of change in the relative price of capital, this capital gain or loss adds

$\pi_k p_k k$ to disposable income. As in Chapter 3, for the time being we assume $\pi_k = 0$ and omit this term. The effects of allowing π_k to be different from zero will be studied in Chapter 14.

(D) EXPECTED CAPITAL GAINS ON THE STOCK OF GOVERNMENT DEBT

The value of the outstanding government debt can change because p_m, the value of money, changes. If p_m is expected to increase or decrease, corresponding to a positive or negative π_m, disposable income will include an additional term, $\pi_m g p_m$, the real value of the expected capital gains or losses on the outstanding government debt. If $\pi_m < 0$, then people expect inflation to occur. $-\pi_m g p_m$ is what is frequently referred to as an inflation tax, with $g p_m$ the base and $-\pi_m$ the rate.

When we sum these terms we get our definition of disposable income:

$$(4\text{–}8) \qquad y = q_C + p_k q_I + i b p_m + (v - t)p_m + \pi_m g p_m.$$

Using equation (4–6), we can also write this as

$$(4\text{–}9) \qquad y = q_C + p_k q_I + d p_m + \pi_m g p_m - e.$$

Collecting the terms which contain p_m and making use of expression (4–7), we have

$$(4\text{–}10) \qquad y = q_C + p_k q_I - e + \left(\frac{\dot g}{g} + n + \pi_m\right) g p_m.$$

Finally, we can write the demand for consumption goods in the general case as

$$(4\text{–}11) \qquad c^d = c[p_k k + p_m g, q_C + p_k q_I + (d + \pi_m g)p_m - e]$$

or alternatively

$$(4\text{–}12) \qquad c^d = c\left[p_k k + p_m g, q_C + p_k q_I + \left(\frac{\dot g}{g} + n + \pi_m\right) g p_m - e\right].$$

4–5   Equilibrium in the Consumption Goods Market

If the consumption goods market clears, we have

$$(4\text{–}13) \quad c^s = q_C - e = c[p_k k + p_m g, q_C + p_k q_I + (d + \pi_m g)p_m - e].$$

In Figures 4–1a and 4–1b, we present supply and demand curves for the consumption goods market as a function of the price of money, given k,

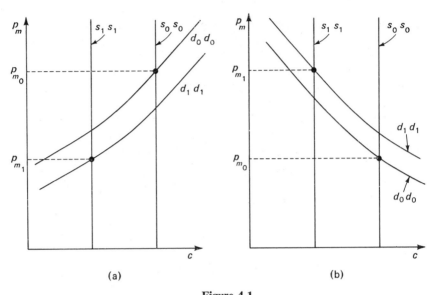

Figure 4-1

g, k, π_m, π_k, d, e are constant. p_k rises from p_{k0} to p_{k1}.

p_k, e, π_m, and d. The supply is not elastic with respect to the price of money and appears as the vertical line ss.

A change in p_m affects the demand for consumption goods through both arguments: wealth and income. The effect through wealth is clear. If private net holdings of government debt are positive, an increase in p_m raises private wealth and raises the demand for consumption. On the other hand, if g is negative, the private sector is a net debtor to the government, and an increase in p_m, raising the value of the debt, reduces private consumption.

The effect through income is more complicated. The change in the price level affects two components of disposable income: the real value of the deficit, dp_m, and the real value of the expected appreciation or depreciation of the outstanding stock of government debt, $\pi_m g p_m$. We assume that an instantaneous change in the level of prices changes the base of the inflation tax but does not affect the expected tax rate; that is, it does not affect people's expectations about the rate of change of prices. We shall postpone further discussion of this question until Chapter 13, where we analyze expectations explicitly.

In the long run, one would expect the economy to reach a state of equilibrium where expected and actual rates of change in prices are equal and all per-capita real variables are constant. This is the way we usually characterize states of steady growth. In this case π_m would equal the actual rate of change in p_m, $\dot{p}_m/p_m$, and the rate of change in the real value of per-capita government debt would be zero. Thus

$$(4\text{–}14) \qquad \frac{\dot{\gamma}}{\gamma} = \frac{\dot{g}}{g} + \frac{\dot{p}_m}{p_m} = 0,$$

where $\gamma = g p_m$ is the real value of the government debt. Together, these steady-state conditions imply that

$$(4\text{–}15) \quad (d + \pi_m g)p_m = \left(\frac{\dot{g}}{g} + n + \pi_m\right)g p_m = \left(\frac{\dot{g}}{g} + n + \frac{\dot{p}_m}{p_m}\right)g p_m = n g p_m .$$

In the long run, the income effect of a change in p_m depends on the sign of g just as the wealth effect does, and the two reinforce each other. In a steadily growing economy with $g > 0$, wealth owners accumulate government debt over time at a positive rate to maintain the per-capita level of real debt. The real value of increase in the debt will exceed the real value of the depreciation of the debt, or alternatively, the rate of inflation will be lower than the rate of expansion in the government debt, the difference being equal to the steady state rate of growth.

In the short run, there is no such systematic relationship between d, g, and π_m. It is possible for $d + \pi_m g$ to be of either sign (or zero) despite a positive or negative value for g. If $d + \pi_m g$ and g are both greater than zero, then an increase in p_m increases demand for consumption goods; the demand curve is upward-sloped, as in Figure 4–1a. If $d + \pi_m g$ and g are both less than zero, an increase in p_m reduces the demand for consumption goods; the demand schedule is downward-sloped, as in Figure 4–1b. When $d + \pi_m g$ and g differ in sign, the slope of the demand curve depends on the relative strengths of the income and wealth effects and may be either positive or negative. The reader should note, however, that a demand as in Figure 4–1b implies that a rise in prices (fall in p_m) increases excess demand.

It is easy to see that, given the stock of capital, the quantity of resources purchased by the government, and the deficit, there are values of p_k for which the consumption goods market cannot clear at a positive price of money. This occurs when the dd schedule intersects the horizontal axis to the right of the supply schedule in Figure 4–1a or to its left in Figure 4–1b.

If we now change p_k and observe the new equilibrium p_m, we shall trace out the (p_m, p_k) pairs that equilibrate the consumption goods market and find the shape of the cc schedule. A rise in p_k reduces the supply of consumption goods according to Proposition 2–1, shifting the ss schedule to the left, from $s_0 s_0$ to $s_1 s_1$, in both parts of Figure 4–1.

When p_k increases, both income and wealth increase for any value of p_m. The wealth increase is straightforward because k is positive. The income increase comes from the fact that the value of output measured in consumption units, $q(p_k, k)$, rises with p_k, as shown in Chapter 3 (see Figure 3–1). On both accounts, demand increases, and the dd curves of Figure 4–1 shift to the right from $d_0 d_0$ to $d_1 d_1$. In Figure 4–1a, where the demand curve slopes upward, the effect is to lower p_m, which falls from p_{m_0} to p_{m_1}. In Figure 4–1b, we see that a rise in p_m from p_{m_0} to p_{m_1} is necessary to clear the market.

Figures 4–2a and 4–2b show schedules of combinations of p_m and p_k that clear the consumption goods market for given stocks of capital and debt, level of government expenditures and deficit, and expected rate of price change when a rise in p_m raises and lowers demand, respectively; this is the cc schedule.

For $p_m = 0$, the equilibrium price of capital is between $\bar{p}_k$ and zero, independent of whether the demand schedule is an increasing or decreasing function of p_m. For $p_k = \bar{p}_k$, the supply of consumption goods to the

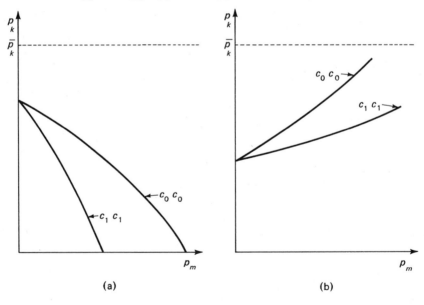

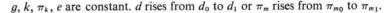

(a)   (b)

Figure 4–2

g, k, π_k, e are constant. d rises from d_0 to d_1 or π_m rises from π_{m0} to π_{m1}.

private sector is zero but demand for them is $c^d(\bar{p}_k k, \bar{p}_k q_I)$. Since both wealth and income are greater than zero, it is reasonable to assume that demand for consumption goods is positive as well, and $c^d(\bar{p}_k k, \bar{p}_k q_I) > 0$. There is, therefore, excess demand for consumption. When both p_k and p_m are zero, wealth is zero; and, since $0 \le p_k$, national income is q_C. The demand for consumption goods is then $c^d(0, q_C)$. Since the value of wealth is zero, the public cannot consume more than total national income. It is reasonable to assume that they save some part of income so that $c^d(q_C)/q_C < 1$. We would therefore have excess supply of goods at $p_k = 0$. So, as we pass from zero to $\bar{p}_k$ at $p_m = 0$, we go from excess supply to excess demand for consumption goods. There is some p_k between zero and $\bar{p}_k$ at which the market for consumption goods clears, with $p_m = 0$.

The slope of the cc schedule depends on the slope of the demand curve and thus on the combined wealth and income effects of changes in p_m. As mentioned above, we generally expect a rise in the price level (fall in p_m) to reduce demand, and require a rise in p_k to restore equilibrium, as pictured in Figure 4–2a. The cc schedule will slope upward only when $d + \pi_m g$ is large in magnitude and negative and g itself is small or negative. The cc schedule determines the consumption goods market equilibrium price of money that is consistent with p_k, k, e, d, π_m, and g:

$$(4\text{–}16) \qquad\qquad p_m = \chi(k, p_k, d + \pi_m g, e).$$

(The existence of this function depends on the existence and uniqueness of the intersections in Figure 4–2.)

4–6 Effects of Changes in Fiscal Policy Through the Deficit

One of the ways the government can influence aggregate demand is through raising or lowering taxes without changing the volume of its expenditures. This has the effect of decreasing or increasing $d + \pi_m g$ because it changes d.

An increase in the expected rate of change in the price of money, π_m, has qualitatively the same effect on the demand for consumption goods as a decrease in taxes. A lower expected rate of inflation reduces the anticipated rate of depreciation of government debt; that is, the inflation tax rate falls, thereby increasing disposable income and raising the demand for consumption goods.

If taxes are cut, the deficit and the demand for consumption goods rise.

To clear the market, p_k must fall in order to increase the supply of consumption goods and to lower demand at a given p_m. The cc schedule shifts downward, as shown in Figures 4–2a and 4–2b.

The value of p_k that clears the market for $p_m = 0$ does not change with a change in $d + \pi_m g$ because this expression enters equation (4–13) only multiplied by p_m. If $p_m = 0$, it has no effect on income or the demand for consumption. The p_k that clears the market is the same one that would clear it if $d + \pi_m g$ were zero. An increase in the deficit rotates the cc schedule clockwise around that point.

When the cc schedule slopes down, an increase in d lowers p_m for any value of p_k. But if the cc schedule slopes upward, a tax cut raises d, lowers the surplus, and requires a higher p_m for each p_k. We can summarize these facts in:

PROPOSITION 4–1 *An increase in the deficit (or a decrease in the expected rate of inflation) lowers the price of capital that clears the market for consumption goods for any given price of money.*

4–7 Effects of Changes in Fiscal Policy Through Expenditures

The second fiscal policy variable is e, the real value of government expenditures. We define a *marginally balanced budget change in expenditure* as a joint change in expenditures, taxes, and transfers that leaves the nominal deficit unaffected. Equilibrium in the consumption goods market implies that

$$(4\text{–}17) \qquad q_C - e = c[p_k k + p_m g, q_C + p_k q_I + (d + \pi_m g)p_m - e].$$

As long as the nominal deficit remains constant, an increase in real expenditures lowers supply by its full amount, Δe, and lowers demand only by $(\partial c/\partial y)\Delta e$, where $\partial c/\partial y$ is the marginal propensity to consume out of income and is less than one. The net effect is to create excess demand for consumption at the old (p_m, p_k). For any given price of money, a lower p_k is required to clear the market for consumption goods. The cc schedule shifts downward, as shown in Figures 4–3a and 4–3b.

PROPOSITION 4–2 *A balanced-budget increase in e, the quantity of expenditure on consumption goods made by the government, lowers the price of capital that clears the consumption goods market for any given price of money.*

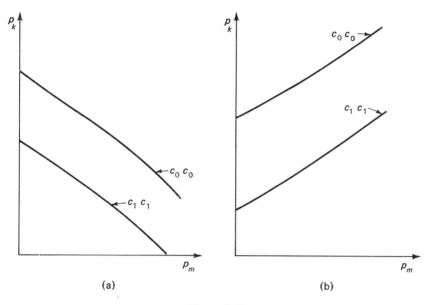

(a)   (b)

Figure 4–3

g, k, π_m, π_k, d are constant. e rises from e_0 to e_1.

4–8 Effects of an Increase in the Stock of Capital

When k increases, we know from Chapter 2 that the supply of consumption goods increases; but income and wealth also both increase so that it is impossible to say whether the cc schedule shifts upward or downward in the general case.

In the special case where the consumption function is linear in income and insensitive to wealth [equation (4–3)], we can write the excess demand in the consumption goods market as

$$(4\text{–}18) \quad c^d - c^s = (1-s)[q_C + p_k q_I + (d + \pi_m g)p_m - e] - (q_C - e)$$
$$= s(e - q_C) + (1-s)p_k q_I + (1-s)(d + \pi_m g)p_m.$$

An increase in k in the usual factor intensity case, according to Proposition 2–4, increases q_C, which will result, from (4–18), in a decrease in excess demand. This can be shown by differentiating (4–18) partially with respect to k:

$$\frac{\partial(c^d - c^s)}{\partial k} = -s\frac{\partial q_C}{\partial k} + (1-s)p_k\frac{\partial q_I}{\partial k} < 0.$$

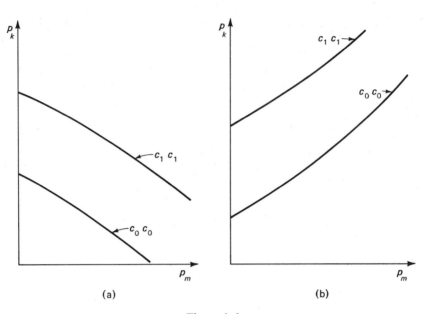

Figure 4-4

g, π_m, π_k, d, e are constant. k rises from k_0 to k_1.

For any p_m, given d, π_m, and e, a higher p_k is necessary if the consumption goods market is to clear. The cc curve, as shown in Figures 4–4a and 4–4b, will shift upward in both cases.

This gives us:

PROPOSITION 4-3   *An increase in the stock of capital may raise or lower the price of capital necessary to clear the consumption goods market for any given price of money. In the special case of the proportional consumption function that does not include wealth as an argument, the consumption market equilibrium price of capital must rise.*

4-9   Effects of an Increase in the Stock of Government Debt

An increase in g affects the demand for consumption goods through both wealth and income. Again, the wealth effect is unambiguous. An increase in the government debt raises the public's wealth holdings and stimulates demand; conversely, a decrease in g lowers wealth and thus demand.

The income effect is more complex and depends on the sign of π_m. If $\pi_m < 0$, that is, if consumers expect inflation, then an increase in the government debt is analogous to an increase in a tax base (discussed above). In this case the rise in g lowers disposable income and, therefore, demand for consumption. If $\pi_m \geq 0$, the inflation tax is a subsidy to the holders of government debt. A rise in the government debt is equivalent to an expansion of the base subsidy; disposable income and demand both rise.

When the wealth and income effects work in the same direction ($\pi_m \geq 0$), the results are clear. A rise in g increases the demand for consumption and a fall in the price of capital is necessary to restore equilibrium. Since g appears in both wealth and disposable income multiplied by p_m, there is no change in the equilibrium p_k at $p_m = 0$ when g rises; the cc curve will rotate downward, as illustrated in Figures 4–2a and 4–2b, for an increase in the deficit. When the two effects work in opposite directions ($\pi_m < 0$), the results of an increase in g depend on their relative strengths; demand may rise, fall, or possibly not change at all. If the net effect should be a fall in demand, a higher p_k is necessary to clear the goods market for each p_m; the cc schedule rotates upward, as illustrated in Figures 4–5a and 4–5b.

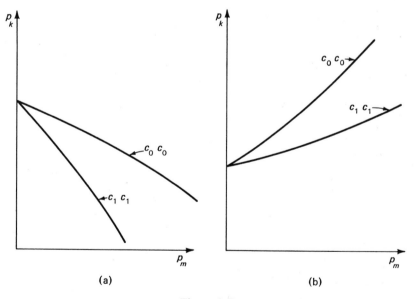

(a)   (b)

Figure 4–5
k, π_m, π_k, d, e are constant. g rises from g_0 to g_1.

In summary:

PROPOSITION 4–4   *If the price of money is expected to rise or stay constant, an increase in the stock of government debt lowers the price of capital that clears the consumption goods market. If the price of money is expected to fall, an increase in g may raise, lower, or leave unchanged the equilibrium p_k in the consumption goods market.*

4–10   Summary

We have derived on the basis of a general consumption function a schedule of (p_m, p_k) pairs that equilibrate the consumption goods market, for given g, k, π_m, e, and d. This schedule usually slopes downward; but in some cases, when the government runs a large surplus or is a net creditor, it may slope upward. We concentrate on the first case, where a rise in the price of consumption goods reduces excess demand.

The results we have derived about movements of the cc schedule carry over in all cases to the simpler consumption function [equation (4–3)]. The next step is to consider how the aa and cc schedules jointly determine a (p_m, p_k) equilibrium and to study the effects on this equilibrium of changes in government policy variables. This is the substance of Chapters 5 and 6.

5 The Complete Model: Statics

5–1 Introduction

Now that we have described the assets and consumption goods markets in detail, we can see how they simultaneously determine the equilibrium prices of money and capital and, in particular, how government policies can affect this equilibrium. Since from Chapter 2 we know that we can view the growth path of the capital stock as depending on the price of capital, we shall be in a position to study the influence government policies have on the economy's rate of growth and on its capital stock.

5–2 Short-Run Equilibrium

In Chapter 3 we studied the *aa* schedule of pairs of p_k and p_m that equilibrate the assets markets. From Proposition 3–2, we know that this schedule is usually upward-sloping if the wealth elasticity of the demand for money is low in relation to the ratio of debt to wealth. A higher value of debt will be absorbed in portfolios only at a lower rate of return to capital and a higher price of capital.

In Chapter 4 we analyzed the *cc* schedule of pairs of p_m and p_k that equilibrate the consumption goods market. This schedule may be upward-sloping or downward-sloping depending on the government deficit, expectations about inflation, and the size of the government debt. We concluded that for an economy with a positive stock of government debt, the schedule will usually slope downward.

The intersection of the aa schedule and the cc schedule gives the equilibrium prices of capital and money for given stocks of capital and debt, composition of the debt, government deficit and expenditures, and expectations of price changes.

In Figures 5–1a and 5–1b, we illustrate this equilibrium for a downward-sloping cc schedule and an upward-sloping cc schedule that intersect the aa schedule from above. There is, however, no guarantee that an intersection does exist. In particular, when the cc schedule has a positive slope, the aa schedule may lie below the cc schedule for all values of p_m. In this case there is no (p_m, p_k) pair that is consistent with equilibrium in both assets and consumption goods markets. It may also happen that there are several crossings of the two schedules, with the aa schedule alternately crossing the cc schedule from above and below, or that there is a tangency g of the two curves. If the economy is at an equilibrium where the aa schedule crosses from above, the effects of the experiments we perform below on p_m and p_k are, in general, different. We do not pursue this case

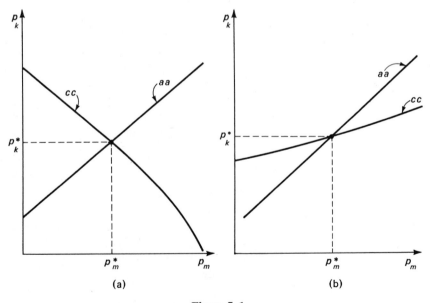

Figure 5–1

$g, k, \pi_m, \pi_k, d, e, x$ are constant.

because it complicates the analysis and is easy for the reader to study himself. As explained in Chapter 4, in the steady state an economy with a positive outstanding stock of government debt will have a positive $d + \pi_m g$ in order to maintain the debt intact over time. This implies a downward-sloping cc schedule, which in turn allows for the existence of only one equilibrium of the usual kind, that is, with the aa schedule crossing from below. We conduct the following analysis under the assumption of a downward-sloping cc schedule. The results are all reconsidered for the case of an upward-sloping cc schedule in Section 5–9.

Given the aggregate stock of capital, government expenditures, the deficit, the expected rate of inflation, and the aggregate nominal stock of debt and its composition, we can determine the equilibrium values of the prices of capital and money. In this chapter we study the effects of changes in policy through the variables d, e and x and the effects of changes in g, π_m, and k on the equilibrium prices of money and capital. We emphasize again the conclusion of Chapter 3 that to each point on the aa schedule there corresponds some rate of interest, but in this chapter we do not pursue the effects of our experiments on the rate of interest.

5–3   Effects of Changes in Fiscal Policy

Tax changes and shifts in the scale of government expenditures directly affect only the consumption market. An increase in the deficit or a rise in the scale of government expenditures with an unchanged deficit shifts the cc curve downward from $c_0 c_0$ to $c_1 c_1$ (see Propositions 4–1 and 4–2). There is no change in the aa schedule, and, as we can see from Figure 5–2, the result must be a lower price of capital and a higher price of consumer goods (lower p_m).

The economics of this experiment are quite simple. The increased deficit or expenditures create excess aggregate demand. In the usual case, this causes a rise in the price level (a fall in p_m). The change in the price level has repercussions in the assets markets because it lowers the real value of government debt. According to Proposition 3–2, the fall in p_m usually lowers the assets markets equilibrium price of capital. The decrease in the price of capital that equilibrates the assets markets in turn helps to eliminate the excess demand created by the expansionary fiscal policy and reduces the rise in the price level that is required to equilibrate the consumption goods market.

We have:

PROPOSITION 5–1 *When the demand for consumption goods is a decreasing function of their price, an increase in the deficit that arises from*

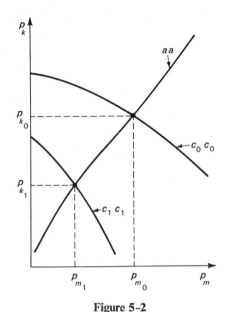

Figure 5-2

g, k, π_m, π_k, x are constant. d rises from d_0 to d_1 or e rises from e_0 to e_1.

lower taxes or higher government expenditures or a rise in the scale of government expenditures with a constant deficit lowers both the equilibrium price of money and the equilibrium price of capital.

5–4   Effects of Changes in Monetary Policy

The government's monetary policy directly affects only the assets markets, given our assumption that savings are insensitive to interest rates. When the aggregate stock of debt is positive, an open market purchase lowers x, the ratio of money to debt, because the authorities buy bonds with money. From Proposition 3–1, we know that a decrease in x raises the price of capital that equilibrates the assets markets for any p_m. In other words, an open market purchase raises the aa schedule from $a_0 a_0$ to $a_1 a_1$.

In Figure 5–3, we can see the effects of an open market purchase on the equilibrium prices of capital and money. When the cc schedule slopes downward, the result must be a higher price of capital and a lower price of money. Again, we can argue this through on the basis of ordinary economic concepts. The open market purchase tends to create excess aggregate demand by raising p_k, thus lowering the supply of consumption goods and

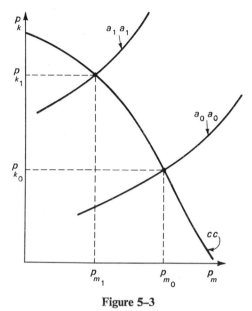

Figure 5–3

g, k, π_m, π_k, d, e are constant. x falls from x_0 to x_1.

raising the value of real income and increasing demand. If excess demand in the consumption goods market is reduced when the price level rises, a lower p_m, that is, a higher price level, will eliminate this excess demand both directly by lowering the demand for consumption goods and indirectly by lowering the value of the government debt, thereby moderating the rise in the price of capital that is necessary to clear the assets markets.

Therefore:

PROPOSITION 5–2   *In the case of a downward-sloping cc schedule, an open market purchase lowers the equilibrium price of money and raises the equilibrium price of capital.*

5–5   Effects of Changes in the Expected Rate of Inflation

If people expect a higher rate of inflation, π_m falls. This affects both the assets and consumption goods markets.

If the stock of government debt is positive, the fall in π_m acts like an increase in taxes, which reduces the aggregate demand for consumption

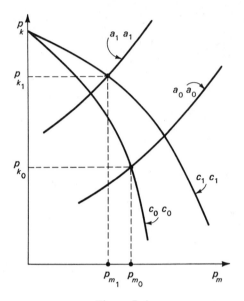

Figure 5–4

g, k, π_k, d, e, x are constant. π_m falls from π_{m_0} to π_{m_1}.

goods. This shifts the cc schedule upward, in Figure 5–4, from $c_0 c_0$ to $c_1 c_1$, according to Proposition 4–1. That is, when g is positive, the effect of a higher expected rate of inflation on the consumption market is deflationary since it is viewed by consumers as decreasing their disposable income because, as indicated earlier, expected capital losses on the debt through inflation are similar to a tax in their effect on demand.

In the assets markets, on the other hand, the higher expected rate of inflation induces wealth owners to shift toward capital and thereby raises the price of capital that equilibrates the assets markets for any p_m (see Proposition 3–4). The aa curve shifts upward from $a_0 a_0$ to $a_1 a_1$. This tends to raise the price of capital, thereby reducing the supply of consumption goods and increasing income and demand.

From Figure 5–4, we can see that the equilibrium p_k rises when the cc schedule slopes downward and there is a positive stock of debt. The price of money may fall or rise depending on the relative shifts of the two schedules.

In more ordinary language, when g is positive, an increase in the expected rate of inflation acts like a tax increase (lowering disposable income) offset by an open market operation (raising the assets markets equilibrium p_k). The uncertainty of the final value of p_m arises from the mixture of the effects described in Section 5–3 and 5–4. Both of these effects tend to increase the price of capital, first by decreasing the demand for consumption goods and second by increasing the price of capital at which wealth owners desire to hold the existing stocks of money, bonds, and capital.

PROPOSITION 5–3   *When the government is a net debtor to the private sector and the demand for consumption goods is an increasing function of the price of money, an increase in the expected rate of inflation raises the equilibrium price of capital, but its effect on the equilibrium price of money is uncertain.*

The fact that the price level may rise or fall as a result of an increase in the expected rate of inflation has important implications for the stability of economies that are subject to inflationary or deflationary pressures. The stability of the system depends heavily on whether a rise in the expected rate of change of a given price increases or decreases that price. If the price rises, this may further increase the expected rate of change and initiate a runaway inflation. We shall study this problem in greater detail in Chapters 12 and 13, where we explicitly analyze the behavior of our model with inflation.

5–6   Effects of an Increase in the Stock of Capital

An increase in the capital stock shifts both the cc and aa schedules.

From Proposition 3–3, we know that wealth owners will hold a larger capital stock only at a lower price of capital for a given p_m. The aa schedule shifts downward, as shown in Figure 5–5, from $a_0 a_0$ to $a_1 a_1$.

The effect of the increase in the capital stock on the market for consumption goods is ambiguous. In the absence of wealth effects on consumption we know that an increase in the stock of capital creates excess supply of consumption goods (see Proposition 4–3); but if wealth affects the demand for consumption goods, the increase in k raises wealth, and this will tend to increase demand. The final position of the cc curve is, therefore, not determined by the restrictions we have placed on the model.

If the cc schedule moves only a little or shifts upward (as would be the case if wealth effects were small), then the price of money must rise; that is, the increase in the capital stock is deflationary, as Figure 5–5 indicates. The equilibrium price of capital may rise or fall in all cases, depending on the relative shifts of the two schedules.

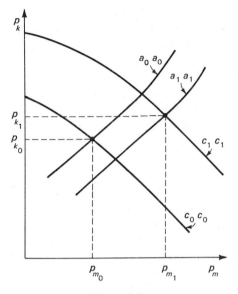

Figure 5–5

g, π_m, π_k, d, e, x are constant. k rises from k_0 to k_1.

5–7   Effects of an Increase in the Stock of Government Debt

As time goes on the stock of debt will change just as the stock of capital will. An increase in g affects both the assets and consumption goods markets.

By Proposition 3–2, we know that an increase in g will in most cases raise the equilibrium price of capital for any price of money, thereby shifting the aa curve upward, as in Figure 5–6.

The increase in g affects both wealth and income. The increase in wealth tends to create excess demand, which means a downward shift of the cc curve. The effect on income depends on the sign of π_m. When inflation is expected, so that π_m is negative, the prospect of capital losses on the larger stock of debt will actually reduce income. When π_m is positive, the increase in g will raise income and reinforce the wealth effect. Net demand for consumption goods is an increasing function of the stock of government debt when the two effects work together or the positive wealth effect outweighs the negative income effect, and the cc schedule will shift downward as a result of an increase in g. If the reduction in demand because of the drop in disposable income dominates the rise in demand due to the

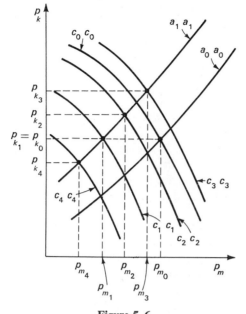

Figure 5–6

k, π_m, π_k, d, e, x are constant. g rises from g_0 to g_1.

increase in wealth, net demand is a decreasing function of the stock of debt, and the cc curve shifts upward when g increases. We shall concentrate our attention on the first case, keeping in mind the fact that the cc curve can conceivably shift either upward or downward as the result of an increase in g.

We can deduce something about the new equilibrium because g enters all the markets multiplied by p_m. What if p_m just changed in inverse proportion to the change in g so that $p_m g$ remained constant? The new pair (p_{m_1}, p_{k_0}), as shown in Figure 5–6, fails to be an equilibrium except when the deficit is equal to zero. When $d = 0$, a constant $p_m g$ will clear both markets, and the equilibrium p_k remains unchanged. When this situation occurs, the government debt is neutral. If d is positive, there will be excess supply at (p_{m_1}, p_{k_0}) since all the expressions in the equilibrium condition for the consumption market will be the same except $p_m d$, which is smaller. When $d > 0$, the new equilibrium must involve a smaller movement of the cc curve downward; indeed, if π_m is sufficiently large in magnitude and negative, the cc curve may shift above its original position. In either situation, p_k and $p_m g$ are both higher. If d is negative, the cc curve moves beyond the neutral point, with $p_m g$ and p_k both lowered.

These four possibilities are shown in Figure 5–6 as $c_1 c_1$, which corresponds to a zero deficit; $c_2 c_2$, which corresponds to a positive deficit; $c_3 c_3$, which corresponds to a very strong income effect with d positive but π_m large in magnitude and negative; and $c_4 c_4$, which corresponds to a negative deficit (a surplus).

We can summarize this as:

PROPOSITION 5–4 *When the demand for consumption goods is a decreasing function of its price, an increase in the stock of government debt will raise, lower, or leave unchanged the price of capital as the deficit is positive, negative, or zero. In most cases the equilibrium price of money will fall. If the deficit is positive and the expected rate of inflation is large, however, the equilibrium price of money may rise.*

Proposition 5–4 may sound strange to those who are familiar with the arguments related to the neutrality of money and government debt. It is well known that if prices are flexible, a change in all components of the government debt in equal proportions lowers the price level by the same proportion and leaves the real variables of the system unchanged. In our model, if the deficit is not zero, this is not the case. A change in g affects the price of capital and modifies the proportion of total resources devoted to producing each type of good.

The difference arises from the fact that since we have taken into account the interaction between the budget constraints of the government and the private sector, the real value of the government deficit, dp_m, appears as an argument in the private demand for commodities. If the deficit is fixed in nominal terms, an equal, proportional increase in g and the price level (fall in p_m) will lower the real value of the government deficit, thereby reducing the demand for commodities by the private sector.

A change in the stock of government debt will have no effect on the real variables of the system only if the nominal deficit, d, also rises in equal proportion to the rise in g, and thus in equal proportion to the fall in p_m. Remembering that $d = \dot{g} - ng$, and thus $d/g = \dot{g}/g - n$, we see that $\dot{g}/g$ will in this case be constant. For an equal, proportional increase in g and the price level to leave q_C and q_I unchanged, the deficit must be adjusted so that the rate of expansion in the government debt remains constant.

5–8   Government Policy

The government controls three important variables: the composition of its debt, x; its deficit, d; and the level of government expenditures, e. The interesting possibility suggested by the study of the effects of the three separately is that the government can mix these policies to determine in the short run both p_k and p_m. In addition, if the public has sufficient confidence in the government's ability to control the price level, the authorities may also be able to determine the expected rate of inflation by announcing their intention to enforce a certain path of prices.

For example, if the government wants a higher p_k, it can, by an open market purchase, decrease x. From Proposition 5–2, we know that when the cc curve slopes downward, this does raise p_k but generally lowers p_m at the same time. If the government wants to, it can get the new higher p_k at the same p_m by offsetting the open market purchase by raising taxes and thereby lowering its deficit. As we can see from Figure 5–7, this will require a smaller open market purchase, since the aa schedule has to move only to $a_1 a_1$ instead of to $a_2 a_2$.

If the government wants a higher level of government expenditures, it can obtain it with p_m and p_k remaining constant. When the government increases e it must simultaneously alter the deficit so as to keep the sum of private and public demand for consumption goods constant.

In fact, the government can in the short run make any (p_m, p_k) pair compatible with any level of e it chooses, given the limitations imposed by the shapes of the schedules and the underlying demand functions. The

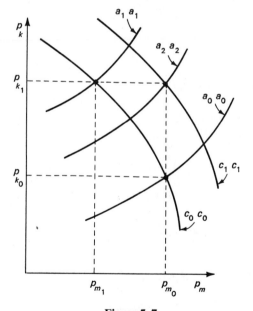

Figure 5–7

g, k, π_m, π_k, are constant. d, e, x vary.

government has enough tools in the short run to meet both an expenditure goal expressed as a target e, an investment goal expressed as a target p_k, and a price stabilization goal expressed as a target p_m.

As time passes, matters are complicated by the fact that g and k will be influenced by past mixes of policy. A tight money, easy fiscal policy will slow the growth of k and accelerate the growth of g, which will change initial conditions at later times. It may be that the changing levels g and k will force a reversal of the short-run policy to meet some goal. What we need now is the conceptual apparatus to study the whole growth path of the economy. This is the subject of Chapter 6.

5–9   Addendum on the Upward-Sloping cc Schedule

We have left to this section the discussion of the case when the demand for consumption goods is a decreasing function of the price of money (an increasing function of the price level). Demand will behave in this fashion if the government is a net creditor rather than a net debtor of the public. There have been periods in the history of the United States when the outstanding stock of government debt was zero or negative. In the 1830's, for instance, a government surplus was held as deposits in state banks.

We confine our analysis to the case where the assets markets equilibrium curve, aa, is steeper than the consumption goods market equilibrium curve, cc, although in some exercises we note the results of the alternative assumption.

(A) EFFECTS OF CHANGES IN FISCAL POLICY

A rise in the deficit or a rise in the scale of government expenditures with an unchanged deficit creates excess demand in the consumption goods market and lowers the consumption goods market equilibrium price of capital for any price of money. This is shown by a downward shift of the cc schedule, in Figure 5–8, from $c_0 c_0$ to $c_1 c_1$. Neither of the two changes affects the assets markets, and, as can be seen from the same figure, the result of an expansionary fiscal policy is a fall in the equilibrium prices of money and capital.

The fall in the price of capital that is required to achieve equilibrium in the consumption goods market will be compatible with equilibrium in the assets markets only if the equilibrium price of money falls. This is because a lower price of money implies a lower stock of real government debt, which in turn usually results in a lower assets markets equilibrium price of capital. The fall in p_m, however, frustrates the adjustment in the consumption goods market because when the cc curve slopes upward,

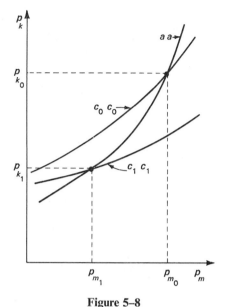

Figure 5–8

g, k, π_m, π_k, x are constant. d rises from d_0 to d_1 or e rises from e_0 to e_1.

excess demand in the market for consumption goods is exacerbated when p_m falls. Equilibrium can still be reached because the indirect effect of the falling p_m through lowering p_k in the assets markets is stronger than the direct effect in the consumption goods market. Geometrically, this means that the *aa* schedule has a steeper slope than the *cc* schedule.

The problems arising when the *aa* curve crosses from above are clearly indicated by this analysis, because in that case the direct effect of a fall in p_m is the stronger, and the excess demand could be eliminated only by a rise in p_m and p_k. This seems very peculiar, but it is possible.

PROPOSITION 5–5   *An increase in the deficit or a rise in the level of government expenditures with a constant deficit lowers both the equilibrium prices of money and capital, provided the aa curve crosses the cc curve from below.*

(B) EFFECTS OF CHANGES IN MONETARY POLICY

An open market purchase lowers the ratio of debt to money and increases the assets markets equilibrium price of capital, thus raising the *aa* schedule from $a_0 a_0$ to $a_1 a_1$ by Proposition 3–1. Changes in the composition of the government debt do not affect equilibrium in the consumption goods

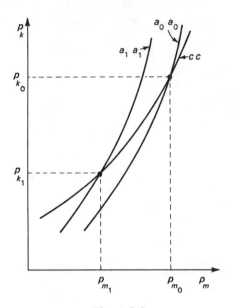

Figure 5–9

g, k, π_m, π_k, d, e are constant. x falls from x_0 to x_1.

market, and the cc schedule stays where it was. In Figure 5–9, we can see that this results in a lower price of money and a lower price of capital.

For a given price of capital, if the assets markets are to return to equilibrium, the price of money has to fall, reducing the real value of the government debt. A fall in p_m creates excess demand for consumption goods, which also makes a lower price of capital necessary for the consumption goods market to return to equilibrium. Thus an open market purchase is inflationary because it lowers the equilibrium price of money, but it also tends to discourage growth by lowering the price of capital. Again, the situation where the aa curve crosses from above if clear: both p_k and p_m must rise after the decrease in x.

PROPOSITION 5–6 *In the case where demand for consumption goods is a decreasing function of the price of money and the aa curve crosses the cc curve from below, an open market purchase lowers both p_m and p_k.*

(C) EFFECTS OF CHANGES IN THE EXPECTED RATE OF INFLATION

We have shown in Chapter 4 that in a long-run steady state the cc schedule will be upward-sloped if and only if the net outstanding stock of debt is negative. In this case an increase in the expected rate of inflation increases the private demand for consumption goods because it increases the rate at which the real value of the private indebtedness to the government is depreciating, thus increasing disposable income and demand. The *cc* line shifts downward from $c_0 c_0$ to $c_1 c_1$ in Figure 5–10 and the price of capital that equilibrates the consumption goods market falls.

In the assets markets the effect of a fall in π_m is the usual one. Wealth owners shift from money and bonds into capital and the assets markets equilibrium price of capital rises. The *aa* schedule shifts upward from $a_0 a_0$ to $a_1 a_1$.

The result of an increase in the expected rate of inflation is, therefore, lower prices for both capital and money. The explanation of this is that the decrease in the consumption goods market equilibrium price of capital will be consistent with equilibrium in the assets markets only if p_m falls, that is, only if the value of the stock of debt falls. The decrease in p_m, however, tends to frustrate the movement toward equilibrium in the consumption goods market because the demand for commodities in this case is a decreasing function of p_m; a fall in the price of money will create additional excess demand for commodities, which in turn requires a further decrease in the price of capital. Since we assume that the *aa* schedule is steeper than the *cc* schedule, the fall in p_k will finally overcome

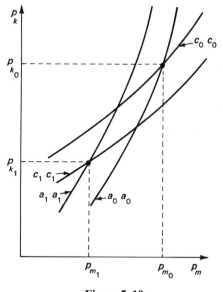

Figure 5–10
g, k, π_k, d, e, x are constant. π_m falls from π_{m0} to π_{m1}.

the effects of a fall in the price of money in the consumption goods market, and equilibrium in all markets will be reestablished at lower prices of money and capital.

When the economy is not in steady-state equilibrium, the fact that the cc schedule is upward-sloped does not imply that g is negative. If the aggregate stock of debt were positive, the demand for consumption goods would decrease with a fall in π_m, and the effects on the price of money and capital would be uncertain.

PROPOSITION 5-7   *In the steady state, an upward-slopping cc schedule implies a negative outstanding stock of government debt. Provided the aa curve crosses the cc curve from below, an increase in the expected rate of inflation lowers the equilibrium prices of both capital and money. In the short run, the effects of a fall in π_m and p_k and p_m are ambiguous.*

(D) EFFECTS OF AN INCREASE IN THE STOCK OF CAPITAL

A larger stock of capital will be held by wealth owners only at a lower price of capital for a given price of money, and so when the stock of capital rises, the aa schedule shifts down by Proposition 3–3. The effect of an increase in k on the consumption goods market is ambiguous. An increase in the capital stock raises the output of consumption goods, but it also increases income and wealth. There is no way to be certain whether or not the supply of consumption goods rises more than the demand for them; so we cannot say which way the cc schedule will move, if at all, or what the changes in the equilibrium prices of capital and money will be.

In the simple case of a proportional consumption function that omits wealth effects [equation (4.3)], the larger stock of capital definitely creates excess supply of consumption goods (see Proposition 4–3), requiring a higher p_k for each p_m in equilibrium. The cc schedule shifts upward from $c_0 c_0$ to $c_1 c_1$ in Figure 5–11. As can be seen from Figure 5–11, the results in this case of an increase in the stock of capital are an unambiguous increase in both p_m and p_k.

With consumption demand an increasing function of the price of consumption goods and a proportional consumption function, the increase in capital means that at each price of money the consumption market will clear only at a higher price of capital. For the assets markets to return to equilibrium, for any given p_k, p_m must rise. The increase in p_m, however, tends to frustrate the movement toward equilibrium in the consumption goods market by reinforcing the effect of the rise in k and increasing the excess supply. If the aa schedule is more steeply sloped than the cc schedule,

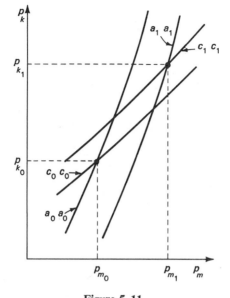

Figure 5–11

g, π_m, π_k, d, e, x are constant. k rises from k_0 to k_1.

the rise in the price of capital along with a rise in the price of money will ultimately succeed in restoring equilibrium in both markets.

PROPOSITION 5–8 *When demand for consumption goods is a decreasing function of the price of money, the effect of an increase in the stock of capital is uncertain. If the consumption function is proportional, or, more generally, if excess demand for consumption goods is a decreasing function of the stock of capital, the rise in k increases both the equilibrium prices of money and capital when the aa curve is more steeply sloped than the cc curve.*

(E) EFFECTS OF AN INCREASE IN THE STOCK OF GOVERNMENT DEBT

An increase in the stock of government debt (or a reduction in the net liability of the public to the government) usually raises the price of capital necessary to clear the assets markets for any given price of money (see Proposition 3–2) and so shifts the *aa* curve upward, in Figure 5–12, from $a_0 a_0$ to $a_1 a_1$. There are again both wealth and income effects in the consumption goods market; however, when g rises, the wealth effect is unambiguous. An increase in the stock of government debt or reduction in

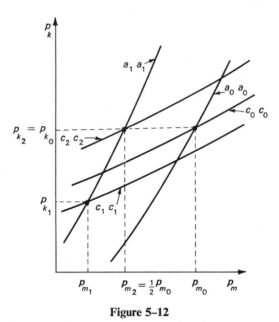

Figure 5–12

k, π_m, π_k, d, e, x are constant. g rises from g_0 to g_1.

the stock of private liabilities to the government raises the net stock of wealth in private hands, which in turn raises consumption demand. If $\pi_m > 0$, that is, the public expects deflation, an increase in g unambiguously raises disposable income; for in that situation either the base on which they are being paid a subsidy through deflation has risen or the base on which they are paying a tax through deflation (since they are the debtors) has fallen (see Chapter 4). If inflation is expected, that is, $\pi_m < 0$, an increase in g will lower disposable income for reasons symmetric to those just given.

When the income and wealth effects work together then demand clearly rises and the equilibrium of capital for any price of money falls in the consumption goods market; the cc curve shifts down from $c_0 c_0$ to $c_1 c_1$. As can be seen in Figure 5–12, the result is a lower equilibrium price of money and of capital.

When $\pi_m < 0$ and the wealth and income effects are in opposition, it is possible that an increase in g will lower the demand for commodities and that the cc curve will shift upward rather than downward. In the steady state an upward-sloping cc schedule implies a negative g. Such a cc schedule means that an increase in p_m reduces excess demand for consumption goods and thus that the following expression holds:

$$(5\text{–}1) \qquad \frac{\partial c}{\partial p_m} = \frac{\partial c}{\partial y}(d + \pi_m g) + \frac{\partial c}{\partial a} g < 0$$

$$\frac{\partial c}{\partial y} d + \left(\frac{\partial c}{\partial y} \pi_m + \frac{\partial c}{\partial a} \right) g < 0.$$

The change in excess demand produced by a change in g is

$$(5\text{–}2) \qquad \frac{\partial c}{\partial y} \pi_m p_m + \frac{\partial c}{\partial a} p_m = \left(\frac{\partial c}{\partial y} \pi_m + \frac{\partial c}{\partial a} \right) p_m .$$

To say that the income effect outweighs the wealth effect and causes the cc schedule to shift upward is to say that excess demand falls when g rises or that expression (5–2) is negative. Since $p_m \geq 0$, and in the steady state $g < 0$, it is clear from equation (5–1) that $(\partial c/\partial y)\pi_m + (\partial c/\partial a)\, p_m$ can be negative only when $d < 0$.

Let us postulate that when g is doubled the cc curve shifts upward to $c_2 c_2$ in Figure 5–12 and thus passes through the point $(\frac{1}{2} p_{m_0}, p_{k_0})$. Since it is the real value of the debt, $p_m g$, that affects the assets markets, we know that the $a_1 a_1$ schedule goes through that point. As in Section 5–7, this configuration can be an equilibrium only if $d = 0$; but we have just shown that in the long run, if the cc curve moves upward at all, it does so only when $d < 0$. When $d < 0$, the points along the $c_2 c_2$ schedule would be points of excess demand. Thus in the long run for $\pi_m < 0$, if an increase in g shifts the cc upward at all, the new equilibrium cc schedule must lie below $c_2 c_2$ in Figure 5–12. Therefore, even when the income effects of an increase in the stock of government debt outweigh the wealth effects, the result of the rise in g is a lower equilibrium price of both money and capital.

In the short run, we cannot infer the sign of g from the slope of the cc schedule and so cannot conclude what the sign of d must be for the cc schedule to shift upward. The effects of an increase in the stock of government debt in the short run on p_k and p_m are uncertain.

PROPOSITION 5–9 *In steady-state equilibrium, the effects of an increase in the stock of government debt are a lower equilibrium price of capital and money when the aa curve is the more steeply sloped one. In the short run, the increase in g has ambiguous effects on p_k and p_m.*

6 The Complete Model: Dynamics

6-1 Introduction

In Chapter 5 we showed how a general equilibrium is established in this model, determining the price level, the price of capital, the rate of interest, the outputs of the two sectors, and the wage and rental rates, given the stocks of capital and debt, the composition of the debt, the magnitudes of the government deficit and expenditures, and expectations about capital gains. Now we must ask what happens as time passes.

At each instant there must be a static equilibrium of the kind described in Chapter 5. The equilibrium prices of money and capital and other variables determined in a succession of instantaneous equilibria trace out paths as functions of time. The static equilibria are tied together by several requirements. For example, the path traced out by the stocks of capital and debt must have derivatives that satisfy the capital accumulation law [equation (2–23)] and the law of accumulation of government debt [equation (4–7)]. At each instant the total capital stock is the integral of past rates of investment and the aggregate stock of government debt is the integral of past government budget deficits.

While these relations are familiar, there may be still other restrictions on the paths of the variables. The expected price changes π_k and π_m may

87

depend in some way on the behavior of prices in the past. All of these restrictions must be met as the economy moves through time.

Our model is a system of differential equations. The paths for the variables must meet both instantaneous requirements and restrictions on their derivatives. Any path for all the variables that meets all the requirements is called a solution to the system.

We should make clear that the kind of dynamics we are talking about has nothing to do with the way the instantaneous prices reach their equilibrium values as of any moment of time. A great deal of what is usually called the dynamics of macroeconomic models is precisely the study of the process by which the system reaches its instantaneous equilibrium prices. The most common of the models of dynamic behavior assumes that a market secretary or auctioneer announces a vector of prices that suppliers and demanders use to calculate the quantities of each commodity or asset they want to buy or sell. If at a given set of prices, some or all of the markets fail to clear, the auctioneer is supposed to vary prices until no excess demand or supply remains. Since most macroeconomic models, like ours, are equilibrium models, it is assumed that no transactions actually take place until the equilibrium vector of prices is found and that all purchases and sales are made at the equilibrium prices.

It is by means of this *tâtonnement* process that the system is supposed to find its equilibrium at any moment. It is, therefore, clear that whether the system converges or does not converge to a set of equilibrium prices depends as much on the particular rules according to which the market secretary varies the vector of prices when markets fail to clear as it does on the characteristics of the demand and supply schedules in the system.

By *dynamics* in this book we *do not mean the study of any tâtonnement process*. We imagine that whatever *tâtonnement* there is takes no time at all or occurs out of time. At each instant all prices meet the complete equilibrium requirements, and we do not rule out any equilibrium vector of prices because under some rules of price adjustment in the underlying *tâtonnement* process the system would not converge to this equilibrium vector. What we are interested in is where the succession of instantaneous equilibria will lead the economy as time passes. As pointed out in Chapter 2, a characteristic long-run outcome is for the economy to settle down to some constant stock of capital per head. We shall most often study solution paths that lead to this outcome in the long run. What we are analyzing is the interaction of government policy, private demand and supply of all commodities, and the accumulation of capital over the whole history of an economy that is at each instant in equilibrium and in which the investment and deficit of each instant affect the initial stocks of capital and debt on which the next instant's equilibrium is based.

6–2   The Model

The requirements of instantaneous equilibrium are that all markets clear as of any moment of time. The prices of money and capital and the rate of interest should be such at every instant that the markets for bonds, capital, money, and consumption goods clear. To determine the equilibrium prices of money and capital and the equilibrium rate of interest, we need three independent equations.

We know that if any two of the assets markets clear, the third one will also clear. In particular, if the money and capital markets are in equilibrium, the bond market is also in equilibrium:

$$(6\text{–}1) \qquad kp_k = J\left(kp_k + gp_m, \; q(k,\, p_k), \; \pi_m, \; i + \pi_m, \; \frac{r(p_k)}{p_k} + \pi_k \right)$$

$$(6\text{–}2) \quad (1/x)gp_m = L\left(kp_k + gp_m, \; q(k,\, p_k), \; \pi_m, \; i + \pi_m, \; \frac{r(p_k)}{p_k} + \pi_k \right).$$

We see that the equilibrium conditions in the markets for assets provide only two of the three independent relationships that are necessary to determine the market clearing triplet $(p_m,\, p_k,\, i)$. The third of these independent equations is the equilibrium condition in the consumption market.

$$(6\text{–}3) \quad q_c(k,\, p_k) - e = c(kp_k + gp_m, \; q(k,\, p_k) + (d + \pi_m g)p_m - e + \pi_k kp_k).$$

Note that while we can eliminate any of the assets markets clearing equations, we cannot eliminate the consumption market clearing equation. This is because there are two different types of decisions in this economy, decisions about stocks and decisions about flows. The consumption market equilibrium is a flow equilibrium, while the assets markets equilibrate the demand and supply for stocks. Two separate budget constraints are involved. First, the total demand for assets equals total wealth. This allows us to eliminate one of the assets markets equations. The second budget constraint is that desired consumption and the value of the desired savings must add up to total income.

Our model separates stock decisions and flow decisions very sharply. The fact that wealth owners are content to hold existing stocks of assets is no guarantee that supply and demand for flows of newly produced consumption goods are equal. We might contrast this with models where consumers decide simultaneously the whole path of their assets holdings and consumption flows on the basis of certain knowledge of all future prices. In these models (which might be called intertemporal equilibrium models in contrast to our instantaneous equilibrium model) stock and flow decisions are two different ways of looking at the same consumption path. In intertemporal equilibrium models one maximizing decision is made at one instant that determines the whole future path of consumption and assets holdings, while in our model consumers make a sequence of short-run decisions based on possibly wrong guesses about the future. We must distinguish between stock and flow decisions and guarantee that both kinds of markets will clear. We therefore need the consumption market clearing equation: it cannot be eliminated.

Having determined the equilibrium values of p_m, p_k, and i as functions of the historically given values of k and g, the expected rate of capital gains of money and capital, π_m and π_k, and the policy variables d, e, and x, we must now add to dynamic restrictions on the paths of k and g that hold at any moment of time.

$$(6\text{–}4) \qquad \qquad \dot{k} = q_I(k, p_k) - nk$$

$$(6\text{–}5) \qquad \qquad \dot{g} = d - ng.$$

Equations (6–1) through (6–5) are the basic five equations of our model. Any path for the ten variables $(g, k, p_m, p_k, i, \pi_m, \pi_k, d, e, x)$ that satisfies these five equations is a solution. It represents a possible course of development for the economy.

Sometimes we choose to present the static equations (6–1) through (6–3) in a slightly different form. Given x, g, k, π_m, and π_k, we can think of p_k and i as being determined for any p_m in the assets markets (assuming that the assets markets equations are invertible). Corresponding to this view we think of p_m as being determined for each p_k in the consumption market given g, k, π_m, π_k, d, and e. These are the aa and cc schedules we have used before, and the final equilibrium involves a (p_m, p_k) pair that is mutually consistent. The basic equations of our model can then be written in the following form:

(1) $\dot{k} = q_I(k, p_k) - nk$

(2) $\dot{g} = d - ng$

(3) $p_k = \Phi(gp_m, k, \pi_m, \pi_k, x)$

(4) $i = \Psi(gp_m, k, \pi_m, \pi_k, x)$

(5) $q_C(k, p_k) - e = c(kp_k + gp_m, q(k, p_k) + (d + \pi_m g)p_m - e + \pi_k k p_k)$

Equation **(3)** is the expression underlying the *aa* schedule as presented in Chapter 3. Equation **(5)** underlies the *cc* schedule, which was discussed in Chapter 4. Equation **(4)** determines the equilibrium rate of interest that corresponds to any point on the *aa* schedule. That is, equations **(3)** and **(5)** determine the equilibrium p_m and p_k (graphically this is the intersection of the *aa* and *cc* schedules), while equation **(4)** determines the equilibrium rate of interest that corresponds to that intersection.

6-3 The Theory of Investment

The theory we have given so far has been couched in the language of general equilibrium. This obscures some of the relationships of our model to other macroeconomic models. In particular the reader may wonder about the "investment function" or "theory of investment" implied by our model.

The investment process in our model can be understood by looking at the two parts of Figure 6-1. In Figure 6-1a we show the supply and de-

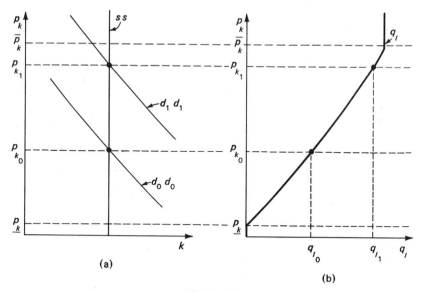

(a)

(b)

Figure 6-1

(a) p_m, π_m, π_k are constant. i falls from i_0 to i_1. (b) k is constant.

mand for capital as a stock. For a given p_m, π_m, and i, this depends on
p_k and is higher the lower is p_k because a lower p_k produces a higher rate
of return to capital.

In Figure 6–1b we plot the supply curve of new investment, which will
be an increasing function of p_k. This is exactly the q_I function we studied
in Chapter 2. The price of capital is determined by the intersection of the
stock supply and demand curves in Figure 6–1a and the rate of investment
by the flow supply schedule of Figure 6–1b. If the interest rate fell and
nothing else changed, the stock demand curve in Figure 6–1a would rise
to $d_1 d_1$ and the higher price of capital, p_{k_1}, would induce a larger flow of
investment, q_{I_1}.

To understand the general spirit of other investment theories, consider
Figure 6–2. This time we have drawn the supply schedule of new investment on the hypothesis that the capital intensities in the two sectors are
the same, so that the model reduces to the one-sector model. Since the
transformation curve is a straight line, only one p_k^* is consistent with production of both investment and consumption. Any lower p_k^* will imply
zero investment and all resources devoted to consumption; any higher
p_k will draw all resources into the investment sector. If $p_k = p_k^*$, producers
will be indifferent between producing consumption and investment goods.

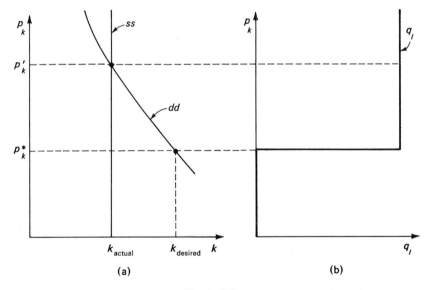

Figure 6–2

(a) i, p_m, π_m, π_k are constant. (b) k is constant.

For the theorist a problem arises if the stock demand for capital curve in Figure 6-2a intersects the stock supply of capital at a p'_k different from p^*_k. It is impossible to achieve consumption market equilibrium at any p_k different from p^*_k because at a higher p_k there will be zero supply of consumption goods and at a lower p_k all the resources of the economy will be drawn into the consumption sector and if there is any saving, there will be excess supply of consumption goods. This leads some theorists to distinguish a *desired* stock of capital, which is the stock that would clear the capital market at p^*_k. Firms invest, according to this view, in order to eliminate the discrepancy between the desired and actual stocks of capital or to prevent it from arising. The rate of investment is limited by rising firm marginal costs to investment, which gives rise to a *distributed lag* investment function that spreads the investment required to eliminate the discrepancy over time.

In considering these two accounts we can see certain characteristic differences. The cost of adjustment view emphasizes equilibrium between a flow demand for investment and a flow supply. Our view emphasizes equilibrium between a stock demand for capital and a stock supply. The cost of adjustment theory depends on rising costs to the individual investing firm to limit and determine the rate of investment, while our model depends on rising costs to the whole economy as resources are shifted to the investment sector. In addition, the cost of adjustment model focuses very strongly on the firm and attributes many of the portfolio decisions about the stock demand for capital to the firm itself. This is not very different from our model since firms may be viewed as the agents of the ultimate wealth owners in holding capital.

We would like to add parenthetically that we believe that the relative importance of the two sets of forces in determining the rate of investment in a real economy is a question that can only be answered empirically. So far as we know, no econometric study has embodied the ideas of our model in a way that clearly measures their importance.

Most theories of investment and most macroeconomic models have assumed an inverse relationship between the rate of interest and the rate of investment. In our model this relationship may not exist. It is true that, other things equal, an increase in the rate of interest lowers the demand for capital on the part of wealth owners, decreasing, thereby, the equilibrium price of capital and thus lowering the level of output of investment goods. Other things, however, are not usually equal. The rate of interest itself is an endogenous variable of the system. For the rate of interest to change, some other variable must have changed, and the change in this variable may have increased the demand for capital; this increase may even outweigh the depressing effect on the demand for capital that resulted from the rise in the rate of interest.

To show that no consistent relationship need exist between the rate of interest and level of investment, consider the effects of a tighter fiscal policy, which may result from a lower deficit or lower government expenditures, while the composition of the debt does not change. A tighter fiscal policy with a constant x shifts the cc schedule upward, while the aa schedule does not move. The result is a higher price of money and, more important from the point of view of the level of investment, a higher price of capital. As a result of this, the level of investment rises. What has happened to the rate of interest? The answer is that we do not know: it may have increased, decreased, or remained constant. In Chapter 3, we showed that an increase in the real stock of government debt has an ambiguous effect on the equilibrium rate of interest; and thus the increase in the real stock of debt that results from the rise in the price of money may have raised or lowered the equilibrium rate of interest.

Given the level of technology and the stock of capital that is a result of past investment, the only variable in our model that is unequivocally related to the level of investment is the price of capital goods. When the price of capital is high, the level of investment is also high; if the price of capital is low, investment is low. The higher the relative price of capital goods, the larger will be the share of the economy's total resources that producers will find it profitable to allocate to the production of investment goods.

6–4 Stock-Flow Equilibrium

After the producers' equilibrium level of output in the investment goods sector is determined, it is natural to ask whether wealth owners will absorb this real capital into their portfolios at the equilibrium prices and interest rate. We can ask the same question about the government deficit, which increases the stock of government debt. The fact that actual and desired stocks of capital, money, and bonds are equal at certain prices does not guarantee that people will be content to absorb any given increases in the stocks, even though the demand and supply of consumption goods are equal. If people are not content to absorb the given additions, how will the new supplies of capital and other assets find room in private portfolios?

To begin with, we note that the private sector income budget constraint requires that private disposable income equal the private demand for consumption goods plus the value of desired additions to assets holdings:

$$(6\text{-}6) \qquad q + z p_m = c^d + \frac{\dot{K}^d}{N} p_k + \frac{\dot{G}^d}{N} p_m,$$

where $G = Ng$ is the total debt and z is the per-capita nominal net transfers to the private sector, including interest on government bonds. By desired additions to assets holdings we mean the amounts of new money, bonds, and capital that would be absorbed in portfolios at current levels of p_m, p_k, and i.

The budget deficit is in turn equal to net transfers plus government expenditures,

$$(6\text{-}7) \qquad d p_m = z p_m + e,$$

and we know that

$$(6\text{-}8) \qquad q = q_c + p_k q_I = q_c + \frac{\dot{K}^s}{N} p_k.$$

Using these two facts in equation (6–6), we obtain

$$(6\text{-}9) \qquad \frac{\dot{K}^s}{N} p_k + q_c - e + d p_m = c^d + \frac{\dot{G}^d}{N} p_m + \frac{\dot{K}^d}{N} p_k.$$

Since the deficit is equal to the rate of increase in the government debt, we can write (6–9) as

$$(6\text{-}10) \qquad \frac{\dot{K}^s}{N} p_k + \frac{\dot{G}^s}{N} p_m + q_c - e = c^d + \frac{\dot{K}^d}{N} p_k + \frac{\dot{G}^d}{N} p_m.$$

When the consumption market clears, $q_c - e$ is equal to c^d, so that we get the equality of total supply of new assets and total desired acquisitions:

$$(6\text{-}11) \qquad \frac{\dot{K}^s}{N} p_k + \frac{\dot{G}^s}{N} p_m = \frac{\dot{K}^d}{N} p_k + \frac{\dot{G}^d}{N} p_m.$$

If we add the capital gains terms to both sides of (6–6), we see that consumption market equilibrium implies that desired and actual savings are equal. Rewriting (6–11), we have

$$(6\text{-}12) \qquad p_k \left(q_I - \frac{\dot{K}^d}{N} \right) = p_m \left(\frac{\dot{G}^d}{N} - d \right) = p_m \left(\frac{\dot{G}^d}{N} - \frac{\dot{G}^s}{N} \right).$$

This indicates that it is possible for individuals to be content to hold existing stocks of capital and debt, to purchase the quantities of consumption goods desired, and therefore to be accumulating in total the value of assets they wish to accumulate and at the same time at the current equilibrium prices to desire to add to their holdings of assets in proportions that are different from the rates at which the stocks of assets are increasing. From (6–12), we see that if the government is increasing the supply of debt more rapidly than wealth holders wish to accumulate it at the current prices, wealth holders will be accumulating capital more slowly than they wish to: a flow excess supply of debt is accompanied by a flow excess demand for capital.

In fact, even if $\dot{G}^d/N = d$, so that wealth holders are accumulating just the amounts of capital and debt that they desire, they may not be accumulating debt in the desired proportions. We have

$$\frac{\dot{G}^d}{N} = \frac{\dot{M}^d}{N} + \frac{\dot{B}^d}{N}$$

and

$$d = \frac{\dot{G}^s}{N} = \frac{\dot{M}^s}{N} + \frac{\dot{B}^s}{N}$$

and the equality of $\dot{G}^d/N$ and d does not imply that the actual rate of change of the quantities of money and bonds are equal to desired rates of change.

The results of any difference between actual and desired rates of change of assets holdings will clearly be changes in the price of capital (and its rate of return), the price of money, and the interest rate over time. If we insist on a complete dynamic model in which the assets markets are always in equilibrium, the supply of capital at every instant is the integral of past investment, and the supply of debt is the integral of past deficit, then the three variables p_k, p_m, and i must follow paths that allow for the voluntary absorption of new capital and new debt. Prices may be changing, but at every instant all markets are in equilibrium and there is a determinate rate of investment.

The growth of portfolios and the absorption of capital and debt by saving are dynamic processes that can be studied only through time and that generally involve changes in the prices of capital and money and the interest rate. The fact that prices have to change to induce wealth owners to hold the new supplies of assets raises the question of expectations. As the economy moves through its succession of instantaneous equilibria, the actual changes in prices will influence expectations about future price changes. There are three popular versions of this process: *static expectations*, *adaptive expectations*, and *perfect foresight*.

Perfect foresight requires that $\pi_m = \dot{p}_m/p_m$ and $\pi_k = \dot{p}_k/p_k$ at each moment on the whole path. If in addition we were to specify equations describing the time paths of the policy variables d, x, and e, we would have a complete system of ten equations in ten unknowns, determining fully the time path of the economy.

While the assumption of perfect foresight in problems of intertemporal economics seems to be a natural extension of the assumption of perfect information usually made in static equilibrium models, it imposes severe restrictions on the system and its path. First, it rules out all notions of uncertainty and portfolio diversification; second, it requires assumptions about information that are unlikely to be met in reality; and, third, and most important, it leaves almost no room for discretionary government policy. A strong condition on government policy that is consistent with perfect foresight is that future government policy is known and therefore unalterable. In this case, the complete paths for policy variables are determined from time zero, and no further change can occur without violating the perfect foresight assumption.

Government discretionary policies are consistent with perfect foresight when they do not induce regrets in economic agents. But even with this weaker condition, most of the policies considered in the analysis of Chapter 5, which seems to be types of policy most governments use to control aggregate demand and its composition, would be excluded because they do induce regrets.

In the other models of expectation formation, where actual price changes influence expected price changes either not at all or with a lag, there will not be an intertemporal competitive equilibrium but only a succession of instantaneous equilibria. There is a larger sphere for discretionary government policy and the set of solution paths becomes wider. There will also be regrets, which imply that individuals and firms are not in intertemporal equilibria. They will be in instantaneous equilibrium given their imperfect information about the future.

It seems to us, then, that the requirement of intertemporal competitive equilibrium is very strong and requires assumptions about information that are unlikely to be met in reality. There seems to be a place for a theory that allows for a lack of intertemporal equilibrium while insisting on instantaneous equilibrium.

Until Chapter 14, we assume that expectations about the price of capital are *static*, that is, people expect whatever price of capital occurs to continue indefinitely. π_k is zero on the basis of this hypothesis, not a very plausible circumstance except in states of steady growth. We make the assumption that $\pi_k = 0$ mostly for pedagogic reasons—so that we can use diagrammatic presentations to study relatively difficult issues. Realizing the limitations that this assumption imposes on our model, we therefore remove it in Chapter 14, where we study some models of the economy's behavior when expectations about the price of capital are based on the past behavior of the price of capital, using a model that allows for errors and attempts to correct errors on the basis of experience.

For most of the book we assume that one of the government policy goals is to maintain a stable price level and that the government, by using monetary and fiscal policy tools, enforces a path on which p_m is constant over time. Since p_m does not change, it is then reasonable to assume that expectations are static, in the sense that π_m is equal to zero. Actually, the government may have a target rate of inflation that is different from zero. If it ensures that the path followed by p_m is one on which the rate of inflation is constant and it announces this target rate to the public, it is reasonable to assume that π_m will be equal to the negative of the target, constant rate of inflation. Governments obviously do not always succeed in maintaining constant target rates of inflation over time, and in Chapter 13 we study the economy's behavior when expectations about the rate of inflation are formed on the basis of information that economic agents can find in the past behavior of the system. This model will allow for error, regrets, and subsequent attempts to correct the errors by learning from experience.

In any case, π_m and π_k have to come from somewhere. They may be exogenously given (as in the static expectations case in which they are assumed to be zero) or determined by the government's announcement of its intentions to enforce some price behavior, or derived from past behavior of the economy. What is important is that this adds two more equations to the five already stated in the basic model. The precise form of these equations will clearly depend on the particular expectations formation model that we are considering.

6–5   Tools and Goals

In the system of seven equations, (6–1) through (6–5) and the two expectations equations (one for π_m and one for π_k), we have ten variables: g, k, p_m, p_k, i, π_m, π_k, d, e, and x. The last three, the deficit, the expenditures, and the composition of the government debt, are government policy tools.

Since we have ten variables and only seven restrictions on their paths, there will be, in general, many different solutions to the system. In fact, we can choose arbitrary paths for the government policy tools and the other variables will be forced through the equilibrium conditions and the restriction on the paths of g, k, π_m, and π_k to follow consistent trajectories. We can make no statement about properties of the model until it is more completely specified. We are free to add three more restrictions on the path as long as these restrictions do not contradict any of the existing conditions. For example, we cannot specify that along the economy's path the price of capital, the price of money, and the rate of interest remain constant over time. In general the capital stock and the stock of debt will be changing over time if the price of money is constant, and changes in the composition of the debt will be able to maintain a constant price of capital or a constant rate of interest but not both simultaneously. Except for states of steady growth, paths on which p_m, p_k, and i are constant are inconsistent with instantaneous equilibrium along the path, one of the requirements of our model. *Except for cases of this kind we can add any three restrictions we choose.*

The new restrictions can be thought of as *goals* of government policy. There are a large number of goals that might be pursued: price stability, a target price of capital to achieve a given rate of growth in the short run, a target interest rate for balance of payments purposes, or a good allocation between private and public consumption. It may also be interesting to study economies in which one or more of the policy tools are inactive, so that the deficit, say, is fixed at some level, or open market policy is passive. Any combination of three of these goals, as long as they are consistent, can be added to the basic model to fill it out. After this is done, it is possible to study the evolution of the economy over time when it sticks to whatever rules have been assigned.

We have an enormous variety of models to study. We analyze in Part II a group of simpler versions, which are used to study some classic propositions about the short-run and long-run effects of open market purchases, government budget deficits, expenditures, levies on the national debt, and related problems.

In Part III, we consider a selection of models that involve current issues in policy and theory: the effects of perfectly and imperfectly anticipated inflations, optimal monetary and fiscal policies, and international capital flows. These models are more complicated but probably more interesting.

Readers, we hope, will come to be able to adapt the model to situations that they may be particularly interested in but that we do not discuss. There is a standing invitation to anyone to roll his own model out of the fixings we have provided.

Dynamic Exercises

Price Stabilization Through
Monetary Policy

7–1 Introduction

In this chapter we analyze the behavior of an economy when fiscal policy is passive and the government uses its monetary tools to maintain stable prices. The central monetary authority continuously performs operations in the open market that change the composition of the outstanding stock of government debt so as to make the assets markets equilibrium price of capital consistent with the price of capital that will clear the consumption goods markets at a constant price level. To make the exercises of this chapter and Chapters 8 and 9 more straightforward and to obtain clear-cut results for illustrative purposes, we use the proportional consumption function [equation (4–3)].

To begin the analysis, it is necessary first to define what we mean by a passive fiscal policy. A fiscal policy that results in an ever-increasing or ever-decreasing nominal per-capital stock of government debt will not be compatible with the economy reaching a steady state equilibrium with stable prices. For prices to be stable on a steady-state growth path, the nominal stock of debt has to grow at the economy's rate of expansion, n, so that the per-capita nominal stock of debt, g, will be constant. Recall from Section 5–7 that any change in g disturbs equilibrium in both the assets and

103

consumption goods markets. A passive fiscal policy that is consistent with steady-state stable prices is one in which the government fixes the scale of its expenditures at some constant level $e = e^*$ and runs a constant budget deficit over time so that $d = d^*$. This is one regime that is consistent with a constant g in the steady state but there are others as well.

To clarify the nature of this policy, we must look back to the government budget constraint as presented in equation (4–6), which together with equation (4–5) gives the following equation:

$$(7\text{--}1) \qquad e^* + z p_m^* = d^* p_m^*.$$

Since

$$(7\text{--}2) \qquad z p_m^* = i b p_m^* + v p_m^* - t p_m^*$$

and $b = [1 - (1/x)]g$,

$$(7\text{--}3) \qquad \{ig[1 - (1/x)] + v - t\} p_m^* + e^* = d^* p_m^*$$

It follows that, having fixed e and d, taxes or transfers will have to vary to provide the government with the revenue required to meet its outlays. With e and d constant, a change in k or p_k affects the real value of government expenditures and requires a change in t or v; or, alternatively, changes in x, g, or i affect the interest cost of the government debt and also require a change in taxes or transfers so that the government budget constraint is satisfied. We describe this type of fiscal policy as passive, but except on the steady-state growth path, transfers minus taxes will be continuously changing so that equation (7–3) is always satisfied.

Any definition of a passive fiscal policy will be somewhat arbitrary. It is possible to hold any three of the four variables e, d, v, and t constant, letting the other vary to satisfy (7–3). One advantage of choosing d to be constant is that it is the link between the creation of new government debt and consumption market equilibrium. If d is constant, g will eventually also be constant, which substantially simplifies matters.

7–2 The Model

In the case of a proportional consumption function, demand for commodities is

$$c^d = (1 - s)y = (1 - s)[q + (d + \pi_m g)p_m - e].$$

Supply is still

$$c^s = q_C(k, p_k) - e.$$

The basic equations of our model are, therefore,

(7–4) $$\dot{k} = q_I(k, p_k) - nk \qquad \text{(1)}$$

(7–5) $$\dot{g} = d - ng \qquad \text{(2)}$$

(7–6) $$p_k = \Phi(gp_m, k, \pi_m, x) \qquad \text{(3)}$$

(7–7) $$i = \Psi(gp_m, k, \pi_m, x) \qquad \text{(4)}$$

(7–8) $$q_C(k, p_k) - e = (1 - s)[q + (d + \pi_m g)p_m - e]. \qquad \text{(5)}$$

The government stabilization policy is aimed at maintaining a constant price of money. This policy goal can be stated as

(7–9) $$p_m = p_m^*.$$

If the price level is constant over time, it is reasonable to assume that people do not expect the price level to change, so that

(7–10) $$\pi_m = 0.$$

The fixing of government expenditures at some constant level gives us an additional equation:

(7–11) $$e = e^*.$$

The deficit is also constant over time:

(7–12) $$d = d^*.$$

Equations (7–4) through (7–12) are a system of nine equations in nine unknowns, g, k, p_m, p_k, i, π_m, d, e, and x, that completely describe the growth path of the economy when aggregate demand is stabilized through the use of monetary policy.

7–3 Static Analysis

At any moment of time, the stock of capital depends on past accumulation. Given the fixed scale of government expenditures and budget deficit, the price of capital that is consistent with a constant price of money p_m^* is then determined by the consumption goods market equilibrium condition, equation (7–8), which now can be written as

$$(7\text{–}13) \qquad q_c(k, p_k) - e^* = (1 - s)[q(k, p_k) + d^* p_m^* - e^*].$$

Given a stock of capital k, government expenditures e^*, and a deficit d^*, the consumption goods market equilibrium price of capital is independent of x and equal to some p_{k_0}, as shown by the vertical cc line in Figure 7–1.

On the other hand, given the stock of capital and the aggregate stock of debt, which is a result of past deficits, the price of capital that clears the assets markets for $p_m = p_m^*$ is a function of the composition of the government debt. According to Proposition 3–1, the higher the ratio of debt to money, the lower the price of capital that clears the assets markets for a given $p_m = p_m^*$. The combinations of (p_k, x) that clear the assets markets for given g, p_m, and k are shown by the aa line in Figure 7–1. Given k, g, p_m, d, and e, Figure 7–1 determines the price of capital that clears the consumption and assets markets and the composition of the government debt that is necessary to attain this p_k.

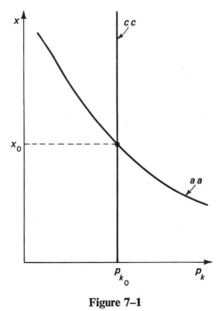

Figure 7–1

g, k, p_m, π_m, π_k, d, e are constant.

What is the effect of a change in the aggregate stocks of capital and debt on the equilibrium price of capital and on the composition of the debt required to maintain a stable price level?

By Proposition 3–2 we know that an increase in the aggregate stock of debt increases the price of capital that equilibrates the assets markets. This means that as g rises, the aa schedule shifts rightward from $a_0 a_0$ to $a_1 a_1$, as shown in Figure 7–2. Since a change in the aggregate stock of debt with an unchanged deficit does not affect the demand for consumption as long as $\pi_m = 0$ and consumption demand does not depend on wealth, the cc schedule is not affected. The increase in g results in an unchanged price of capital and a higher ratio of debt to money, the latter being necessary to counteract the inflationary effect of an increase in the aggregate stock of debt in the assets markets. When g rises, the government has to make an open market sale to maintain a constant equilibrium price of capital in the assets markets.

An increase in the aggregate stock of capital affects both the consumption market and the assets markets. In Proposition 4–3 we have shown, on the hypothesis of a proportional consumption function, that an increase in k creates excess supply in the consumption goods market and raises the consumption goods market equilibrium price of capital The cc schedule

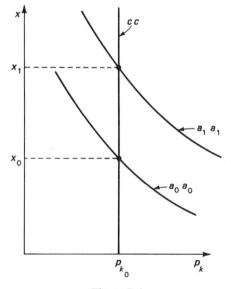

Figure 7–2

$k, p_m, \pi_m, \pi_k, d, e$ are constant. g rises from g_0 to g_1.

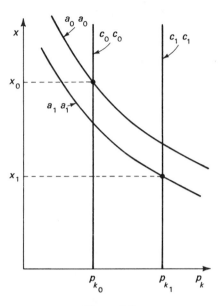

Figure 7–3

$g, p_m, \pi_m, \pi_k, d, e$ are constant. k rises from k_0 to k_1.

shifts rightward from $c_0 c_0$ to $c_1 c_1$ as k rises, as shown in Figure 7–3. On the other hand, from Proposition 3–3, we know that given the supply of other assets, wealth owners will hold a higher stock of capital in their portfolios only if the price of capital falls. The aa schedule shifts leftward as a result of the increase in the stock of capital from $a_0 a_0$ to $a_1 a_1$, as shown in Figure 7–3. It follows from Figure 7–3 that the increase in the stock of capital raises the equilibrium price of capital and lowers the equilibrium ratio of debt to money. In other words, since the consumption goods markets equilibrium p_k rises and the assets markets equilibrium p_k would fall in the absence of an open market operation, a reconciliation of the two is necessary to ensure that the consumption goods market p_k also clears the assets markets at p_m^*. An easy monetary policy (lower x) increases p_k in the assets markets so that this p_k is consistent with the higher equilibrium price of capital in the consumption goods market. An open market purchase is required for the ratio of debt to money to fall from x_0 to x_1, as shown in Figure 7–3.

The dynamic analysis of this model is simply the description of a sequence of short-run solutions of the sort described here, and this is the topic of Section 7–4.

7-4   Dynamic Analysis

In Section 7-3 we showed that with the per-capita deficit and scale of government expenditures fixed at d^* and e^*, and the government committed to a monetary policy that maintains a stable price level through time so that $p_m = p_m^*$ and $\pi_m = 0$, the equilibrium price of capital, as indicated by the consumption goods market clearing equation, is a function only of the aggregate stock of capital, given at any moment of time by past accumulation. We saw that the price of capital is, in fact, an increasing function of the capital stock.

In Figure 7-4 we plot the cc schedule, which shows the price of capital goods that clears the consumption goods market for each value of k. The cc schedule is the locus of pairs (k, p_k) for which equation (7-8) is satisfied. The cc schedule cannot start from the origin when d is positive because when $k = 0$ the output of consumption goods is zero but their demand is $(1 - s)d^*p_m^* > 0$. The schedule therefore starts at some positive value of k. Since a change in the price of capital does not affect q_C and q when the economy is specialized to the production of consumption goods, the cc schedule is vertical as long as it is in the region below the p_k line. Finally, in the region of nonspecialization, the slope of the cc line is positive because, as we have shown in Chapter 4, the increase in k creates excess

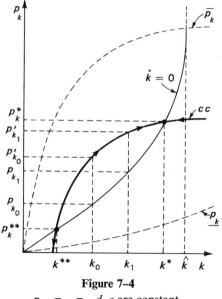

Figure 7-4

p_m, π_m, π_k, d, e are constant.

supply in the consumption goods market. If the price level is to remain constant, the excess supply has to be eliminated by a rise in p_k.

That the slope of the cc schedule is positive can be shown by rewriting the consumption goods market clearing equation as

$$sq_C - e^* = (1 - s)(q_I p_k + d^* p_m^* - e^*)$$

and differentiating this equation with respect to k and p_k. Thus we have

$$\left.\frac{\partial p_k}{\partial k}\right|_{cc} = \frac{(1 - s)p_k(\partial q_I/\partial k) - s(\partial q_C/\partial k)}{s(\partial q_C/\partial p_k) - (1 - s)[q_I + p_k(\partial q_I/\partial p_k)]} > 0.$$

In Figure 7–4 we also plot the $\dot{k} = 0$ schedule of Figure 2–7. As shown in Chapter 2, this line indicates the price of capital that, given any stock of capital k, will induce a level of output in the investment goods sector just sufficient to maintain a constant ratio of capital to labor through time. The cc schedule indicates the price of capital that will prevail in the market for any given capital stock, and the $\dot{k} = 0$ schedule indicates the price that has to prevail for the capital stock to remain unchanged over time. Since the consumption market always clears, we would only observe (k, p_k) pairs that are on the cc schedule. As time passes, the economy moves along the cc schedule.

Given, for example, a stock of capital $k = k_0$, we find that the price of capital goods p'_{k_0} that clears the consumption goods market is higher than the price of capital p_{k_0} for which $\dot{k} = 0$. This means that when $k = k_0$ the rate of change in the ratio of capital to labor is positive because investment is higher than nk. This is indicated by the arrow pointing east on the cc schedule. As time goes on, the capital stock increases, say from k_0 to k_1. At k_1 the equilibrium price of capital as indicated by the cc line is p'_{k_1}, while the price of capital for which $\dot{k} = 0$ is p_{k_1}. This means that at k_1 the rate of change in the ratio of capital to labor is still positive, and capital will further accumulate until k reaches the value k^*, for which the equilibrium market price of capital and the p_k required for $\dot{k} = 0$ are equal.

Since at any point to the right of k^* the rate of change in k is negative, while at any point between k^{**} and k^* this rate of change is positive, given any initial stock of capital $k(0)$ such that $k(0) > k^{**}$, the system will approach a state of steady growth with constant prices and a ratio of capital to labor of k^*. For any $k(0) < k^{**}$, the economy will continuously shrink to lower and lower capital stocks, until there is no positive price p_k at which the consumption goods market can clear. We have two equilibrium stocks of capital that determine a consumption market clearing price of capital that also makes $\dot{k} = 0$, but only one of them is stable.

We leave it to the reader to verify that cases may exist in which there is no steady-state value of k because the cc and $\dot{k} = 0$ schedules do not intersect; that only one steady state may exist, with this value of k stable to the right and unstable to the left (this is the case of tangency of the cc and $\dot{k} = 0$ schedules); and, finally, that more than one stable steady-state capital stock may exist when there are multiple intersections of the cc and $\dot{k} = 0$ lines. In what follows we analyze only the case where a stable steady state exists.

The behavior of the per-capita stock of debt over time is straightforward. Having fixed the budget deficit at the level d^*, from equation (7–5) we have

$$(7\text{--}14) \qquad\qquad \dot{g} = d^* - ng$$

That is, the rate of change in the per-capita stock of debt is a function only of the deficit, d^* and the labor force growth rate, n — both constants — and the value that g takes at any moment. In Figure 7–5, we represent the rate of change in g as a function of these variables. It follows from Figure 7–5 that since at any point to the left of g^* the actual deficit d^* is higher than the deficit ng required to maintain a stable g over time, that is, $d^* - ng > 0$, the stock of debt will be growing. To the left of g^* the actual deficit is

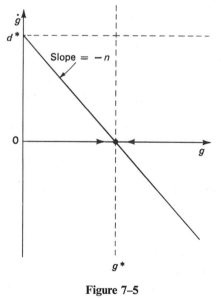

Figure 7–5
d^* is constant.

smaller than ng and hence $\dot{g} < 0$. This means that with a constant deficit the per-capita stock of debt will in the long run approach a steady-state value g^*, which is determined only by the size of the deficit and the long-run growth rate and is independent of the initial value of g.

Let us now consider the effects of a discrete change in the variables that we have assumed constant and that are not involved in the stabilization process, d and e, on the economy's short-run rate of growth and its steady state stock of capital.

7–5   Effects of a Decrease in the Deficit with a Constant Scale of Expenditures

We shall begin with d. To study the effects of a decrease in the deficit from d_0 to d_1 on the economy's growth rate in the short run, we must consider the effect of a cut in the budget deficit on the consumption goods market equilibrium price of capital. As shown in Chapter 4, a decrease in the deficit that results from a tax increase with unchanged government expenditures lowers private disposable income and reduces the demand for consumption goods. To eliminate the resulting excess supply in the consumption goods market, the price of capital has to rise, both to increase income and demand and to lower output in the consumption goods sector. This is indicated by an upward shift of the cc schedule from $c_0 c_0$ to $c_1 c_1$, as in Figure 7–6.

Since d does not enter equation (7–4), the decrease in the budget deficit does not affect the price of capital which exactly maintains a given k, and the $\dot{k} = 0$ schedule does not shift with the change in d. The initial increase in the market price of capital requires a sudden jump from the old equilibrium to the new $c_1 c_1$ schedule at the same k_0^* and then a gradual movement along the $c_1 c_1$ schedule to the new equilibrium. From Figure 7–6, we can see that the decrease in the deficit raises the long-run capital intensity; since the equilibrium price of capital rises for all values of k, at k_0^* the rate of change in the ratio of capital to labor is now positive, and the long-run per-capita capital stock increases to k_1^*. As the economy moves from one state to another, it always stays on the cc schedule because the consumption market must clear at every instant.

The effect of the decrease in the deficit on the aggregate stock of debt is straightforward. A decrease in the deficit lowers the rate of increase in the nominal stock of debt. Given an unchanged rate of population growth, the rate of change in the per-capita stock of debt at g_0^* becomes negative, and the economy will end up with a lower long-run per-capita stock of govern-

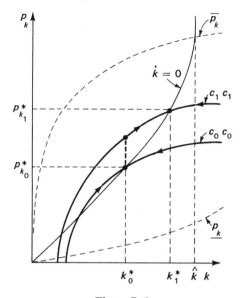

Figure 7–6

p_m, π_m, π_k, e are constant. d falls from d_0 to d_1.

ment debt, as shown in Figure 7–7. A decrease in the deficit from d_0^* to d_1^* shifts the $\dot{g}$ line downward for any given g and hence reduces the long-run stock of debt from g_0^* to g_1^*.

We therefore find that the decrease in the deficit lowers the long-run aggregate stock of debt and increases the long-run capital intensity. When monetary policy is used to stabilize the price level, a lower long-run stock of debt is associated with a higher long-run stock of capital.

To determine the behavior of other variables in the system, we must consider the equilibrium conditions in the assets markets and the action that the government must take to achieve its policy objective of stable prices. The decrease in the government deficit lowers aggregate demand and raises the price of capital that clears the consumption goods market for any given price of money. For the assets markets to clear at the higher price of capital, the government will have to perform an open market purchase, which, according to Proposition 3–1, increases the assets markets price of capital and lowers the equilibrium rate of interest. The higher price of capital in the assets markets in turn raises the rate of capital accumulation, thereby generating further reactions.

The increasing stock of capital and the decreasing stock of government debt, the result of a lower government deficit, combine to lower the assets

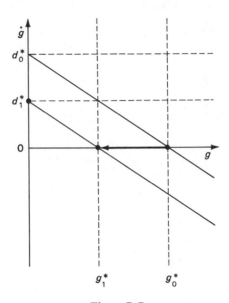

Figure 7–7
d^* falls from d_0^* to d_1^*.

markets equilibrium price of capital. The accumulation of capital raises the consumption goods market equilibrium price of capital, however, by increasing the supply of consumption goods by more than it increases their demand. Thus the secondary effects of the increase in k are to widen further the gap between the equilibrium price of capital in the consumption goods market and in the assets markets first opened by the deficit itself. The government will have to increase continuously the proportion of the government debt that is monetized (i.e., continuously lower x) in order to raise the assets markets price of capital and make it compatible with the price of capital that clears the consumption goods market at the target p_m^*.

If wealth owners are to assimilate a continuously rising stock of capital with its price increasing over time at the same time that the stock of government debt is decreasing, the rate of return on the alternative assets to real capital will have to fall. Since the price level is pegged by an active monetary policy, the rate of return to money is zero, and the adjustment comes through a continuous fall of the rate of return on bonds. This is shown in Figure 7–8. Suppose we start from an equilibrium pair (i_0, p_{k_0}) and assume that the increase in k from k_0 to k_1 raises the consumption goods market equilibrium price of capital from p_{k_0} to p_{k_1} and that the increase in k and the fall in g from g_0 to g_1 shift the kk and mm schedules downward from

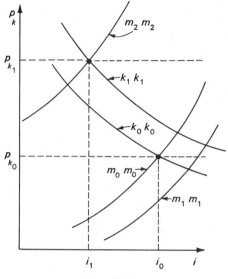

Figure 7–8

p_m, π_m, π_k are constant. g falls from g_0 to g_1 and k rises from k_0 to k_1, then x falls from x_0 to x_2.

$k_0 k_0$ to $k_1 k_1$ and from $m_0 m_0$ to $m_1 m_1$, clearly a disequilibrium situation. As can be seen in Figure 7–8, for the assets markets to come into equilibrium at p_{k_1}, the interest rate has to fall from i_0 to i_1, a fall achieved by a decrease in the ratio of debt to money from x_0 to x_2. It follows that as the economy approaches a new higher stock of capital, the stock of debt, the ratio or debt to money, and the rate of interest will be continuously falling.

7–6   Effects of an Increase in the Scale of Expenditures with a Constant Deficit

In the preceding sections we considered the effects of a change in taxes with a constant level of expenditures. Now we analyze the effects on the short-run growth rate and on the steady-state stock of capital of a simultaneous change in taxes and expenditures that keeps the size of the deficit constant. This is in the spirit of balanced-budget exercises.

An increase in total resources purchased by the government reduces the privately available per-capita supply of consumption goods, but it leaves unchanged the supply of investment goods. In Figure 7–9, the $\dot{k} = 0$ schedule remains unchanged after the increase in e.

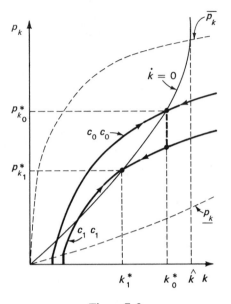

Figure 7–9

p_m, π_m, π_k, d are constant. e rises from e_0 to e_1.

As shown in Proposition 4–2, when the government is running a deficit, an increase in government expenditures with no change in the deficit creates excess demand in the consumption goods market because it reduces the supply of consumption goods more than it reduces the demand for them. This means that the price of capital that equates supply and demand in the consumption goods market at an unchanged price level has to fall to eliminate the excess demand by reducing income, and hence the demand for consumption goods, and by increasing their supply. This results in a downward shift of the cc shedule, in Figure 7–9, from $c_0 c_0$ to $c_1 c_1$.

We can see from Figure 7–9 that an increase in government expenditures lowers the equilibrium price of capital, reduces the steady-state capital stock, and slows the short-run rate of growth. The result of the change must be a decrease in the steady-state capital stock from k_0^* to k_1^*, and as the economy moves from k_0^* to k_1^*, the rate of growth is lower than at k_0^* or k_1^*.

Since the increase in government expenditures creates excess demand in the consumption goods market, monetary policy will initially have to be tightened to avoid an increase in prices. The excess demand for commodities can be eliminated by an increase in the price level or by a fall in the price of capital. If the government maintains a constant price level, it will have to increase the ratio of debt to money through an open market sale to lower the equilibrium price of capital.

As the capital stock falls due to the increase in government expenditures, excess demand in the consumption goods market will threaten to appear. If the price level is to remain constant, a further decrease in the equilibrium price of capital will be necessary. In the assets markets, on the other hand, the decrease in the stock of capital increases the assets markets equilibrium price of capital. Since this price has to fall to avoid inflation, the government will have to tighten its monetary policy even further.

The result of the increase in government expenditures is a fall in the equilibrium price of capital, which causes the stock of capital to decrease. To maintain stable prices, the price of capital has to fall even more. If wealth owners are to be satisfied with a lower share of capital in their portfolios, the rate of return on alternative assets has to increase. Since the rate of inflation is not allowed to change, the rate of interest will have to rise. The economy will, after the increase in e, end up on a new steady-state growth path with a lower stock and price of capital goods and a higher rate of interest.

7–7 Summary

In the case where the government commits itself to a given level of expenditures and deficit and relies on monetary policy to maintain price stability, the steady-state stock of capital depends on the level chosen for expenditures and deficit. A lower deficit or lower expenditures leads to a higher steady-state stock of capital. The stock of government debt is determined in the steady state by the deficit.

Price Stabilization Through a Deficit-Financed Fiscal Policy

8–1 Introduction

In Chapter 7 we analyzed the behavior of an economy with a passive fiscal policy when monetary policy is used to stabilize aggregate demand at a constant price level. Now we reverse the roles of monetary and fiscal policy. We assume that monetary policy is passive and that fiscal tools are used to check inflationary or deflationary pressures.

We can distinguish stabilizing fiscal policies that involve changes in the size of the deficit from those that do not affect the size of the deficit. If expenditures and net taxes vary by equal amounts, the deficit does not change, and we call this a marginally balanced-budget change. Stabilization in this case is achieved through the differential effects of taxes and expenditures on aggregate demand. This balanced-budget type of stabilizing fiscal policy is analyzed in Chapter 9; here we consider stabilizing fiscal policies that involve changes in the size of the deficit.

The government may, for example, fix the scale of government expenditure at some constant level e^* and stabilize aggregate demand through changes in net taxes; or, alternatively, it may fix its net taxes at a constant level and control demand by continuously changing the rate of government expenditures. What is important here is that the per-capita deficit changes for

119

stabilization purposes, thereby affecting the time path of the stock of government debt. Changes in the stock of government debt, in turn, modify the price of capital at which assets owners are willing to hold a given stock of capital and hence affect the economy's rate of growth for any given capital stock.

In this chapter we choose to analyze only the case where the scale of expenditures is fixed at some level e^* and aggregate demand is controlled by changes in the level of taxes. This is possibly the most interesting of all cases. It is the type of stabilization policy that modern economists, educated in the "new economics," find attractive, first, because of the relative flexibility of tax rates and, second, because of the presumably short lag with which this type of policy affects aggregate demand.

Finally, we must define what we mean by a passive monetary policy. Since monetary policy works in our model through changes in the ratio of debt to money that result from open market purchases and scales, it seems natural to define a passive monetary policy as one that keeps a constant ratio of debt to money over time. In this case, with x pegged at some constant level, the number of assets in our model is effectively reduced to two: debt, which consists now of a dose of money and a dose of bonds, and capital.

This definition of a passive monetary policy, although natural in our model, is not the only one available. Many economists believe that monetary policy essentially affects aggregate demand through changes in the rate of interest and suggest the interest rate as an indicator of monetary ease or restriction. These economists would define a passive monetary policy as one that maintains a constant interest rate over time. There are still others who believe that monetary policy affects aggregate demand only through changes in the money supply, independently of how these changes come about. For these economists, a passive monetary policy consistent with long-run stable prices would be one that maintains a constant per-capita money supply, that is, one that increases the money stock at a constant rate n.

The choice of the definition of a passive monetary policy is not a trivial one because the results of some of the experiments we perform may depend on this definition. We choose to use the first definition, that is, a constant ratio of debt to money, and we leave it to the reader to analyze the sensitivity of our results to a change in the definition.

8–2   The Model

Retaining our assumptions of a proportional consumption function and no expected capital gains on capital ($\pi_k = 0$), we begin with the five basic equations:

(8–1)
$$\dot{k} = q_I(k, p_k) - nk \qquad (1)$$

(8–2)
$$\dot{g} = d - ng \qquad (2)$$

(8–3)
$$p_k = \Phi(gp_m, k, \pi_m, x) \qquad (3')$$

(8–4)
$$i = \Psi(gp_m, k, \pi_m, x) \qquad (4')$$

(8–5)
$$q_C(k, p_k) - e = (1 - s)[q(k, p_k) + (d + \pi_m g)p_m - e]. \qquad (5')$$

We specify the passivity of monetary and expenditure policy by requiring that the ratio of debt to money and the size of government expenditure stay fixed at some given level:

(8–6)
$$e = e^*$$

(8–7)
$$x = x^*.$$

We shall study in this chapter paths on which the government enforces a constant price level, and we assume that since the price level does not change over time, people do not expect it to change. That is,

(8–8)
$$p_m = p_m^*$$

(8–9)
$$\pi_m = 0.$$

We now have a system of nine equations in nine unknowns: g, k, p_m, p_k, i, π_m, d, e, and x. These completely describe the growth path an economy will follow when the price level is stabilized through an active tax policy.

8–3 Static Analysis

At any moment the price level that the government wants to enforce is given by equation (8–8), while the per-capita government debt, g, and the per-capita stock of capital, k, are determined by past savings and past government budget deficits. With the ratio of debt to money pegged at the level x^*, there is only one price of capital that clears the assets markets, as indicated by equation (8–3). The government must adjust the level of taxes and, therefore, the size of its deficit so that the market for consumption goods also clears at the p_k determined by equation (8–3).

In Figure 8–1, we illustrate the determination of this deficit. The vertical *aa* schedule shows the assets markets equilibrium price of capital, when $k = k_0$, $g = g_0$, $x = x^*$, and $p_m = p_m^*$. For each p_k there is some deficit that will clear the consumption goods market. From (8–5) and (8–9) we can write this as

$$(8\text{–}10) \qquad d = \frac{q_c - se^* - (1 - s)q}{(1 - s)p_m^*}.$$

The locus of (p_k, d) points that imply such equilibrium in the consumption goods market is labeled *cc*.

If for a given price of capital the supply of consumption goods exceeds the proportion $1 - s$ of total rewards to factors employed in the private sector, the government has to run a deficit and raise demand in order to avoid deflation. On the other hand, if output of consumption goods is lower than the propensity to consume times total factor rewards in the private sector, the government has to run a surplus to avoid an instantaneous rise in prices. It should be noted that as the price of capital rises, the

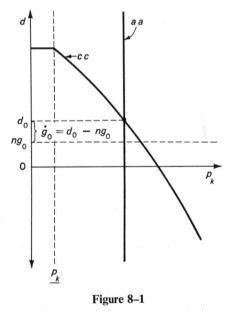

Figure 8–1

g, k, p_m, π_m, π_k, e, x are constant.

supply of consumption goods falls and factor rewards in the private sector, measured in consumption goods units, and thus demand, rise. This means that as the price of capital rises, the deficit required to avoid price level changes falls. This is shown by the segment of the cc schedule that has a negative slope in Figure 8–1. The cc line has a horizontal segment up to $\underline{p}_k$ because for any p_k lower than $\underline{p}_k$, q_c and $\dot{q}$ are equal and constant. The economy is specialized in the production of consumption goods, and the output of consumption goods is equal to total factor rewards in the private sector. Any change in p_k, for p_k less than $\underline{p}_k$, does not affect the level of output in the consumption goods sector, nor does it change the value of factor rewards measured in consumption goods units. Hence, such a change does not modify the deficit required to maintain a constant price level.

On the vertical axis in Figure 8–1, we show the deficit d_0 that the government has to run in order to make $p_m = p_m^*$, when $k = k_0$, $g = g_0$, and $x = x^*$. On the other hand, given values of the aggregate stock of debt, g_0, the government would have to run a deficit equal to ng_0 to maintain a constant per-capita debt. The difference between the actual deficit d_0 and ng_0, as indicated by equation (8–2), is equal to the growth of the per-capita stock of debt, $\dot{g}_0$.

What is the effect of changes in the stocks of capital and debt on the budget deficit required to maintain a stable price level? Consider first the effect of an increase in the stock of government debt. We have shown in Proposition 3–2 that an increase in the stock of government debt generally increases the demand for capital and thus raises the price of capital at which wealth owners are willing to hold the higher stock of government debt. This means that the aa line shifts to the right, from p_{k_0} to p_{k_1}. Since $\pi_m = 0$, an increase in the stock of government debt has no direct effect on consumption demand, and the cc schedule does not shift.

A higher price of capital reduces the supply of consumption goods but increases demand for consumption because the consumption goods value of factor payments rises. It follows that the deficit necessary to maintain stable prices falls from d_0 to d_1, as indicated in Figure 8–2. The increase in the stock of government debt not only reduces the size of the deficit but also increases the deficit required to maintain a constant per-capita stock of debt from ng_0 to ng_1. Both the decrease in the actual deficit and the increase in the deficit required to maintain a constant per-capita debt result in a lower rate of growth of the per-capita stock of debt, which is reduced from $\dot{g}_0$ to $\dot{g}_1$. We conclude that an increase in the aggregate stock of debt reduces the rate of change in the stock of debt that is consistent with stable prices.

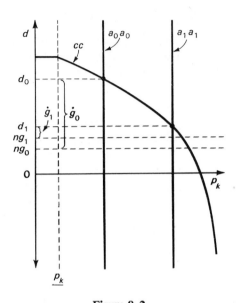

Figure 8–2

$k, p_m, \pi_m, \pi_k, e, x$ are constant. g rises from g_0 to g_1.

Assume now that while $g = g_0$, $e = e^*$, and $x = x^*$, the capital stock increases from k_0 to k_1. As shown in Proposition 3–3, the increase in the aggregate supply of capital reduces the equilibrium price of capital in the assets markets; given the supplies of alternative assets, the price of capital must fall to induce wealth owners to hold a higher stock of capital. This is shown by a leftward shift of the aa schedule from $a_0 a_0$ to $a_1 a_1$ in Figure 8–3. In addition, the increase in the stock of capital raises both the supply of consumption goods and factor payments in the private sector. But an increase in the capital stock lowers output in the investment sector for a given p_k, so that total factor payments rise by less than the increase in the output of consumption goods. The increase in k creates excess supply of consumption goods. This is shown by a rightward shift of the cc schedule from $c_0 c_0$ to $c_1 c_1$ in Figure 8–3. As k increases, the price of capital that clears the consumption goods market for a given deficit also increases. Both the decrease in the assets markets equilibrium price of capital and the increase in the price of capital that clears the consumption goods market for any given deficit increase the deficit necessary to maintain stable prices from d_0 to d_1. Since the stock of debt is constant at $g = g_0$, the increase in the stabilizing deficit raises the rate of change in the outstanding stock of debt from $\dot{g}_0$ to $\dot{g}_1$, as shown in Figure 8–3.

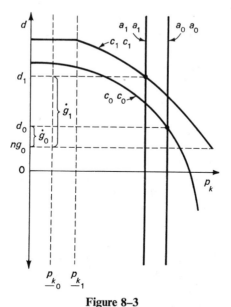

Figure 8–3

$g, p_m, \pi_m, \pi_k, e, x$ are constant. k rises from k_0 to k_1.

A succession of equilibria of the kind just described is a solution to the system (8–1) through (8–9). In Section 8–4, we study these solutions.

8–4 Dynamic Analysis

We considered in Section 8–3 the relationship between the stabilizing deficit and the stocks of capital and government debt. Now we study the behavior of the system (8–1) through (8–9) over time. This is just the study of a system of differential equations given a number of parameters and a set of initial conditions.

This set of differential equations (8–1) through (8–9) has a very simple structure because so many of the variables are constant or follow an exponential path. First, we substitute the equilibrium price of capital, as determined in expression (8–3), into equation (8–1), which describes the rate of capital accumulation as a function of the stock of capital and its equilibrium price. We obtain

(8–11) $$\dot{k} = q_I(k, \Phi(g p_m^*, k, x^*)) - nk.$$

The important thing about (8–11) is that it involves only two variables that actually vary on the growth path, g and k. Then, substituting expressions (8–2) and (8–3) into equation (8–10), which relates the stabilizing deficit to the per-capita stock of capital and its equilibrium price, we have another equation that has this same property:

$$(8\text{--}12) \quad \dot{g} = [1/(1 - s)p_m^*][q_C(k, \Phi(gp_m^*, k, x^*))$$
$$- se^* - (1 - s)q(k, \Phi(gp_m^*, k, x^*))] - ng.$$

If we can find paths of g and k that have derivatives that satisfy these equations, we can derive the paths of all the other variables from them. The time path of the price of capital, the rate of interest, and the stabilizing deficit we can find from equation (8–3), (8–4), and (8–10). We can then confine ourselves to studying solutions to (8–11) and (8–12), which considerably simplifies the analysis.

In the economy, since x is fixed and π_m is equal to zero, p_k at any moment is determined in the assets markets by the target price level, p_m^*, and the historically given values of g and k. If the government is to have the market for consumption goods clear at $p_m = p_m^*$, it is forced to adjust its own deficit to achieve equilibrium at the given p_k. Equation (8–12) shows how large an addition to the outstanding per-capita stock of debt the government must make to clear the consumption market.

The price of capital and the historically given stock of capital also determine the amount of investment, as (8–11) indicates. From the fact that the consumption goods market clears, we know that the total value of new assets is equal to the amount people want to save; but at existing rates of return they may not want to hold the new capital and debt in the proportions that are being produced. The result will be a new price of capital and interest rate in the assets markets. The changes in g and k given by equations (8–11) and (8–12) determine the next instant's stocks, and the whole process starts again.

8–5   Graphical Study of the System

It is interesting for several reasons to study combinations of g and k that produce either $\dot{k} = 0$ or $\dot{g} = 0$ in equations (8–11) and (8–12). Before we do this, however, we should note that there are some restrictions placed on the values that certain variables of our model can take. In particular, suppose that we analyze an economy that starts with a positive stock of debt and a ratio of debt to money fixed at some constant positive level x^*. Suppose now that stabilization requires a tight fiscal policy that results in a continuously falling stock of debt over time. If g were to approach zero or become negative as a result of the required fiscal policy, a constant x would imply that the money supply would also go to zero or negative over time, and according to the assumptions we made in Chapter 3, assets markets would not clear with a zero money supply. Thus if we start with a positive g and x is fixed at some constant level, g cannot become negative with all markets clearing; or if we start with a negative g and we fix x at some constant negative value, g cannot become positive with all markets clearing. Here we confine ourselves to analyzing economies with positive stocks of debt and positive ratios of debt to money.

We now begin our graphical analysis of the system of differential equations (8–1) through (8–9) by considering the $\bar{g}$ and $\underline{g}$ curves in Figure 8–4. These lines are similar to the $\bar{p}_k$ and $\underline{p}_k$ lines in Figure 2–7. Given any stock of capital, they indicate the values of g that will produce equilibrium prices of capital at which the economy will be specialized in the production of only one of its outputs.

We have proved in Chapter 2 that under the usual capital intensity assumption the specialization prices $\underline{p}_k$ and $\bar{p}_k$ are increasing functions of the stock of capital. In Section 8–3, however, we have shown that the equilibrium price of capital actually falls with an increase in k but rises with an increase in g. It follows that, given any pair (k, g) for which p_k is such

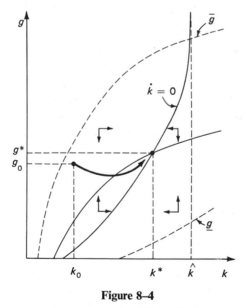

Figure 8–4

p_m, π_m, π_k, e, x are constant.

that the economy is just specialized in the production of one of the commodities, if the economy is to remain specialized, g has to rise when k increases. This shows that both the $\bar{g}$ and g lines are upward-sloped.

We analyze now the $\dot{k} = 0$ schedule in Figure 8–4, which depicts the pairs (k, g) for which the level of output in the investment goods sector is just enough to maintain a constant k; it consists of (k, g) pairs for which the right-hand side of equation (8–11) vanishes. This schedule is similar to the $\dot{k} = 0$ in Figure 2–7, except for the change in the variable measured along the vertical axis. $\hat{k}$ in Figure 8–4 indicates the maximum capital stock that this economy can sustain when all its resources are allocated to the production of investment goods. At any point to the left of $\hat{k}$ the $\dot{k} = 0$ schedule lies above the g schedule because some investment (positive q_I) is always required to maintain a constant k over time.

Why is $\dot{k} = 0$ upward-sloping? Consider any pair (k, g) for which $\dot{k} = 0$. As k increases in equation (8–11), several things happen. The size of nk increases, requiring more investment to keep k constant; but the increase in k at a constant p_k, by Proposition 2–4, actually decreases investment output. In addition, Proposition 3–3 states that assets markets will clear at a lower p_k when k arises, which further cuts back production of investment goods. To counter these effects and increase the output of investment goods so that $\dot{k}$ remains equal to zero, p_k must rise, and this requires an increase in g.

Setting equation (8–11) equal to zero and differentiating partially with respect to k and g, we have

$$(8–13) \qquad \left. \frac{\partial g}{\partial k} \right|_{\dot{k}=0} = -\frac{[(\partial q_I/\partial k) + (\partial q_I/\partial p_k)(\partial p_k/\partial k)] - n}{(\partial q_I/\partial p_k)(\partial p_k/\partial g)} > 0,$$

which proves that the $\dot{k} = 0$ schedule has a positive slope.

Now look at the $\dot{g} = 0$ schedule, which consists of pairs (k, g) that make the right-hand side of equation (8–12) vanish. If $g = \bar{g}$ for some k, the economy is specialized in investment and $q_C = 0$. If $g > 0$, at the same time, it is clear that the right-hand side of equation (8–12) will be negative. That is, for a positive g, the $\dot{g} = 0$ schedule must lie below $\bar{g}$. It may, however, cross the g schedule.

The $\dot{g} = 0$ schedule is also upward-sloping. From any (k, g) point, an increase in k causes g to rise for two reasons. First, given p_k and g, by Proposition 4–3 we know that an increase in k creates excess supply in the consumption goods market; this raises the size of the deficit that will clear the consumption goods market and raises $\dot{g}$. Second, the increase in k lowers the assets markets equilibrium p_k and generates additional excess supply of consumption goods, which tends to raise d and g even further. If $\dot{g}$ is to remain equal to zero, the forces tending to increase it must be offset by a rise in g. Such a change in g causes the equilibrium p_k to increase and reverses the effects just described of the lower equilibrium p_k due to the increase in k. In addition, the increase in g raises the deficit that is required to maintain a constant per-capita debt over time, which, for a given d, lowers $\dot{g}$. Thus k and g must rise together if $\dot{g}$ is to remain at zero.

That the $\dot{g} = 0$ schedule is also upward-sloped can be shown by setting equation (8–12) equal to zero, substituting $q_C + p_k q_I$ for q, and differentiating partially with respect to k and g:

$$(8\text{–}14) \quad \left.\frac{\partial g}{\partial k}\right|_{\dot{g}=0}$$

$$= \frac{\dfrac{s}{(1-s)}\left(\dfrac{\partial q_C}{\partial k} + \dfrac{\partial q_C}{\partial p_k}\dfrac{\partial p_k}{\partial k}\right) - p_k\left(\dfrac{\partial q_I}{\partial k} + \dfrac{\partial q_I}{\partial p_k}\dfrac{\partial p_k}{\partial k}\right) - q_I \dfrac{\partial p_k}{\partial k}}{\dfrac{s}{(1-s)}\left(\dfrac{\partial q_C}{\partial p_k}\dfrac{\partial p_k}{\partial g}\right) - p_k\left(\dfrac{\partial q_I}{\partial p_k}\dfrac{\partial p_k}{\partial g}\right) - q_I \dfrac{\partial p_k}{\partial g} - np_m^*} > 0.$$

As the schedules are plotted, they have a single intersection at a positive g, with the economy not specialized. This may not be the case, because the $\dot{g} = 0$ schedule may lie completely below the $\dot{k} = 0$ schedule. They may also intersect at a negative g, but we have shown that this is not permissible if $x^* > 0$. (If $x^* < 0$, the kind of intersection shown in Figure 8–4 where $g > 0$ is not permissible.) Finally, they may intersect more than once.

Consider now the stability of the system. Suppose we are to the right of the $\dot{k} = 0$ schedule. Then the capital stock exceeds the stock that would just maintain itself at that g and k. The result must be a fall in the capital stock and a negative $\dot{k}$, as the arrows in Figure 8–4 show. At points to the left of $\dot{k} = 0$, $\dot{k}$ must be positive. Likewise, if we are below the $\dot{g} = 0$ schedule, $\dot{g}$ is positive, first, because the deficit that is required to maintain a constant g falls, and, second, because the lower g lowers p_k and creates excess supply in the consumption goods market, thereby raising d and $\dot{g}$. Thus at a point like this $\dot{g} > 0$, we tend to move toward the $\dot{g} = 0$ schedule. Similarly, the system tends to move downward from any point above the $\dot{g} = 0$ schedule.

It is clear that the system, starting from initial values k_0 and g_0 close enough to (k^*, g^*), will move toward the intersection (k^*, g^*). This property is called local stability, and the pair (k^*, g^*) is called a steady-state solution, because if we started there, neither g nor k would change at all.

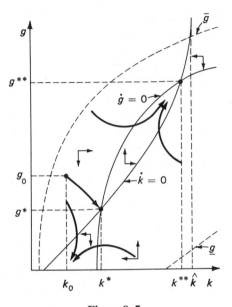

Figure 8–5

p_m, π_m, π_k, e, x are constant.

It is important to note, however, that only where the $\dot{g} = 0$ schedule intersects the $\dot{k} = 0$ line from above will the intersection be a stable steady state. If, as shown in Figure 8–5, the $\dot{g} = 0$ line has a steeper slope at the intersection, the steady-state solution (k^*, g^*) is a saddle point. From an initial k_0 there is only one initial g_0 from which the economy will converge to (k^*, g^*). From any other g_0 the system will finally move away from (k^*, g^*). Note, however, that since the $\dot{g} = 0$ schedule cannot cross the $\bar{g}$ line if an intersection like (k^*, g^*) in Figure 8–5 exists, then there must be at least one stable steady state like (k^{**}, g^{**}). In what follows we consider the behavior of the economy in a neighborhood of a stable steady-state equilibrium.

8–6   Effects of an Open Market Purchase with a Constant Scale of Expenditures

When the government increases the money supply through an open market purchase, it lowers x and thereby changes the relation between g and k to p_k for a given price level. By Proposition 3–1, we know that as x falls, the equilibrium price of capital rises. This means that the *aa* schedule shifts rightward from $a_0 a_0$ to $a_1 a_1$. A change in x does not disturb equilibrium in the consumption goods market, so the cc schedule does not shift.

As shown in Figure 8–6, the increase in the assets markets equilibrium price of capital lowers the size of the equilibrating deficit from d^* to d_1. Hence, given the initial stocks of debt and capital, g^* and k^*, the decrease in x raises the equilibrium price of capital, resulting in a positive rate of change in the stock of capital. It also lowers the deficit required to maintain a stable price level, thereby producing a negative $\dot{g}$.

In terms of Figure 8–7, this means that a pair (k, g) on the original $\dot{k} = 0$ schedule will now produce more investment, and the result will be a positive $\dot{k}$. For $\dot{k}$ to return to zero, p_k must be depressed, and this can be accomplished by lowering g according to Proposition 3–2. The $\dot{k} = 0$ schedule, therefore, shifts downward from $(\dot{k} = 0)_0$ to $(\dot{k} = 0)_1$.

Now consider the $\dot{g} = 0$ schedule. At the old (k^*, g^*), $\dot{g}$ is now negative. If g were lower, p_k would fall and ng would become smaller, so that $\dot{g} = 0$ could be achieved. This means that the $\dot{g} = 0$ schedule also moves downward from $(\dot{g} = 0)_0$ to $(\dot{g} = 0)_1$, as shown in Figure 8–7. Since, given any (k, g) pair, p_k rises as x falls, the $\underline{g}$ and $\bar{g}$ lines shift downward as x falls. When the proportion of the debt that is monetized rises, a lower stock of debt is sufficient to produce the specialization prices $\underline{p}_k$ and $\bar{p}_k$ for each k.

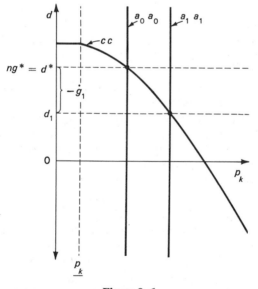

Figure 8–6

$g, k, p_m, \pi_m, \pi_k, e$ are constant. x falls from x_0 to x_1.

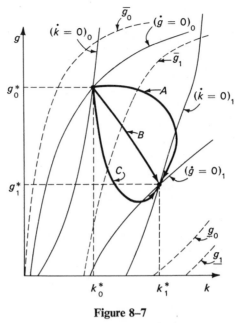

Figure 8–7

p_m, π_m, π_k, e are constant. x falls from x_0 to x_1.

The new steady-state k will depend on whether the $\dot{k} = 0$ or $\dot{g} = 0$ schedule shifts farther. We can see that the new steady-state k_1^* must be higher if at the old k_0^* the new $\dot{k} = 0$ schedule lies below the new $\dot{g} = 0$ schedule.

To prove that the $\dot{k} = 0$ schedule does shift downward farther than the $\dot{g} = 0$ schedule, suppose that we take the g that makes $\dot{k} = 0$ on the new locus $(\dot{k} = 0)_1$ at the old k_0^* point. This g leaves p_k and the output of consumption and investment goods constant by definition of the $\dot{k} = 0$ locus. We can see from equation (8–12) that $\dot{g}$ depends only on these variables and on g itself. At the g that keeps p_k, q_I, and q_C the same after the increase in x, ng will be smaller, and $\dot{g}$ must be positive. This shows that at the new x_1 and the old steady-state k_0^*, the g that makes $\dot{k} = 0$ makes $\dot{g}$ positive, so that the new $\dot{g} = 0$ schedule lies above the new $\dot{k} = 0$ schedule at k_0^*.

From this we can conclude that the long-run effect of an open market purchase is to increase the steady-state capital stock. The effect on g is uncertain. The steady-state value of the stock of government debt may rise or fall; that is, the higher stock of capital that results from the open market purchase may be accompanied by a higher or lower stock of government debt in the long run.

In the short run, as we know from Proposition 3–1, the open market purchase raises p_k and stimulates investment, thereby increasing the rate of growth. The easy monetary policy requires a tighter fiscal policy if the price level is to be kept on its predetermined path. The tight fiscal policy begins to extinguish some of the government debt, and as this process continues, p_k starts falling. The approach to the new long-run values may then continue with g and k being monotonic functions of time, as indicated by the path B in Figure 8–7; or one of the variables may overshoot its long-run value, as indicated by the paths A and C. The long-run effect is always a higher k, whatever happens to g. Figure 8–7 shows the case where g falls.

8–7   Effects of an Increase in the Scale of Expenditures with a Constant Monetary Policy

An increase in the scale of government expenditures does not affect the assets markets equilibrium price of capital; the aa schedule in Figure 8–8 does not shift as a result of the higher e. Since we are starting from a steady-state equilibrium with a positive stock of government debt, the government must be running a deficit to maintain the per-capita debt over time. By Proposition 4–2 the increase in government expenditures creates

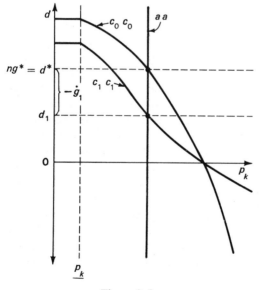

Figure 8–8

$g, k, p_m, \pi_m, \pi_k, x$ are constant. e rises from e_0 to e_1.

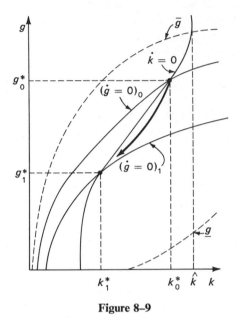

Figure 8–9

p_m, π_m, π_k, x are constant. e rises from e_0 to e_1.

excess demand in the consumption goods market, which lowers the price of capital at which the consumption goods market clears. This is shown by a shift of the cc schedule from $c_0 c_0$ to $c_1 c_1$. To stabilize the price level, the budget deficit has to fall from $d^* = ng$ to $d_1 < ng$; that is, taxes have to rise by more than the value of government expenditures. This is not a balanced-budget change since we depend on changes in the deficit to stabilize prices. If we started in a state of steady growth with $\dot{g} = 0$, the rate of change in the stock of debt would now be negative. Thus for any k, the g at which $\dot{g} = 0$ is lower, and the ($\dot{g} = 0$) locus has shifted downward in Figure 8–9. In addition, since the equilibrium price of capital did not change and the quantity of total resources going to investment has not changed, the $k = 0$ schedule is not affected by the change in e.

As a result of the increase in government expenditures, the economy will approach a new steady-state growth path that is characterized by a lower stock of capital and a lower stock of government debt; the capital stock falls from k_0^* to k_1^* and the stock of debt decreases from g_0^* to g_1^*. In this case the stocks of capital and debt per capita move in the same direction in the long run: the lower the debt, the lower the steady-state capital stock.

8–8 Summary

When the government systematically varies taxes and the deficit to maintain stable prices, the steady-state stocks of capital and debt are determined by the ratio of debt to money and the scale of government expenditures. A lower ratio of debt to money gives rise to a higher per-capita stock of capital in the steady state (if the steady state is stable), while the per-capita stock of debt may rise or fall. An increase in the scale of expenditures on the same assumptions reduces the per-capita stock both of capital and of debt in the steady state.

Price Stabilization Through
a Balanced-Budget Fiscal Policy

9–1 Introduction

In this chapter we study an economy where the government achieves price
stability by constantly varying the scale of government expenditures, at the
same time manipulating taxes so as to keep the deficit constant. We again
employ the assumption of a proportional consumption function.

If demand for consumption goods is deficient for some price of capital
and deficit, the government can always clear the consumption goods
market by increasing the proportion of the economy's resources that it
absorbs. This leaves less capacity for producing private consumption
goods, reduces the output of these goods, and eliminates their excess
supply.

It is obvious that this policy has limits in the other direction. If the
government denies itself the options of changing the deficit or using open
market policy, it can reduce excess demand only by releasing resources to
the private sector. This is not an open-ended procedure, since the government can release only resources that it is currently contracting for; and if
these are not sufficient to soak up the excess demand, the consumption
market can clear only if p_k or p_m changes. A change in p_k without a change
in p_m, given the stocks of debt and capital, is possible only through an

137

open market purchase. The government that eschews both deficit manipulation and open market policy may be unable to check excess demand.

The important thing to realize in this model is that taxes always change
with expenditures so as to leave the deficit constant. For this reason we
call this type of fiscal policy *marginally balanced budget* or in a fit of
informality *balanced budget*.

9–2   The Model

To start with, we have, as usual (assuming $\pi_k = 0$):

$$(9\text{–}1) \qquad\qquad \dot{k} = q_I(k, p_k) - nk \qquad\qquad (1)$$

$$(9\text{–}2) \qquad\qquad \dot{g} = d - ng \qquad\qquad (2)$$

$$(9\text{–}3) \qquad\qquad p_k = \Phi(gp_m, k, \pi_m, x) \qquad\qquad (3')$$

$$(9\text{–}4) \qquad\qquad i = \Psi(gp_m, k, \pi_m, x) \qquad\qquad (4')$$

$$(9\text{–}5) \qquad q_C(k, p_k) - e = (1 - s)[q(k, p_k) + (d + \pi_m g)p_m - e]. \qquad (5')$$

Since monetary policy is passive, we require that the ratio of debt to
money stay fixed at a given level:

$$(9\text{–}6) \qquad\qquad\qquad x = x^*.$$

The government is committed to paths on which the price level is
constant, and we assume that people expect no inflation or deflation:

$$(9\text{–}7) \qquad\qquad\qquad p_m = p_m^*$$

$$(9\text{–}8) \qquad\qquad\qquad \pi_m = 0.$$

The deficit itself is also maintained constant by changes of taxes to
finance expenditures:

$$(9\text{–}9) \qquad\qquad\qquad d = d^*.$$

Notice that these equations are exactly like equations (8–1) through (8–9)
except that $d = d^*$ is substituted for $e = e^*$, and exactly like equations (7–4)
through (7–12) except that $x = x^*$ replaces $e = e^*$. As in Chapter 8, we
have a system of nine equations in nine unknowns: g, k, p_m, p_k, i, π_m, d,
e, and x. These equations completely describe the growth path, after the
initial conditions are given, of an economy that is stabilized by a balanced-
budget fiscal policy.

9–3   Static Analysis

At any moment of time the stocks of capital and debt are determined by past history. The stock of capital is a result of past savings and the stock of debt a result of past deficits. Thus, with the composition of the debt fixed at some level x^*, there is only one price of capital that clears the assets markets at the target price of money p_m^* for the historically given stocks of g and k. This price is shown by the aa line in Figure 9–1; the line is vertical because a change in the scale of government expenditures does not affect the assets markets equilibrium price of capital.

Given the size of the government budget deficit fixed at some constant level d^* and the stock of capital that is inherited from the past, there are different combinations of e and p_k that clear the consumption market goods at a price level $p_m = p_m^*$. From the consumption market goods equilibrium condition we find the size of expenditures necessary to clear the consumption goods market for each price of capital, given k and d:

$$(9\text{--}10) \qquad e = (1/s)[sq_C - (1 - s)(p_k q_I + d^* p_m^*)].$$

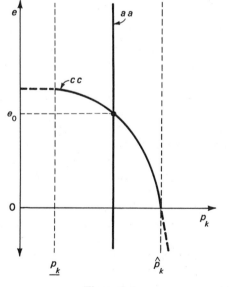

Figure 9–1

$g, k, p_m, \pi_m, \pi_k, d, x$ are constant.

Before we proceed with our analysis, we should note that $0 < e < q_C$. Negative values of e are not allowed because $e < 0$ implies that the government is a net supplier of private consumption goods in the market, while we assumed that all factors of production are owned by the private sector. Values of e greater than q_C are not allowed because if $e > q_C$, the production of private consumption goods would be negative.

In Figure 9–1, we plot the cc schedule, which indicates the pairs (p_k, e) for which the consumption goods market clears for given d^* and k. Since $0 < e < q_C$, the only relevant range of the cc schedule is the one that lies to the left of $\hat{p}_k$, the price at which e must be zero for consumption market clearing. For any $p_k > \hat{p}_k$, the value of e required to clear the consumption goods market is negative. Note that $\hat{p}_k < \bar{p}_k$; for at $p_k = \bar{p}_k$, $q_C = 0$ and e is already unambiguously negative.

An increase in the scale of government expenditures creates excess demand for consumption goods and lowers the consumption market equilibrium price of capital. Thus the cc schedule is downward sloped for all $p_k > \hat{p}_k$. This can be shown by differentiating (9–10) partially with respect to e and p_k:

$$(9\text{–}11) \qquad \left.\frac{\partial e}{\partial p_k}\right|_{cc} = \frac{\partial q_C}{\partial p_k} - \frac{(1-s)}{s}\left(q_I + p_k \frac{\partial q_I}{\partial p_k}\right) < 0 \quad \text{for } p_k > \underline{p}_k.$$

When p_k is lower than $\underline{p}_k$, changes in p_k do not affect the level of excess demand in the consumption goods market, and there is only one e that clears the market for all $p_k < \underline{p}_k$.

It follows from Figure 9–1 that, given x, there are only certain pairs (k, g) that will be compatible with equilibrium in all markets at $p_m = p_m^*$ when a balanced-budget fiscal policy is used for stabilization. There are certain combinations (k, g) that produce an assets markets equilibrium p_k that is too high to have zero excess demand for consumption goods when the government is running a deficit. Even when there is a zero deficit, some high values of p_k may produce excess demand.

The intersection of the cc and aa schedules determines the equilibrium price of capital and the scale of government expenditures that is required to clear all markets at the target price level p_m^*, when $d = d^*$, $x = x^*$, $g = g_0$, and $k = k_0$. What is the effect of changes in the stocks of capital and debt on the equilibrium values of p_k and e?

Given a constant deficit d^* and $\pi_m = 0$, an increase in the aggregate stock of debt has no effect on the equilibrium price of capital in the consumption goods market and hence does not affect the cc schedule. From

Proposition 3–2 we know, however, that given the stock of capital, wealth owners will hold a higher stock of debt in their portfolios only if the price of capital is also higher. Thus the *aa* schedule in Figure 9–2 shifts to the right as g increases. The result is a lower scale of government expenditures e_1 required to maintain a stable price level. We see, then, that an increase in the stock of debt raises the economy's rate of growth. By increasing p_k, it shifts resources to the investment goods sector.

An increase in the stock of capital affects both the *aa* and *cc* schedules. In the assets markets the higher per-capita stock of capital reduces the price of capital at which wealth owners are content to hold the existing stock of government debt, according to Proposition 3–3. This shifts the *aa* curve to the left, from $a_0 a_0$ to $a_1 a_1$ in Figure 9–3. The higher stock of capital, by Proposition 4–3, also increases the supply of consumption goods more than it increases the demand, for any given p_k. This means that the government must absorb more resources to keep the price level stable, so the *cc* curve shifts upward, from $c_0 c_0$ to $c_1 c_1$. The result is a lower p_k and a higher e, as is clear from Figure 9–3. The fall in the equilibrium price of capital lowers the rate of capital accumulation by shifting resources from the investment to the consumption goods sector.

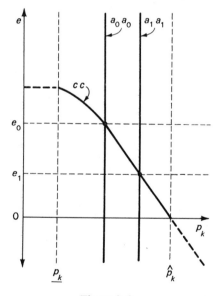

Figure 9–2
$k, p_m, \pi_m, \pi_k, d, x$ are constant. g rises from g_0 to g_1.

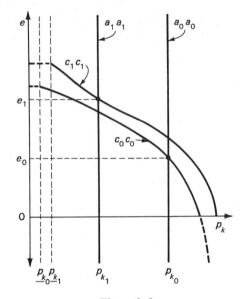

Figure 9–3

$g, p_m, \pi_m, \pi_k, d, x$ are constant. k rises from k_0 to k_1.

As the economy moves through time with a fixed deficit and fixed ratio of debt to money, it will pass through a sequence of short-run equilibria of this kind. We study the paths of the variables in this economy in Section 9–4.

9–4 Dynamic Analysis

As was the case in Chapters 7 and 8, the system of equations (9–1) through (9–9) has a simple solution because some of the variables in the system are either constant or grow at a constant rate. The system can be reduced to two equations in two unknowns, g and k. The problem is to eliminate both p_k and e.

It is easy to see that, since x, π_m, and p_m are constant through time, equation (9–3) gives p_k as a function only of g and k. We can use this in equation (9–10) to find e as a function of g and k, since

$$(9\text{–}12) \quad e = (1/s)[sq_C(k, \Phi(g p_m^*, k, x^*))$$
$$- (1-s)(\Phi(g p_m^*, k, x^*)q_I(k, \Phi(g p_m^*, k, x^*)) + d^* p_m^*)].$$

As shown in Section 9–3, e increases with an increase in k but decreases with an increase in g.

We can rewrite equation (9–1) as an expression in g and k:

(9–13) $$k = q_I[k, \Phi(g p_m^*, k, x^*)] - nk.$$

Equations (9–12) and (9–9) give us the other of our pair of dynamic equations:

(9–14) $$\dot{g} = d^* - ng.$$

Any solution path for g and k that satisfies (9–13) and (9–14) will produce paths for p_k, e, and i that are consistent with a constant deficit, a constant price level, a constant composition of the debt, and a zero rate of expected inflation.

In Figure 9–4 we show the $\dot{g} = 0$ and $\dot{k} = 0$ schedules for these two equations. As in Chapter 8, these schedules depict the pairs (g, k) for which the rates of change in the per-capita stocks of debt and capital are, respectively, equal to zero.

If $\dot{g} = 0$, then g must equal d^*/n, from equation (9–14). This equation has very simple behavior: whenever g is below $g^* = d^*/n$, the current deficit d^* is larger than the deficit ng required to maintain a constant

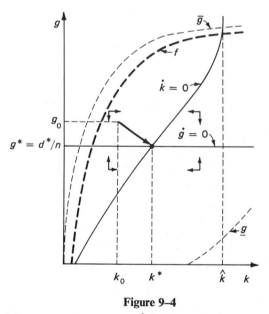

Figure 9–4

p_m, π_m, π_k, d, x are constant.

per-capita stock of debt when population grows at the rate n, and g will be rising. If g is larger than g^*, it will be falling. Only at $g = g^*$ will g be constant over time, and this is completely independent of k. The $\dot{g} = 0$ schedule is, therefore, a horizontal line in Figure 9–4, and the movements of g are shown by the arrows pointing up and down in the figure.

Once again we must note that if the government runs a surplus rather than a deficit, the long-run per-capita stock of debt will be negative. Of course, if g^* is negative, x^* must also be negative to maintain a positive supply of money. In Figure 9–4 and in the rest of this chapter, we analyze cases in which g^* is positive; that is, where the government has fixed d at some positive value.

The $k = 0$ schedule is somewhat more complicated. An increase in k in equation (9–13) has several effects. First, from Proposition 2–4, it reduces q_I. Second, as shown in Section 9–3, it lowers the equilibrium price of capital, which accentuates the decline in q_I arising from the higher capital stock. Third, it increases nk; that is, it increases the level of investment necessary to maintain a constant ratio of capital to labor over time. This all has the effect of lowering k. To keep $k = 0$, the stock of debt must also rise. The higher g, according to Section 9–3, will increase p_k, which counters the effect of the higher k. The $k = 0$ schedule in Figure 9–4 is thus upward-sloping. This can be shown by setting equation (9–13) equal to zero and differentiating partially with respect to g and k:

$$(9\text{–}15) \qquad \left. \frac{\partial g}{\partial k} \right|_{k=0} = - \frac{(\partial q_I/\partial k) + (\partial q_I/\partial p_k)(\partial p_k/\partial k) - n}{(\partial q_I/\partial p_k)(\partial p_k/\partial g)} > 0.$$

Just as in Chapter 8, the $k = 0$ schedule lies between the specialization schedules $\bar{g}$ and g up to a maximum capital stock $\hat{k}$.

For any g, a lower k than the one corresponding to $k = 0$ will mean a positive k. The low k will mean a higher p_k, a higher q_I, and a smaller nk, which must give $k > 0$. In just the opposite case, if the (k, g) pair is to the right of the $k = 0$ schedule, k will be negative. These facts are indicated by the arrows pointing east and west in Figure 9–4.

There are some (k, g) pairs, as shown in Section 9–3, that are not compatible with short-run solutions because they lead to so much excess demand that e would have to be negative to clear the consumption market. These pairs correspond to high g and low k, so that p_k is very high; the region in Figure 9–4 above and to the left of the heavy dashed line f contains these points.

The point (k^*, g^*) is the steady-state solution, and it is clear from the laws of motion indicated by the arrows in Figure 9–4 that starting at any feasible (k, g) pair like (k_0, g_0) in Figure 9-4, the economy will move toward (k^*, g^*). Thus the long-run solution (k^*, g^*) is always stable. Furthermore, since the $\dot{g} = 0$ schedule is horizontal and the $\dot{k} = 0$ schedule is always upward-sloped, there can be only one intersection; if a feasible steady-state pair (k^*, g^*) exists, it is unique.

Since at g_0 the size of the deficit required to maintain a constant g over time, that is, ng_0, is larger than the actual deficit, the stock of government debt will be falling through time, moving smoothly toward g^*. In addition, (k_0, g_0) is to the left of the $\dot{k} = 0$ line, and this means that the equilibrium price of capital and level of expenditures determine a rate of investment that is higher than the investment level nk_0 required to maintain a constant ratio of capital to labor over time. Thus at (k_0, g_0) the ratio of capital to labor is growing. As k increases and g decreases, the equilibrium price of capital falls, and the quantity of total resources hired by the government rises to check the deflationary pressure of a falling stock of debt and a rising capital stock. As k rises and p_k falls, the level of output in the investment goods sector declines; at the same time the rising k requires a larger level of investment to maintain a constant k. Thus, starting from (k_0, g_0), the rate of change in the ratio of capital to labor declines steadily, and k moves smoothly toward k^*.

9-5   Effects of an Open Market Purchase with a Constant Deficit

Suppose the economy is at its long-run equilibrium (k^*, g^*) and the government changes the composition of the government debt once and for all by making an open market purchase. We choose to start at (k^*, g^*) for convenience. The analysis also applies to any feasible initial (k_0, g_0).

As shown in Section 5-4, a change in the composition of the government debt does not have a direct effect on the consumption goods market, so that the cc schedule in Figure 9-5 is not affected by the change in x. The increase in the proportion of the debt that is monetized does affect the assets markets equilibrium price of capital. By Proposition 3-1, we know that a decrease in x raises the assets markets equilibrium price of capital, thereby shifting the aa schedule to the right, in Figure 9-5, from $a_0 a_0$ to $a_1 a_1$. The increase in the equilibrium price of capital is inflationary, and to maintain stable prices the government will have to lower taxes and expenditures until e falls from e_0 to e_1. The effect of the open market purchase is, therefore, to raise the equilibrium price of capital, shifting resources from the production of consumption goods to the production of investment goods, and to lower the amount of resources employed by

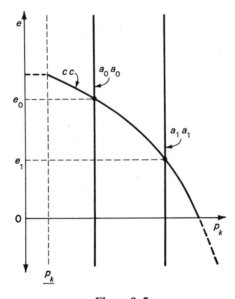

Figure 9–5

g, k, π_m, π_k, d are constant. x falls from x_0 to x_1.

the government for stabilization purchases. The result is an acceleration of the rate of growth in the short run.

In analyzing the long-run effects of an open market purchase, we first notice that the change in x does not affect the $\dot{g} = 0$ schedule at all, since its height depends only on the deficit and the rate of population growth. The $\dot{k} = 0$ schedule, on the other hand, will shift because p_k will rise for any (k, g) combination. For a given g, at the k corresponding to the $\dot{k} = 0$ schedule, there will now be more investment than is needed to maintain k. The old $\dot{k} = 0$ schedule is now in the $\dot{k} > 0$ area. At the given g, an increase in k will lower q_I and p_k and raise nk, so that $\dot{k} = 0$ will hold once again. The open market purchase shifts the entire $\dot{k} = 0$ schedule to the right, as shown in Figure 9–6, from $(\dot{k} = 0)_0$ to $(\dot{k} = 0)_1$.

After the open market purchase, the economy will accumulate capital until it reaches a new higher steady-state capital stock k_1^*. The stock of government debt remains constant through the whole process at its original g^*.

From the behavior of g and k, we can deduce the behavior of the other variables. Since g does not change, the increase in k will tend to require a higher e after its initial reduction in order to avoid a fall in the price level that would result from the increase in the stock of capital. The

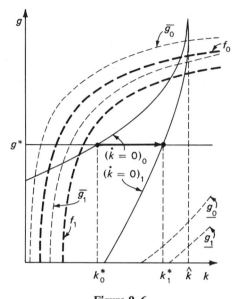

Figure 9–6

p_m, π_m, π_k, d are constant. x falls from x_0 to x_1.

path of p_k falls after its initial rise because the change in x that raises p_k originally tends to be offset as time goes on by the higher k. After its initial change, x remains constant and so does g. Wealth owners will then be willing to hold a larger stock of capital in their portfolios only if the price of capital falls.

9–6   Effects of a Decrease in the Deficit with a Constant Monetary Policy

The other policy tool that the government controls and that it is not using in this economy is its deficit. In this section we study the consequences of a decrease in the deficit. We start from some long-run pair (k_0^*, g_0^*) and we assume that the government raises the level of taxes for every scale of expenditures to achieve a smaller deficit. This will clearly create excess supply in the consumption goods market at the original e, and the government will then have to raise both taxes and expenditures simultaneously to avoid a fall in the price level that would result from the lower deficit. Given any p_k, the decrease in d increases the scale of expenditures necessary to equilibrate the consumption goods market at a constant p_m. The cc schedule shifts upward from $c_0 c_0$ to $c_1 c_1$ in Figure 9–7.

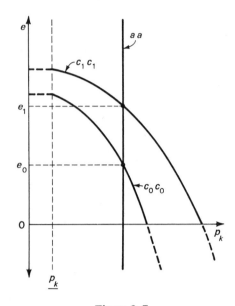

Figure 9–7
$g, k, p_m, \pi_m, \pi_k, x$ are constant. d falls from d_0 to d_1.

The assets markets equilibrium price of capital depends on the total supply of assets and not on their rates of change. The increase in the deficit is equivalent to a rise in the rate of change in the stock of government debt and therefore has no effects on the assets markets equilibrium p_k. The aa schedule does not shift. The result of the decrease in the deficit, as shown in Figure 9–7, is an unchanged price of capital and a higher scale of government expenditures, $e_1 > e_0$.

To analyze the long-run effects of the lower deficit, we consider the $\dot{k} = 0$ and $\dot{g} = 0$ schedules in Figure 9–8. A decrease in the deficit does not affect the $\dot{k} = 0$ schedule since it is a function solely of g and k. The smaller deficit clearly can support only a smaller long-run stock of government debt, so the $\dot{g} = 0$ schedule shifts downward from $g_0^* = d_0/n$ to $g_1^* = d_1/n$, where d_1 is the new, lower deficit.

As shown clearly by Figure 9–8, the new long-run equilibrium capital stock k^* is smaller, as is the new equilibrium stock of government debt. At the instant when the deficit is changed, e must increase to eliminate the threatened excess supply of consumption goods. The lower d at the given g means that $\dot{g}$ suddenly changes from zero to a negative value. As g decreases, p_k falls, and the lower p_k in turn induces a reduction in the output

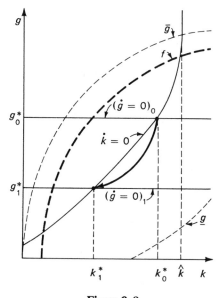

Figure 9–8

p_m, π_m, π_k, x are constant. d falls from d_0 to d_1.

of investment goods. The immediate short-run result is then a decline in the rates of net investment and growth.

Over time the system moves smoothly to the new equilibrium, investment being too low to maintain k and the deficit too low to maintain g. The stocks of capital and debt shrink toward their new steady-state values. The paths of p_k and e after this experiment are ambiguous since both k and g are falling, and they have opposite effects on both e and p_k. Given different functions, many different final configurations are possible.

This is an interesting experiment because the lower deficit leads to a lower stock of both debt and capital when stabilization is carried on in this particular way. In an economy stabilized by balanced-budget manipulations, debt and capital in the long run rise and fall together. This example indicates how tricky it is to generalize about the effects of the government debt without clearly specifying the policies that produced the debt.

9–7 Summary of Chapters 7, 8, and 9

It is possible now to give the results of the chief experiments of Chapters 7, 8, and 9 in tabular form (Table 9–1). There is an important distinction between the short-run and the steady-state columns. The short-run

Table 9-1

STABILIZATION TOOL	EXPERIMENT	EFFECT ON		
		SHORT-RUN GROWTH	STEADY-STATE CAPITAL STOCK	STEADY-STATE STOCK OF DEBT
Monetary policy	Decrease deficit	Faster	Higher	Lower
	Increase scale of government expenditure	Slower	Lower	Same
Deficit-financed fiscal policy	Open market purchase	Faster	Higher	Ambiguous
	Increase scale of government expenditure	Slower	Lower	Lower
Balanced budget fiscal policy	Open market purchase	Faster	Higher	Same
	Decrease deficit	Slower	Lower	Lower

column indicates the effect in our economy of the change in a policy variable when its price effects are offset by the corresponding stabilizing variable. These results are general for any experiment that pairs policy variables in this way. The steady-state effects on the other hand, depend crucially on the assumption that the government, after the experiment, allows only the stabilizing variable to change and keeps the others constant. The steady-state columns are the result of applying these imaginary constraints to the government. In general, we would expect governments to exercise all their available tools all the time to achieve different purposes. The steady-state effects apply only to a very particular behavior of the government.

10 Dynamic Exercises with Wealth Effects on Consumption

10–1 Introduction

The exercises of the last three chapters are supposed to point the way to more complicated and realistic specifications of government goals. In each of these three simple models we made the simplifying assumption that consumption was a fixed fraction of income. This type of consumption function is inadequate because there is substantial evidence that the fraction if income consumed depends on wealth. In many discussions of the theoretical issues we have raised, arguments about the existence and consequences of wealth effects have held center stage.

It would perhaps be best to carry out all of our experiments with wealth effects explicitly accounted for, but we will content ourselves in this chapter with repeating some of the exercises of Chapters 7, 8, and 9. There are two reasons for doing this. First, the versions of the model considered up to this point have some interest in their own right, and one interesting fact about the conclusions we have drawn is that they are often unaffected by the inclusion of wealth in the consumption function. Our second purpose is pedagogical. The exercises in Chapters 7, 8, and 9 are intended as analytical paradigms for a broad range of possible versions of the model, and this chapter will serve to show how wealth effects can be studied in these paradigm cases and to suggest techniques for other cases.

151

The reason the inclusion of wealth does not upset our conclusions is itself enlightening. The long-run stocks of debt and capital are endogenous in our system. After the deficit, for instance, is fixed, the stock of debt must ultimately conform to it. A higher steady-state stock of debt must be maintained by a higher steady-state deficit. The higher deficit has an income effect on consumption that is qualitatively similar to the wealth effect of the larger stock of debt. The wealth effect can produce no surprises, at least in steady-state analysis, because we have included the income effect all along.

To begin with, recall from Chapter 4 that equilibrium in the consumption goods market when wealth is explicitly included in the demand function requires

(10–1)

$$q_C - e = c(kp_k + gp_m, q_C + p_k q_I + dp_m^* - e), \quad \frac{\partial c}{\partial a} > 0, \ 1 > \frac{\partial c}{\partial y} > 0.$$

10–2 Price Stabilization Through Monetary Policy

In this model the deficit is fixed, so that the price of capital is determined by the clearing of the consumption market. This means that for any g, k, p_m^*, d, and e, there is a particular p_k that the government must enforce by monetary policy. In Figure 10–1, which is similar to Figure 7–4, we plot the pairs of k and p_k that satisfy this relationship for a given g, d, and e. There are two differences from the situation described in Chapter 7. First, in Chapter 7 a rise in k always created excess supply of consumption goods, which had to be removed by an increase in p_k, so that the cc curve was everywhere upward-sloping.

Since we assume $\partial c/\partial a > 0$, an increase in k may raise demand by as much as or more than it increases the supply in the consumption goods market. The cc curve in Figure 10–1 is drawn with one upward-sloping section and one downward-sloping one, but there may be several such regions in alternation. We do know that the cc curve begins by sloping upward near $p_k = 0$, since if $p_k = 0$, the wealth effect of the increase in k is nonexistent.

The second difference from the previous model is that in Chapter 7 the stock of debt g had no influence on the level of the cc curve. Under the present assumption, increases in g will increase demand, requiring a lower p_k for any k to clear the consumption market. This shift is shown in Figure 10–1 by the $c_1 c_1$ schedule, which corresponds to a higher g.

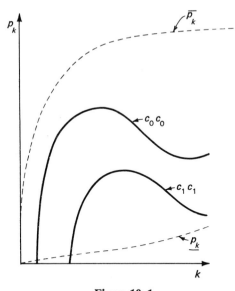

Figure 10–1

p_m, π_m, π_k, d, e are constant. g rises from g_0 to g_1.

Since g has effects on both consumption and assets markets, we have two joint differential equations:

(10–2) $$\dot{k} = q_I[k,\ p_k(k,\ g p_m^*,\ d^*,\ e^*)] - nk$$

(10–3) $$\dot{g} = d^* - ng.$$

We want eventually to study pairs (k, g) at which $\dot{k} = 0$. The first step is to look in Figure 10–2 at the pairs (k, p_k) at which $\dot{k} = 0$, derived in Chapter 2. Also drawn in Figure 10–2 is the cc schedule of pairs (k, p_k) for which the consumption market clears. The economy must stay on the cc schedule at all times to maintain price stability.

For each level of g there will be a separate cc schedule. As drawn in Figure 10–2, there are two points of intersection of the $\dot{k} = 0$ and cc schedules for each level of g. As g rises from g_0 to g_1, the cc schedule falls from $c_0 c_0$ to $c_1 c_1$, moving the intersections closer together until, if g rises high enough, there may be a point of tangency. For high enough values of g the cc schedule may lie entirely beneath the $\dot{k} = 0$ schedule. Of course the cc schedule may cross the $\dot{k} = 0$ schedule more than twice, giving more than two intersections.

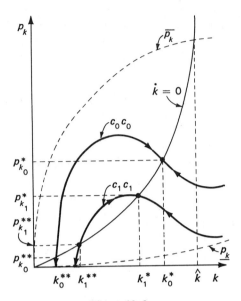

Figure 10–2

p_m, π_m, π_k, d, e are constant. g rises from g_0 to g_1.

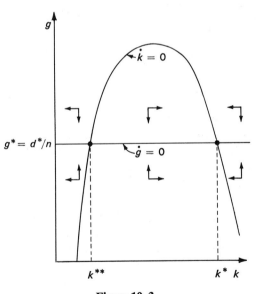

Figure 10–3

p_m, π_m, π_k, d, e are constant.

The intersections correspond to (k, g) pairs at which $\dot{k} = 0$. In Figure 10–3, we draw this locus, which for any g has either two (or possibly more) corresponding k's, or if g is very high, none at all. In this way we derive the $\dot{k} = 0$ schedule in (k, g) space from the $\dot{k} = 0$ and cc schedules in (k, p_k) space.

The $\dot{g} = 0$ schedule is just a straight line of height d^*/n. The laws of motion of this system are shown by the arrows in Figure 10–3. k tends to move toward the downward-sloping part of the $\dot{k} = 0$ schedule and away from the upward-sloping part. To see this, consider Figure 10–2 again. For g_0 corresponding to $c_0 c_0$, the system must be on the $c_0 c_0$ schedule. If $k > k_0^{**}$ but $k < k_0^*$, the (k, p_k) pair is to the left of the $\dot{k} = 0$ schedule so that k is increasing, that is, moving toward k_0^*. If $k > k_0^*$, the system is right of the $\dot{k} = 0$ schedule, and k will be falling toward k_0^*. For $k < k_0^{**}$ the system is to the right of $\dot{k} = 0$, and k will be falling, that is, moving away from k_0^{**}. In the (k, g) plane the system will clearly always move toward the $\dot{g} = 0$ line.

As we can see from Figure 10–3, only (k^*, g^*) is stable, but it is not globally stable. There may be a succession of stable and unstable equilibria if the cc schedules alternately have positive and negative slopes in Figure 10–2.

Now we are in a position to study the policy manipulation experiments. Consider a decrease in the deficit. A lower deficit will maintain only a lower long-run stock of debt, and therefore the $\dot{g} = 0$ schedule shifts downward, as shown in Figure 10–4. In addition, the lower deficit decreases the demand for consumption goods, increases the equilibrium price of capital, and raises k, as shown in Figure 10–4. The $\dot{k} = 0$ line shifts upward because for p_k to remain unchanged after the decrease in d, the stock of debt has to rise to increase the demand for consumption goods.

The long-run effect of a decrease in the deficit at a stable equilibrium is to lower the stock of debt and to increase the stock of capital, while in the short run it raises the rate of capital accumulation. These conclusions are qualitatively the same as the ones we arrived at when we did not consider the influence of wealth on aggregate saving. The recognition of the effect of wealth on saving does not modify the qualitative results of Chapter 7 because the result of a lower deficit is a lower stock of debt in the long run, and this reinforces the effect of a decrease in the deficit on the equilibrium price of capital. The lower deficit decreases disposable income and lowers the demand for consumption goods for any given stock of wealth, and in addition, the lower outstanding stock of debt decreases wealth and hence reduces consumption for any given level of disposable income.

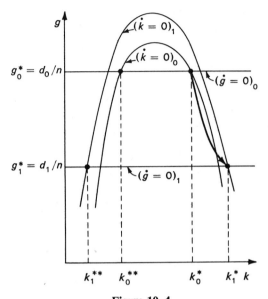

Figure 10–4

p_m, π_m, π_k, e are constant. d falls from d_0 to d_1.

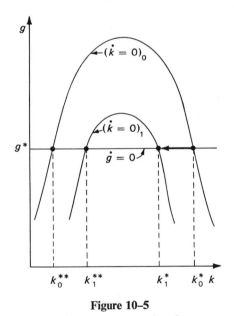

Figure 10–5

p_m, π_m, π_k, d are constant. e rises from e_0 to e_1.

As a second experiment, suppose expenditures increase with a constant deficit. The $\dot{g} = 0$ locus remains unchanged because the deficit is the same, while the $\dot{k} = 0$ locus shifts downward, as illustrated in Figure 10-5. This occurs because an increase in e at any (k, g) increases excess demand for consumption goods. The p_k that clears the consumption market is lower, and so is investment. If investment had been exactly enough to maintain $\dot{k} = 0$, it would not be sufficient to do so after the increase in expenditures. We need a lower g at each k to keep $\dot{k} = 0$.

The results are the same as in Section 7-6 for a stable equilibrium, a constant steady-state stock of debt, and a lower steady-state capital stock.

We conclude that when monetary policy is used to stabilize aggregate demand, the inclusion of wealth in the saving function does not modify qualitatively the conclusions that we summarized in the first row of Table 9-1.

10-3   Price Stabilization Through a Deficit-Financed Fiscal Policy

To analyze the behavior of an economy in which a deficit-financed fiscal policy is used to stabilize the price level when consumption is a function of wealth and disposable income, we first have to rewrite equation (8-12) to include the effects of wealth on the consumption function and thus on the stabilizing deficit. The deficit has to be adjusted at each instant to equilibrate the consumption goods market; it will accordingly depend on the stock of capital, the price of capital, and the stock of government debt, that is, the variables that enter the consumption market clearing equation [equation (10-1)]. We ask what change in the stabilizing deficit a change in any of these variables will induce.

If k rises, it is not certain whether fiscal policy will have to be eased or tightened. On the one hand, the higher k increases the supply of consumption goods; on the other it raises both income and wealth. The deficit may have to rise or fall to compensate, depending on which effect is stronger. An increase in p_k certainly requires a smaller deficit, since it simultaneously reduces supply and raises demand by increasing wealth and income. Similarly, when g increases, it raises demand through the wealth effect and requires a smaller deficit.

To sum up, we can write

$$(10\text{-}4) \qquad d = d(g, k, p_k), \quad \frac{\partial d}{\partial g} < 0, \frac{\partial d}{\partial k} \gtrless 0, \frac{\partial d}{\partial p_k} < 0.$$

Substituting this into the second of the five basic differential equations of the system, we obtain

$$(10\text{–}5) \qquad \dot{g} = d(g, k, \Phi(g p_m^*, k, x^*)) - ng.$$

The other equation of the system is again

$$(10\text{–}6) \qquad \dot{k} = q_I(k, \Phi(g p_m^*, k, x^*)) - nk.$$

The only difference between this model and the one in which the saving rate is constant is that an increase in k may create excess demand for consumption goods rather than excess supply, so that the $\dot{g} = 0$ schedule may be downward-sloping. When an increase in k creates excess demand, the deficit must fall to clear the consumption market. If originally (k_0, g_0) were a pair for which $\dot{g} = 0$, it is clear that at the new (k_1, g_1) pair with a higher k, the lower deficit will support only a lower g_1. The $\dot{g} = 0$ schedule, instead of sloping upward everywhere, may slope downward.

If a case like the one presented in Figure 10–6 exists, then as the economy approaches its stable steady-state (k^*, g^*), there may be fluctuations in the ratio of capital to labor and in the aggregate stock of debt. Consider an

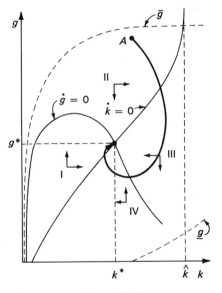

Figure 10–6

p_m, π_m, π_k, e, x are constant.

economy at a point like A. The actual deficit is too small to maintain a constant debt over time, and investment is higher than nk so that the capital stock is growing. As the capital stock rises, excess demand for consumption goods is created. To avoid inflation, the deficit falls, and $\dot{g}$ becomes more negative.

In region II the fall in g and the increase in k steadily lower k, and the economy approaches the $k = 0$ schedule. On this schedule $q_I = nk$, but the deficit that is required to maintain a stable price level is lower than ng, and $\dot{g}$ is still negative. As g falls, we enter region III, where k becomes negative because the fall in g has lowered p_k, thus decreasing the output of investment goods. The process continues in this fashion as the system approaches the steady-state values g^* and k^*.

It is clear that around a stable equilibrium, where $\dot{g} = 0$ crosses $k = 0$ from above, the results of the policy changes discussed in Chapter 8 are the same. An open market operation that lowers x shifts $k = 0$ to the right, as it did in Chapter 8, for the same reasons; a decrease in x raises the equilibrium p_k and thus the rate of capital accumulation for each g. The former $k = 0$ schedule now lies in the $k > 0$ region, and the new $k = 0$ locus is to the right, as in Figure 10–7. As before, the decrease in x requires that the government reduce the size of its deficit to maintain a stable price

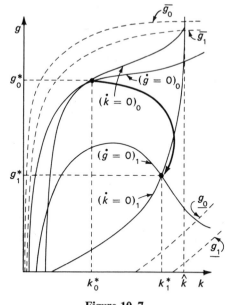

Figure 10–7

p_m, π_m, π_k, e are constant. x falls from x_0 to x_1.

level. The lower d means that at each former $\dot{g} = 0$ point, $\dot{g}$ is negative. For each k, a lower g, which reduces both p_k and ng, is necessary for $\dot{g} = 0$, and the $(\dot{g} = 0)_0$ locus shifts downward to $(\dot{g} = 0)_1$.

As in Chapter 8 we can show that the new intersection will be at a higher capital stock. At the point on the new $\dot{k} = 0$ corresponding to k_0^*, p_k, q_I, and q_C are unchanged, but g has decreased so that $\dot{g}$ will be positive. The $(\dot{g} = 0)_1$ schedule must be above the $(\dot{k} = 0)_1$ at k_0^*, so the new equilibrium will be farther to the right. The results of an open market purchase are a higher steady-state stock of capital and an uncertain change in the stock of government debt. This is the same result we found in Chapter 8.

The results of an increase in government expenditure when the economy begins with a positive stock of debt are straightforward and the same as they were in Chapter 8. The increase in e does not affect the assets markets equilibrium or the rate of capital accumulation, and the $\dot{k} = 0$ locus remains unchanged. The rise in expenditures creates excess demand in the consumption goods market and lowers the price of capital that equilibrates the consumption goods market. The government must lower the deficit in order to stabilize the price level, and the lower d in turn means that $\dot{g}$ is now negative at the points along the $(\dot{g} = 0)_0$ locus in Figure 10–8. The $\dot{g} = 0$ locus again shifts downward from $(\dot{g} = 0)_0$ to $(\dot{g} = 0)_1$. As we can

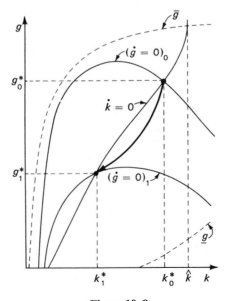

Figure 10–8

p_m, π_m, π_k, x are constant. e rises from e_0 to e_1.

see from Figure 10–8, the results are a fall in both the steady-state equilibrium stock of capital and the steady-state equilibrium stock of government debt. There is no ambiguity about the latter because the slope of the $k = 0$ locus is known.

10–4 Price Stabilization Through a Balanced-Budget Fiscal Policy

Finally, we analyze the behavior of an economy in which a balanced-budget fiscal policy is used to stabilize aggregate demand and consumption is a function of income and wealth.

In this case the equilibrium price of capital is determined in the assets markets as a function of the stocks of capital and government debt and the composition of the government debt. The consumption goods market equilibrium condition determines only the level of taxes and expenditures necessary, given the size of the deficit, to clear the consumption market at a constant price level. The introduction of wealth in the saving function may affect the level of taxes and expenditures necessary to maintain a constant price level over time, but it does not affect the relationship between the equilibrium price of capital, the stocks of both assets, and the composition of the debt.

With wealth affecting saving, equations (9–13) and (9–14) are still the two basic differential equations, and the behavior of the capital stock is the same whether wealth is or is not an argument in the saving function. All of the results in the third section of Table 9–1 hold when we recognize the effect of wealth on saving.

10–5 Summary

The analysis of this chapter has shown two things. First, the results of the experiments we have repeated are unaffected by the inclusion of wealth in the consumption function. Second, the techniques of studying the model we developed in Chapters 7, 8, and 9 are easily modified to handle wealth effects. Usually nothing changes but the shapes of some schedules.

We emphasize that while the long-run qualitative results are the same, the paths the variables follow will be different when wealth effects are included. As we saw, there may be cyclical approaches to equilibrium in some cases. In other versions of the model and for other experiments, wealth effects may produce more novel and fundamental changes in the behavior of the model.

The Burden of the Public Debt

11–1 Introduction

In this chapter we analyze the relationship between the stock of government debt, the short-run rate of capital accumulation, and the long-run stock of capital. This issue has been widely discussed in the " burden of the debt " literature. We leave it to the reader to compare our conclusions with those reached by others. In this chapter we ignore the distortions created by the taxes necessary to pay interest on the debt. (We refer the reader to the Bibliography for some reference to the work of other economists on this question.)

To begin with we must distinguish two different experiments that have been considered in the literature. Some economists analyze the relationship between the total stock of government debt, money plus bonds, and the stock of capital, while others study the relationship between the stock of government bonds and the stock of capital. The results of these two exercises are in general different, and we shall, therefore, keep their discussion separate. We consider first the effects of the stock of government debt, bonds, and money on the stock of capital.

It is often argued that the existence of a positive stock of government debt tends to lower the economy's stock of capital in the long run. If

163

saving is a decreasing function of wealth, the existence of a positive stock of government debt makes private wealth larger than the stock of capital and thus reduces the amount of saving forthcoming from any given level of national income. The result is a lower rate of capital accumulation in the short run and a lower stock of capital in the long run. This argument has led many economists to the conclusion that the extinction of part or all of the government debt will encourage growth in the short run and will increase the long-run stock of capital.

This view is correct as far as it goes, but it is incomplete. The reduction in private wealth that results from a decrease in the stock of government debt also lowers the demand for all assets, including the demand for real capital. As shown in Chapter 3, a reduction in the demand for capital in general lowers the price of capital at which wealth owners are willing to hold the existing stock of capital. While the increase in saving that results from the fall in the stock of government debt tends to increase the equilibrium price of capital, the decrease in the demand for capital that is caused by the same decrease in the debt tends to lower the equilibrium price of capital, for a given price of money.

In what follows we study the effects of a reduction in the debt in an economy in which the government is committed to maintaining a constant price level, and we find that the net effect of a decrease in the stock of government debt on the short-run rate of growth, as well as on the long-run stock of capital, is ambiguous. Whether the effect of saving or the effect on the demand for capital dominates depends on the particular policy the government uses to offset the deflationary pressure of a reduction in the aggregate public debt.

The assumption that the government maintains a constant price level is not merely an attempt to introduce some "realistic" features into the model. If the government lets the price level be determined by the market and tries to lower the stock of government debt by imposing a levy on the holders of the debt and by permanently lowering its deficit, without changing any other variable under its control, the only effect in the long run will be a decrease in the price level. The aggregate real stock of debt and the rest of the real variables of the system will remain unchanged. If prices are completely flexible, the debt and deficit are neutral, since halving the debt and deficit results only in halving the price level. The government must maintain a constant price level through its policy actions if the change in the nominal stock of debt is to change the real stock of debt.

In any case, if the government desires to maintain a constant price level, a decrease in the stock of bonds or in the total stock of debt can be accomplished only if at least one other variable in the system also changes.

We should, therefore, expect that the effects on capital accumulation of a decrease in the debt will depend on the variable or variables that the government chooses to vary in order to maintain stable prices as well as on the methods by which the stock of government debt is reduced. The analysis of the possible results is the subject of this chapter.

11–2 Short-Run Effects of Changes in the Stock of Government Debt, Including Money

In Chapter 3 we have shown that a decrease in the aggregate stock of government debt usually lowers the price of capital at which wealth owners are willing to hold the existing stock of capital for any price of money. This is shown in Figures 11–1a and 11–1b by the upward-sloping aa schedules, which in this case indicate the pairs of g and p_k for which the assets markets are in equilibrium for given k, p_m, and x.

In Chapter 4 we indicated that an increase in the stock of debt affects the demand for consumption goods through two different channels: an income effect and a wealth effect. Since in this chapter we always assume that the price level is stable and that the expected rate of inflation is zero, we

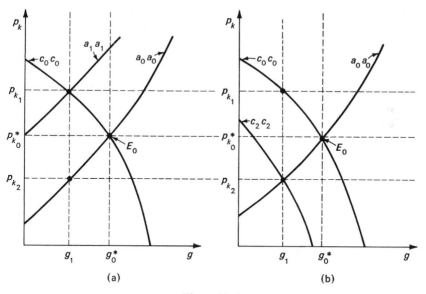

Figure 11–1

(a) $k, p_m, \pi_m, \pi_k, d, e$ are constant. x falls from x_0 to x_1. (b) k, p_m, π_m, π_k, x are constant. d rises from d_0 to d_2 or e rises from e_0 to e_2.

are left only with the wealth effect because the expected inflation tax is zero. An increase in the stock of government debt raises private wealth, increase the demand for consumption goods, and lowers the price of capital that clears the consumption goods market for any p_k. This is shown by the downward sloping cc schedules in Figures 11–1a and 11–1b, which depict the pairs of g and p_k that equilibrate the consumption goods market for given k, p_m, d, and e.

Consider now an economy that is at steady-state equilibrium with a stable price level; its stocks of capital and debt are k^* and g_0^*; the equilibrium prices of capital and money are $p_{k_0}^*$ and p_m^*; the expected rate of inflation is constant and equal to zero; and the policy variables, d, e, and x are fixed at the levels d_0^*, e_0^*, and x_0^*. Such a state of affairs is described by the point E_0 in Figures 11–1a and 11–1b. Suppose now that the outstanding stock of debt is reduced from g_0^* to g_1, as shown in the figures. We can think of this reduction as the result of a capital levy imposed on the holders of government debt.

When the stock of debt is reduced from g_0^* to g_1, the consumption market equilibrium price of capital rises from $p_{k_0}^*$ to $p_{k_1}^*$, while the assets markets equilibrium price of capital falls from $p_{k_0}^*$ to $p_{k_2}^*$. Unless some other variable in the system changes, neither p_{k_1} nor p_{k_2} will be consistent with equilibrium in all markets if the price of money is to remain constant at the original level p_m^*. If the government takes no action to stabilize the price level, the price of money would rise because of the deflationary effect of the reduction in the stock of debt.

The government could maintain a stable price level after the reduction in the debt by using either its monetary or its fiscal tools. If it chooses to use monetary policy, it will have to perform open market purchases until the aa schedule shifts rightward from $a_0 a_0$ to $a_1 a_1$ and intersects the $c_0 c_0$ schedule at (g_1, p_{k_1}), as in Figure 11–1a. The result of the decrease in the stock of government debt in this case is a higher equilibrium price of capital and a higher rate of investment in the short run. When monetary policy is used to stabilize the price level, the wealth effect on saving dominates in the short run, and a reduction in the stock of debt stimulates the rate of capital accumulation.

The deflationary effects of a reduction in the aggregate stock of debt might also be avoided by the use of fiscal tools. The government would have to follow an expansionary fiscal policy to make the cc schedule shift from $c_0 c_0$ to $c_1 c_1$ and intersect the $a_0 a_0$ schedule at (g_1, p_{k_2}), as shown in Figure 11–1b. The expansionary fiscal policy may be of the balanced-budget type, so that expenditures and taxes rise by the same amount, or it may take the form of a higher deficit with the same expenditures. In any case, the wealth effect on the demand for capital dominates and the reduction in the stock of government debt results in a lower equilibrium price of capital and in a lower rate of growth in the short run.

11–3   Long-Run Effects of Changes in the Stock of Government Debt, Including Money

In Section 11–2 we analyzed the short-run effects of a once and for all decrease in the stock of debt. A levy raises the short-run rate of capital accumulation when monetary policy is used to stabilize the price level, but it reduces the rate of accumulation when fiscal policy is used for stabilization. We now ask whether these changes in the short-run rate of capital accumulation are reflected in the steady-state stock of capital.

Consider first the case in which the price level is stabilized through monetary policy. The behavior of the system in this case is depicted in Figure 10–3, reproduced here as Figure 11–2. Suppose that there is only one long-run stable equilibrium, (k^*, g^*); that the economy is at this equilibrium; and that the government imposes a levy on the holders of government debt that reduces the stock of government debt from g^* to g_0. The economy suddenly moves to (k^*, g_0). It follows from the laws of dynamics of the system, as represented by the arrows in Figure 11–2, that

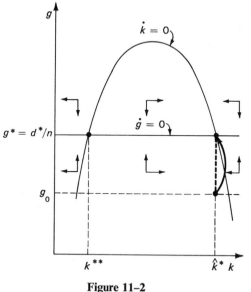

Figure 11–2

p_m, π_m, π_k, d, e are constant.

at (k^*, g_0) the rate of change in the stock of capital is positive. This corresponds to our finding in Section 11-2 that a levy increases the short-run rate of growth when monetary policy has stabilized prices because it raises the price of capital at which the consumption market clears. However, since we have assumed that the deficit remains constant, it follows from Figure 11-4 that at (k^*, g_0) the rate of change in the stock of debt is positive. Thus at (k^*, g_0) both $\dot{k} > 0$ and $\dot{g} > 0$.

From Figure 10-2 and from its underlying differential equations (10-2) and (10-3), we see that the levy affects neither the $\dot{k} = 0$ nor the $\dot{g} = 0$ schedule. Given the long-run rate of growth n, as long as the system remains in the area of local stability, the long-run stock of debt is completely determined by the deficit, which in this case has not changed. The imposition of a once and for all levy is merely a change in initial conditions that increases the short-run rate of growth but has no effect on the steady-state stock of capital when monetary policy is used to stabilize the price level. The decrease in the stock of government debt increases the equilibrium price of capital instantaneously; but as the stock of debt returns to its original value g^*, so does the equilibrium price of capital, leaving unaffected the steady-state stock of capital.

At this point is is easy to see that whenever the level of the deficit is fixed, a similar argument will hold. Figure 11-3 shows the dynamic behavior of a system when a marginally balanced-budget fiscal policy is used to stabilize aggregate demand.

Figure 11-3 is similar to Figure 9-4 because the laws controlling g and k are not affected by introducing wealth as an argument in the consumption function, as shown in Chapter 10.

Suppose the economy is in long-run equilibrium and a levy is imposed that reduces the stock of debt to g_0, but the deficit remains constant. As shown in Figure 11-3, the stock of debt will in the long run move back to its initial value g^*.

When monetary policy is used to stabilize prices, the price of capital is determined by the equilibrium condition in the consumption market and therefore rises with a fall in the stock of government debt. When fiscal policy of either type is used to stabilize the price level, the price of capital is given by the equilibrium condition in the assets markets and therefore falls with a decrease in the debt. This difference is reflected only in the short-run effects of the levy, for in the long run all effects vanish.

If a deficit-financed fiscal policy is used to stabilize the price level, the result is still the same: a once and for all levy on the holders of government debt has no long-run effects. The reasons, however, are different. Consider for this purpose Figure 11-4, which is the same as Figure 10-6 and which

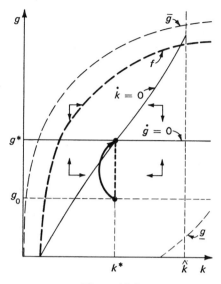

Figure 11–3

p_m, π_m, π_k, d, x are constant.

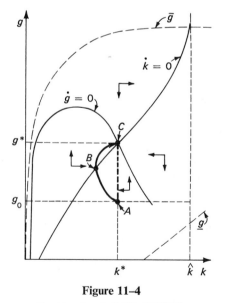

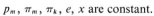

Figure 11–4

p_m, π_m, π_k, e, x are constant.

describes the behavior of the system when a deficit-financed fiscal policy is used to stabilize prices.

Suppose now that there is only one stable state of steady growth, (k^*, g^*), and that the system is at that point. Assume that a levy is imposed on the holders of government debt and that this levy reduces the stock of debt from g^* to g_0 while the capital stock is still k^*. As the arrows in Figure 11–4 show, at the point (k^*, g_0) the rate of change in the ratio of capital to labor is negative. This confirms the conclusions we reached when we examined the short-run effects of a levy. The decrease in the debt is deflationary; if the government wants to avoid deflation, it will have to follow an easy fiscal policy that stimulates consumption, lowers the equilibrium price of capital, and reduces the rate of capital accumulation. The easy fiscal policy necessary to avoid deflation will also increase the deficit and produce a growing per-capita stock of debt over time.

As the stock of capital falls and the stock of debt rises over time, the price of capital will steadily rise. Eventually, for a low enough capital stock and a high enough stock of debt (point B in Figure 11–4), the level of investment will exceed what is required to maintain a constant k, and the capital stock will start growing. This process will continue until the system returns to its original equilibrium position, (k^*, g^*). Again, a once and for all levy on the holders of total government debt has no long-run effect.

In the previous two cases we concluded that if the size of the budget deficit remains unchanged, the stock of debt will converge to its prelevy value, and the levy will have had no effect on the long-run stock of capital. In the last case the deficit does vary, but it varies in order to maintain stable prices; the government cannot choose freely the size of the deficit. Unless the government changes the composition of the debt or the scale of expenditures, it cannot control the long-run stock of debt or capital.

What can the government do to influence the long-run stock of debt? Let us first consider the cases of stabilization through a balanced-budget fiscal policy and through monetary policy. In both these cases the law of accumulation of government debt is

$$(11\text{–}1) \qquad\qquad \dot{g} = d^* - ng.$$

Given the long-run rate of growth n, the long-run stock of debt $g^* = d^*/n$ depends only on the level of the per-capita deficit. We have already examined the effects of reducing the deficit under these two stabilization policies in Chapters 7 and 9 and will not repeat these arguments here. The important point is that the capital levy adds nothing in these cases to the effects on the steady-state capital stock of the lower deficit. This is true despite the fact that the levy has separate short-run effects.

If the deficit is the instrument used to compensate for changes in other variables and to prevent changes in the price level, in order to change the deficit and the long-run stock of debt, the government must change some other variable in the system. The two variables that the government is free to vary are the composition of the debt and the level of government expenditures. We have already shown in Section 10–3 that a decrease in the ratio of debt to money brought about by an open market purchase increases the steady-state stock of capital while it may raise or lower the steady-state stock of debt and that a rise in government expenditures lowers both steady-state stocks. There is no unambiguous relationship between the steady-state stocks of debt and capital that is independent of the policy procedure used. A higher debt does not necessarily imply a lower steady-state stock of capital. In addition, while our purpose in considering these two experiments is to determine the relationship between the steady-state stocks of debt and capital, the experiments basically describe the relationship between the steady-state stock of capital, the composition of the debt, and the scale of government expenditures.

11–4   Short-Run Effects of Changes in the Stock of Government Bonds

To the extent that government bonds are part of private wealth, as they are in our model, the effect of a decrease in stock of government bonds on the demand for consumption goods is qualitatively the same as the effects of a reduction in the aggregate stock of debt, provided that the deficit remains constant. The reduction in the stock of bonds lowers private wealth; it decreases the demand for consumption goods and increases the consumption goods market equilibrium price of capital for the existing price of money.

The effects of a decrease in the stock of government bonds in the assets markets are more complicated. While the decrease in wealth that results from a reduction in the stock of bonds lowers the demand for capital, the reduction in the rate of interest that has to occur for the bond market to return to equilibrium with a lower stock of bonds increases the demand for capital. The equilibrium price of capital that equilibrates the assets markets may fall, rise, or remain unchanged. Since the effect of a decrease in the stock of bonds unambiguously increases the consumption goods market equilibrium price of capital while its effect on the asset markets equilibrium price of capital is ambiguous, there is no presumption that the net effect of a decrease in the stock of bonds is to stimulate the rate of growth.

A sudden decrease in the supply of government bonds can result from either an open market operation or a capital levy on bond holders. In earlier chapters we dealt with the first type of change in the stock of bonds and concluded that in general an open market purchase lowers the equilibrium price of money and raises the equilibrium price of capital, thus raising the rate of growth. Here we analyze the second type of decrease in the stock of bonds.

There is a distinctive difference between these two cases that is very important to keep in mind. The fall in the stock of bonds that results from a levy represents a net subtraction from the private sector's stock of non-human wealth. It reduces the private sector's net claims on the government. On the other hand, a decrease in the supply of bonds that results from an open market purchase does not, directly, reduce the private stock of wealth. The open market operation can change the value of private wealth through its effects on the prices of money and capital, but there is no net change in the nominal value of the government debt since the private sector releases bond holdings of value exactly equal to the increase in the money supply.

To analyze the effects of this type of change in the stock of bonds, we use as usual a pair of aa and cc schedules, which in this case will show the combinations of b and p_k that equilibrate the assets and consumption markets goods for given k, m, p_m, d, and e. To know how to draw these schedules, we must analyze the effects of a change in b in all assets markets as well as in the market for consumption goods. We begin with the assets markets.

(A) EFFECTS OF CHANGES IN THE STOCK OF GOVERNMENT BONDS IN THE ASSETS MARKETS

A decrease in b lowers the private stock of wealth and, therefore, under our assumptions, the demand for money and capital, thus creating excess supply in these markets. Given any price of capital, the decrease in the demand for real cash balances lowers the rate of interest at which the money market is in equilibrium. This means that the mm schedule of money market (i, p_k) equilibrium points (see Section 3-3) shifts from $m_0 m_0$ to $m_1 m_1$, as indicated in Figure 11-5. On the other hand, the decrease in the demand for real capital lowers the price of capital that equilibrates the capital goods market for any given rate of interest. The kk schedule in Figure 11-5 shifts downward to the left from $k_0 k_0$ to $k_1 k_1$.

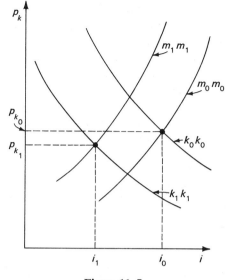

Figure 11-5

m, k, p_m, π_m, π_k are constant. b falls from b_0 to b_1.

It follows from Figure 11–5 that a decrease in the stock of government bonds necessarily lowers the rate of interest at which wealth owners will hold the lower stock of bonds, but may result in a lower or a higher assets markets equilibrium price of capital, depending on whether as a result of the fall in the stock of bonds the kk schedule shifts to the left by more or by less than the mm schedule. The leftward shift of these schedules, in turn, depends on two factors: the wealth elasticity of the demand for capital and money and the degree of substitutability of money and capital for bonds.

A high wealth elasticity of demand for capital, for example, means that as the stock of bonds falls there is a substantial decrease in the demand for capital. Other things equal, there will then have to be a substantial fall in the rate of interest to eliminate the excess supply in the capital market; that is, there will be a large leftward shift of the kk schedule. The leftward shift, however, does not depend only on the excess supply created by the reduction in b but also on how sensitive the excess demand for capital is with respect to changes in the rate of interest. If the demand for capital is not very responsive to changes in the rate of of return on bonds, that is, if capital is not a good substitute for bonds, the change in i necessary to eliminate any excess supply of capital will have to be even larger, thereby increasing the leftward shift of the kk schedule. If bonds are a good substitute for money and not for capital, and if the demand for capital has a high wealth elasticity compared to the wealth elasticity of the demand for money, the decrease in the stock of bonds results in a lower assets markets equilibrium price of capital. This case is shown in Figure 11-4. While the decrease in the stock of bonds results in a lower assets markets equilibrium rate of interest, the assets markets equilibrium price of capital may rise or fall as a result of the reduction in b.

We can prove these results by differentiating any two of the equilibrium conditions in the assets markets. We use for this purpose equations (3–8) and (3–10).

$$(11\text{–}2) \qquad \frac{\partial i}{\partial b} = \frac{p_m}{\Delta}\left[\left(\frac{\partial J}{\partial p_k} - k\right)\frac{\partial L}{\partial a} - \frac{\partial L}{\partial p_k}\frac{\partial J}{\partial a}\right] > 0$$

where

$$(11\text{–}3) \qquad \Delta = \frac{\partial L}{\partial p_k}\frac{\partial J}{\partial \rho_b} - \left(\frac{\partial J}{\partial p_k} - k\right)\frac{\partial L}{\partial \rho_b} < 0$$

and

$$(11\text{–}4) \qquad \frac{\partial p_k}{\partial b} = \frac{p_m}{\Delta}\left(\frac{\partial J}{\partial a}\frac{\partial L}{\partial \rho_b} - \frac{\partial L}{\partial a}\frac{\partial J}{\partial \rho_b}\right) \gtreqless 0.$$

$$(11\text{–}5) \quad \frac{\partial p_k}{\partial b} = \left(\frac{p_m}{\Delta}\right)\left(\frac{J}{L}\right)\left(\frac{\partial L}{\partial \rho_b}\frac{\partial L}{\partial a}\right)\left[\frac{(a/J)(\partial J/\partial a)}{(a/L)(\partial L/\partial a)} - \frac{(\rho_b/J)(\partial J/\partial \rho_b)}{(\rho_b/L)(\partial L/\partial \rho_b)}\right]$$

$$= \left(\frac{p_m}{\Delta}\right)\left(\frac{J}{L}\right)\left(\frac{\partial L}{\partial \rho_b}\frac{\partial L}{\partial a}\right)\left(\frac{\eta_{ka}}{\eta_{ma}} - \frac{\eta_{k\rho_b}}{\eta_{m\rho_b}}\right) \gtreqless 0,$$

where η stands for elasticity, the first subscript refers to the asset, and the second subscript to the variable in the demand functions. Since the expression outside the parentheses is positive in equation (11–5), the increase in the stock of bonds will raise or lower the equilibrium price of capital depending on whether the ratio of the wealth elasticity of demand for capital to the wealth elasticity of the demand for money is greater or smaller than the ratio of the elasticity of demand for capital with respect to the rate of return on bonds to the elasticity of the demand for money with respect to the rate of return on bonds.

It follows that the aa schedules in Figures 11–6 and 11–7, which depict the combinations of p_k and b that equilibrate the assets markets for given

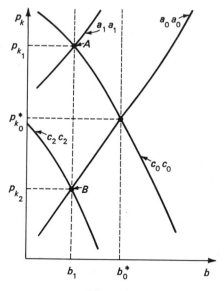

Figure 11–6

m, k, p_m, π_m, π_k are constant. x falls from x_0 to x_1 or d rises from d_0 to d_2 or e rises from e_0 to e_2.

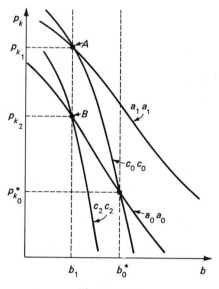

Figure 11–7

m, k, p_m, π_m, π_k are constant. x falls from x_0 to x_1 or d rises from d_0 to d_2 or e rises from e_0 to e_2.

p_m, k, and m, may be upward- or downward-sloped, depending on whether an increase in the stock of bonds raises or lowers the price of capital at which wealth owners are willing to hold the existing stocks of capital and money.

(B) EFFECTS OF CHANGES IN THE STOCK OF GOVERNMENT BONDS IN THE CONSUMPTION GOODS MARKET

We now consider the effects of a change in the stock of bonds in the consumption goods market. Given a constant deficit, a decrease in the stock of bonds affects the demand for consumption goods in the same way that a decrease in the aggregate stock of debt does. In general there are two channels: an income effect and a wealth effect. Since the expected rate of inflation is zero, the income effect does not exist and we are left with a wealth effect, which decreases the demand for consumption goods by reducing private wealth. The *cc* schedule, which in this case shows the combinations of the outstanding stock of government bonds and the price of capital for which the consumption goods market clears, is downward-sloped, as shown in Figures 11–6 and 11–7.

(C) OVERALL SHORT-RUN EFFECTS OF A DECREASE IN THE STOCK OF GOVERNMENT BONDS

Two possible intersections of the *cc* and *aa* schedules are shown in Figures 11–6 and 11–7, and in each of these cases the effect of a decrease in the stock of government bonds is different.

Consider first Figure 11–6 and suppose that the stock of bonds falls from b_0^* to b_1. As a result of this, the demand for consumption goods decreases, thus raising the consumption goods market equilibrium price of capital from $p_{k_0}^*$ to p_{k_1}. On the other hand, the decrease in b has lowered the assets markets equilibrium price of capital from $p_{k_0}^*$ to p_{k_2}, thereby further increasing the level of excess supply in the consumption goods market. If the government does not accompany the decrease in the stock of bonds by a change in its monetary or fiscal policy aimed at restraining aggregate demand, the price level will fall.

If the government uses monetary policy to stabilize the price level, it must make an open market purchase to lower the rate of interest and raise the demand for capital until the *aa* schedule shifts rightward from $a_0 a_0$ to $a_1 a_1$ the $c_0 c_0$ schedule at A. The result of this policy will be a higher equilibrium price of capital and a higher rate of growth in the short run. The effect of a decrease in the stock of debt in this case is to encourage growth.

On the other hand, if the government uses fiscal policy to stabilize the price level, whether by reducing taxes and increasing its deficit or by increasing taxes and expenditures with a constant deficit, it will have to shift the cc schedule leftward from $c_0 c_0$ to $c_1 c_1$, so that for each b the consumption goods market p_k and thus private demand is lower, until this schedule intersects the $a_0 a_0$ schedule at B. The result of this stabilization policy is to decrease the price of capital and to reduce the economy's rate of growth in the short run.

When the aa schedule is downward-sloped, that is, when a decrease in the stock of bonds raises the assets markets equilibrium price of capital, but the slope of this schedule is steeper than the slope of the cc schedule, the decrease in the stock of bonds is also potentially deflationary (see Figure 11–7). This is because at the lower stock of debt b_1 the price of capital that clears the assets markets, p_{k_2}, is lower than the price of capital, p_{k_1}, that clears the consumption goods market. If the government does not use its monetary or fiscal tools, the excess supply would have to be eliminated by a rise in the price of money.

If the government wants to avoid a rise in the price of money, it will have to use fiscal policy to shift the cc schedule leftward from $c_0 c_0$ to $c_1 c_1$ until it intersects the $a_0 a_0$ line at A or it will have to use monetary policy to shift the aa schedule rightward from $a_0 a_0$ to $a_1 a_1$ until it intersects the $c_0 c_0$ schedule at B in Figure 11–7. In both cases the result is a rise in the equilibrium price of capital and a higher rate of capital accumulation. The increase in the rate of capital accumulation is larger when the government uses a tight monetary policy for stabilization. The reader can work out the case in which both the aa and cc schedules have a negative slope and the aa schedule intersects the cc schedule from below.

We can summarize the short-run effects of a decrease in the stock of government bonds as follows. If the decrease in the stock of bonds lowers the price of capital at which wealth owners desire to hold the existing stocks of money and capital, the decrease in the stock of bonds is deflationary and an easy monetary or fiscal policy is required to avoid a decrease in the price level. If the government chooses an easy monetary policy, the price of capital rises and so does the rate of growth. If fiscal policy is used for stabilization, whether by changing the deficit or by changing the level of taxes and expenditures with a constant deficit, the price of capital falls and growth slows. We emphasize that these short-run effects will not necessarily hold in the long run.

11–5 Long-Run Effects of Changes in the Stock of Government Bonds

In Section 11–4 we analyzed the short-run effects of a change in the stock of government bonds. We now consider whether or not these effects hold for the long run. As explained in the beginning of this chapter, the effects of changes in stock of both bonds and debt depend crucially on the stabilization policy being used by the government. We shall again consider the three polar cases, beginning with that of a deficit-financed fiscal policy.

The imposition of a levy on the holders of government bonds is equivalent to a reduction in the aggregate stock of debt. Remembering that $x = g/m$, we can see that a levy on bond holders reduces the numerator while the denominator remains unchanged; that is, the ratio of debt to money is reduced. Figures 11–8a and 11–8b show the two possible patterns of dynamic behavior of an economy in which aggregate demand is stabilized by using a deficit-financed fiscal policy (see Chapter 10). If we start from the state of steady growth (k_0^*, g_0^*), we can see that a levy on bond holders means that the economy at the time of the levy jumps from E_0 to a point with a lower g, E_1, E_2, or E_3. In addition both the $\dot{g} = 0$ and the $\dot{k} = 0$ lines shift downward as a result of the fall in x, with the $\dot{k} = 0$ locus shifting farther downward than the $\dot{g} = 0$ locus, as proved in Chapter 10.

The long-run outcome is an increase in the stock of capital. The reason for this is easy to see if we decompose the levy on bond holders into two separate components, a reduction in the aggregate stock of debt and a

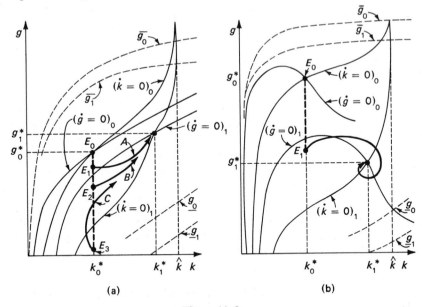

Figure 11–8

p_m, π_m, π_k, e are constant. x falls from x_0 to x_1.

decrease in the ratio of debt to money. As shown earlier in this chapter, the reduction in the stock of debt has only temporary effects, representing a change in initial conditions; it has by itself no effect on the steady-state stock of capital. The fall in x has a permanent effect, just like an open market purchase, which we know already leads to a higher long-run stock of capital. The long-run effect of a levy on bond holders, when a deficit-financed fiscal policy is used to stabilize the price level, is to increase the long-run capital stock because of the change in the composition of the stock of government debt.

While in the steady state the only change that has a permanent effect is the change in the composition of the debt, in the short run both the change in the composition and the initial decrease in the aggregate stock of debt affect the rate of growth. Since they have opposite effects on the assets markets price of capital, we can see why we were unable in Section 11–4 to find an unambiguous short-run effect on the rate of growth from a levy on bond holders when fiscal policy is used to stabilize the price level. The paths that the economy may follow to reach the higher stock of capital k_1^* may involve a steady rise in the stock of capital (arrows A and B in Figure 11–8a), or first a decline and then a rise in the capital stock (arrow C in Figure 11–8a), or fluctuations (Figure 11–8b). The direction in which the economy tends to move in the short run may not be a good indicator of where it is going in the long run. Some policy changes that lower the short-run rate of capital accumulation may actually raise the economy's steady-state stock of capital.

The imposition of a levy on bond holders increases the steady-state stock of capital, and this higher long-run stock of capital may be associated with a higher aggregate stock of government debt. This case is shown in Figure 11–8a in which $g_1^* > g_0^*$. This may occur when an increase in the stock of capital creates excess supply in the consumption goods market. As k rises, an expansionary fiscal policy is needed to stabilize aggregate demand; the government runs higher deficits and the economy may end up with higher stocks of both capital and debt.

Now consider fiscal policy stabilization through marginally balanced-budget changes in expenditures and taxes. It follows from our discussion in Section 11–3 that the long-run stock of debt will not be affected unless the levy on bonds is accompanied by a reduction in the deficit. Therefore the $\dot{g} = 0$ schedule in Figure 11–9, which depicts the dynamic behavior of the system (see Chapter 9), does not shift as a result of the levy on bond holders. The levy can again be thought of as a combination of a reduction in the aggregate stock of debt and a change in its composition. The fall in the ratio of debt to money raises the price of capital, which in this case is

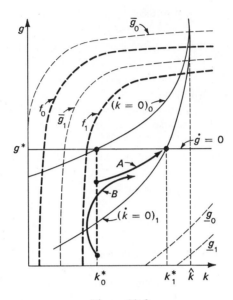

Figure 11–9

p_m, π_m, π_k, d are constant. x falls from x_0 to x_1.

determined in the assets markets, and the output of investment goods for each g. The $(\dot{k} = 0)_0$ locus is now in the $\dot{k} > 0$ region, and the locus shifts rightward to $(\dot{k} = 0)_1$. As can be seen in Figure 11–9, the result of the levy on bond holders is a higher steady-state stock of capital.

The explanation of this result is similar to the one we gave for the effects of a bond levy when a deficit-financed fiscal policy is used to stabilize the price level. Since the deficit is constant, the reduction in the aggregate debt due to the levy has only temporary effects; through time the debt moves back to its original level. The change in the composition of the debt has temporary as well as permanent effects, and again it is the resulting change in the composition of the debt that produces the change in the steady-state stock of capital.

In the short run the reduction in the aggregate debt and the change in its composition push the equilibrium price of capital in opposite directions. The short-run rate of capital accumulation may as a consequence fall or rise depending on the strength of the two effects. The economy may approach the higher steady-state stock of capital with steadily rising stocks of capital and debt (arrow A in Figure 11–9), or it may approach it with first a declining and then an increasing stock of capital but a constantly increasing stock of debt (arrow B).

When any kind of fiscal policy is used to stabilize the price level, a once and for all levy on bond holders will increase the steady-state stock of capital because it unambiguously lowers the ratio of debt to money. It is equivalent to an open market purchase, which, as we have seen, increases the steady-state stock of capital. In the short run, the levy is equivalent to a combination of a levy on the total debt, which according to Section 11–2 reduces the short-run rate of growth, and an open market purchase, which stimulates accumulation in the short run. It is for this reason that when fiscal policy of either type is used to stabilize the price level, the short-run effects of a levy on bond holders are ambiguous.

Finally, we are left with only one of the polar stabilization policies to consider, the case in which the government uses monetary policy to regulate aggregate demand. In this case, as before, a levy on the holders of government bonds that is not accompanied by a change in the deficit has no effect on the position of the $\dot{g} = 0$ schedule. This is shown in Figure 11–10, which illustrates the dynamic behavior of a system in which open market operations stabilize aggregate demand. In addition, in this case the equilibrium price of capital is determined in the consumption goods market as a function of the stocks of capital and debt, government expenditures, and the deficit. Under our assumption the equilibrium price of capital in the consumption goods market does not depend on the composition of the debt so that a levy on bond holders, which is a combination of

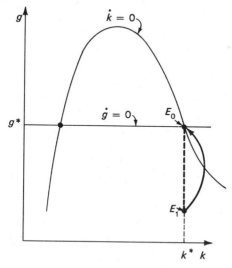

Figure 11–10

p_m, π_m, π_k, d, e are constant.

a reduction on the total debt and a change in its composition, does not affect the position of the $k = 0$ locus either. The only effect of the levy on bond holders is to make the system jump from E_0 to E_1.

The levy on bond holders is in this case merely a change in initial conditions. The reduction in the debt lowers consumption by reducing private wealth, and the rate of capital accumulation accelerates. But as time passes the stock of debt returns to its original value g^* and so does the stock of capital. The composition of the debt cannot be freely chosen by the monetary authorities. The composition of the debt is determined by the government's commitment to a stable price level. There is no difference in this case between a levy on bond holders and a levy on the holders of the aggregate debt. Since the deficit is unchanged and the government cannot freely choose the composition of the debt, the steady-state stocks of debt and capital cannot be affected.

When a deficit-financed fiscal policy is used to stabilize aggregate demand, a levy on bond holders may increase or decrease the short-run rate of growth, but it unambiguously increases the steady-state stock of capital. When a balanced budget policy is used to stabilize the price level, and the levy is not accompanied by a reduction of the deficit so as to keep the debt constant at the new level, the same results hold. In both cases the steady-state is due to the change in the composition of the debt that is brought about by the levy on bond holders, while the short-run result is due to the change in the composition and the initial reduction in the aggregate stock of debt. When monetary policy is used for stabilization, the composition of the debt cannot be changed at the discretion of the government, so that if the deficit remains constant, the steady-state composition of the debt will be unchanged, as will the steady-state stock of capital. In the short run the reduction in the aggregate debt that results from the levy does stimulate capital accumulation; but if the deficit is unchanged, these results disappear over time.

When monetary policy or a marginally balanced-budget fiscal policy is used for stabilization, we can perform a slightly different experiment from the one we performed here. What happens if the government imposes a levy on bond holders and at the same time reduces the deficit to maintain a constant postlevy aggregate stock of debt? When we considered this experiment in connection with levies on the aggregate stock of debt, we concluded that as far as long-run effects are concerned, a levy on the aggregate debt that is accompanied by a change in the deficit is indistinguishable from a simple reduction in the deficit. The reason for this was that the levy itself has no long-run effect. In this case, however, the conclusion is different. A levy on bond holders that is accompanied by a reduction in the deficit may have long-run effects different from a reduction in the deficit. The reason for this is that in some cases the levy by itself, by changing the composition of the debt, will affect the stock of capital in the steady state. In this case a levy on bond holders coupled with a reduction in the deficit has effects on the stock of capital that are the sum of the independent effects of the two experiments. When monetary policy is used to stabilize aggregate demand, the long-run effect of the levy is nil, while the reduction in the deficit raises the capital stock, so that the net effect of a simultaneous levy and reduction in the deficit is an increase in the stock of capital. This is also the effect of a simple reduction in the deficit. When a marginally balanced budget is used to stabilize aggregate demand, the effect of the levy is an increase in the steady-state capital stock, but the effect of the lower deficit is a decrease in it. The effect of both of them combined is ambiguous as opposed to the simple decreases in the deficit, which lower the capital stock in the steady state.

11–6 Summary

The principal conclusion we can draw from the rather long and involved analysis of this chapter is that the effects of a change in the stock of debt depend crucially on exactly how the change is performed, on whether only the stock of bonds or bonds plus money is involved, and on whether any other variable is changed. In addition, the stabilization policy being pursued by the government determines both what the government can do and what the results of its actions will be.

The discussion also suggests that the concept of the "burden" of the public debt is ill-posed. The question is what the consequences of a given mix of government policies will be on the capital stock. The spirit of the "burden" literature is that the way to answer this question is to see what the effects of the policy will be on the debt, with the presumption that anything that increases the debt lowers the capital stock. This is an appealing short cut, but, at least in our model, it does not invariably lead to the truth.

Issues in Theory and Policy

Perfectly Anticipated Inflation

12-1 Introduction

We are now in a position to extend our analysis to more complicated problems. The first kind of complication we consider is the possibility that the government may choose rates of inflation that are different from zero.

The inflation we are talking about is not a result of disequilibrium in any market. At each instant the economy comes into equilibrium with all markets clearing at some set of prices and interest rates, and the rate of inflation is the rate at which the price level has to change for all markets to clear at each point in time. Up to this point we have studied paths on which the equilibrium price was constant through time. Now we consider paths on which p_m rises or declines steadily from instant to instant. Ours is an equilibrium theory of inflation. Each time a price is registered it is an equilibrium price, and we do not discuss the process by which this price is found or its stability.

In this chapter we are concerned only with the effects of a perfectly anticipated inflation, that is, an inflation in which everyone expects the rate of change in prices that actually occurs. This essentially requires that the government announce its target rate of inflation, that everyone believe it, and that the government then manipulate its policy tools to achieve that rate, taking into account what people believe. Changes in the expected rate of inflation, as shown in Section 5–5, affect both the assets markets and the consumption goods market. The government must take account of and counteract these shifts in the *aa* and *cc* schedules to achieve at each instant the desired p_m.

The effects of a perfectly anticipated inflation and an imperfectly anticipated inflation are only different in the short run. In the long run, after everybody has time to adjust his expectations to a constant sustained rate of price increase, the effects will be quite similar.

In Sections 12–2 through 12–5 we analyze the behavior of the economy when inflation occurs at a constant rate that is perfectly anticipated by consumers and wealth owners, while the government uses different policies to maintain a constant rate of inflation over time.

12–2   Stabilization of the Rate of Inflation Through a Deficit-Financed Fiscal Policy

When the rate of inflation is perfectly foreseen by the private sector and is maintained at a constant level by manipulation of the size of the deficit, the system behaves very much as it does when the government maintains a constant price level by using a deficit-financed fiscal policy.

The equation describing the growth of the capital stock is, as usual,

$$(12\text{–}1) \qquad \qquad k = q_I(k, p_k) - nk.$$

The price of capital that clears the assets markets depends only on the real stock of debt, $\gamma = gp_m$; the composition of the debt, x; the stock of capital, k; and the expected rate of deflation, π_m. The composition we assume in this section remains constant at x^*. If inflation is perfectly foreseen, π_m is equal to the actual rate of inflation ($\dot{p}_m/p_m$), and this in turn, we assume, is constant at some level $(\dot{p}_m/p_m)^* = \pi_m^*$.

We can write

$$(12\text{–}2) \qquad \qquad p_k = \Phi(\gamma, k, \pi_m^*, x^*).$$

Substituting equation (12–2) into (12–1), we express the rate of change in per-capita stock of capital as a function of the stocks of capital and real government debt and the constant composition of the debt and rate of inflation:

$$(12\text{–}3) \qquad \qquad k = q_I[k, \Phi(\gamma, k, \pi_m^*, x^*)] - nk.$$

Since x and π_m are constant, the only thing that we need to close our system is an equation describing the time path of the real stock of government debt. We again make use of the simplifying assumption of the proportional consumption function [equation (4–3)] and have for equilibrium in the consumption goods market:

(12–4) $q_C[k, \Phi(\gamma, k, \pi_m^*, x^*)] - e^*$

$$= (1 - s)\{q[k, \Phi(\gamma, k, \pi_m^*, x^*)] + dp_m + \pi_m^* \gamma - e^*\}.$$

where $dp_m + \pi_m^* \gamma$ sums up the net effect on disposable income of the creation of government debt and changes in the value of money. We assume that expenditures are constant at e^*. Since the expected and actual rates of inflation are the same, $dp_m + \pi_m^* \gamma$ is equal to the real value of the change in the debt. We can write

(12–5) $$dp_m + \pi_m^* \gamma = (\dot{g}/g + n + \pi_m)\gamma = \dot{\gamma} + n\gamma.$$

(12–6) $q_C(k, \Phi(\gamma, k, \pi_m^*, x^*)) - e^*$

$$= (1 - s)(q(k, \Phi(\gamma, k, \pi_m^*, x^*)) + \dot{\gamma} + n\gamma - e^*).$$

Solving this for the rate of change in the per-capita real government debt, we obtain

(12–7) $\dot{\gamma} = [1/(1 - s)][q_C(k, \Phi(\gamma, k, \pi_m^*, x^*))$

$$- se^* - (1 - s)q(k, \Phi(\gamma, k, \pi_m^*, x^*))] - n\gamma.$$

Since n, s, e^*, x^*, and π_m^* are constants, we have also expressed the rate of change in the per-capita real stock of government debt as a function of the stocks of capital and real debt. Equations (12–3) and (12–7) are a system of two differential equations in two unknowns, k and γ, which, given the initial conditions k_0 and γ_0, completely describe the time path of the stocks of capital and real debt. Given these paths, we can determine the behavior of the other variables in our model: the rate of interest and the price of capital.

Except for the constant π_m^* and for the substitution of the real stock of debt γ for the nominal stock g, equations (12–3) and (12–7) are identical to equations (8–11) and (8–12), so that the behavior of the economy when the government maintains a constant rate of inflation is described by a figure similar to Figure 8–4 in which γ replaces g on the vertical axis. It follows that everything we said about the existence, uniqueness, and stability of the steady-growth path in Chapter 8 also applies here.

12–3   Effects of Changes in the Rate of Inflation

We now analyze the effects of an increase in the target rate of inflation. Since we want to consider a perfectly anticipated inflation, we assume that as the government adjusts its policy tools to achieve the higher rate of inflation, it also announces to the public the new higher target rate of inflation. We also assume that the private sector believes what it has been told by the government and adjusts its expectations instantaneously.

If we were to look at the time path of this economy's price of money on a semilogarithmic scale diagram, the picture would look like Figure 12–1. The change in the target rate of inflation is reflected by a change in the slope of the $p_m(t)$ line at time T, but there is no jump in p_m at time T. If, when the government announces a change in the rate of inflation, it does not want to disappoint private expectations about the course that p_m will follow, then no jump in p_m can be allowed at $t = T$. Otherwise, the rate of change of p_m at $t = T$ would be infinite.

What is the effect of the change in the expected rate of inflation on the market equilibrium prices and rates of interest, and what kind of action on the part of the government is required to assure that the growth of p_m, as shown in Figure 12–1, will actually be followed?

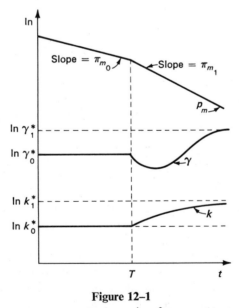

Figure 12–1

π_k, e, x are constant. π_m rises from π_{m_0} to π_{m_1}.

Suppose that we start from a state of steady growth with a given rate of inflation, $-\pi_{m_0}$; a stock of capital, k^*; and a positive outstanding stock of real debt, γ^*. If γ is constant at γ^*, we have $\dot{\gamma} = 0$. From equation (12–5) we can write $\dot{\gamma}$ as $p_m d + \pi_m^* \gamma = n\gamma$. This shows that in a steady state the deficit must be large enough to offset both the depreciation of the debt caused by inflation and to maintain the per-capita magnitude in the face of population growth.

The $c_0 c_0$ and $a_0 a_0$ lines in Figure 12–2 indicate the combinations of γ and p_k that clear the consumption goods and assets markets, respectively, when $k = k^*$, $\pi_m = \pi_{m_0}$, $\pi_k = 0$, $e = e_0$, and $x = x_0$. As shown in Section 5–5, the increase in the expected rate of inflation, that is, the fall in π_m, shifts both of the schedules rightward. The price of capital rises, while the price of money, and the real stock of debt, may either rise or fall. If the government wants the price level to follow a path like the one indicated in Figure 12–1, it will have to change the size of its deficit so that the cc schedule shifts to $c_1 c_1$ and intersects the $a_1 a_1$ schedule at (γ^*, p_{k_1}). If this is done, no jump in p_m occurs at time T and the price level starts moving along a path like the one indicated in Figure 12–1. It is important to note, however, that although the actual deficit may have to rise or fall to make the $c_1 c_1$ schedule intersect the $a_1 a_1$ line at (γ^*, p_{k_1}), $p_m d + \pi_m \gamma$ has to fall for

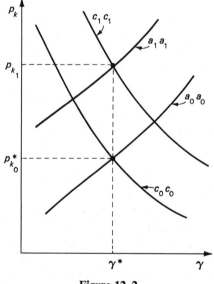

Figure 12–2

g, k, π_k, e, x are constant. π_m falls from π_{m_0} to π_{m_1}.

the cc line to shift rightward. This means that as a result of the increase in the rate of inflation, the rate of change in the real stock of debt becomes negative, while the increase in the price of capital raises the rate of change in the per-capita stock of capital by shifting resources from the consumption to the investment goods sector.

The explanation for the fall in $\dot{\gamma}$ at the moment when π_m rises is that a rise in π_m acts in the assets markets like an open market purchase. Since p_m cannot move *instantaneously* on the path pictured in Figure 12–1, something like an increase in taxes is required to clear the consumption-goods market. The increase in π_m acts like an increase in taxes if g is positive, but it may be too large or too small a change. The change in d reinforces or offsets the change in g to make $\dot{\gamma}$ fall enough to clear the consumption market.

In terms of Figure 12–3, where we plot the $\dot{\gamma} = 0$ and $\dot{k} = 0$ lines for the two different rates of inflation $-\pi_{m_0}$ and $-\pi_{m_1}$, the increase in the expected rate of inflation shifts the $\dot{k} = 0$ line downward and to the right, from $(\dot{k} = 0)_0$ to $(\dot{k} = 0)_1$, because for any (k, γ) pair the increase in the expected rate of inflation has increased the equilibrium price of capital, thus making $\dot{k}$ positive whenever it was previously equal to zero. Given any stock of debt γ, the economy can now sustain a higher stock of real capital; or alternatively, to sustain any given stock of capital k, the required stock of debt is now lower because p_k has increased as a result of the higher rate of inflation.

On the other hand, since to maintain the economy on a path like the one indicated in Figure 12–1, $p_m d + \pi_m \gamma$ has to fall when the higher rate of inflation is announced, at any k the economy will now be able to maintain a lower stock of real government debt. The $\dot{\gamma} = 0$ line shifts downward, from $(\dot{\gamma} = 0)_0$ to $(\dot{\gamma} = 0)_1$.

It may seem odd that a higher rate of inflation is associated with smaller increments to the real value of the government debt. This is attributable to the fact mentioned above that a higher expected rate of inflation has by itself an expansionary effect in the capital market, tending to raise p_k. If expectations were not operating, a larger deficit would be necessary to push up the price level faster at the start. This situation is studied in more detail in Chapter 13.

It is easy to show that the downward shift of the $\dot{\gamma} = 0$ line is smaller than that of the $\dot{k} = 0$ lines, and, therefore, that the increase in the rate of inflation raises the long-run stock of capital. Suppose that π_m falls and that γ also falls, so as to maintain a constant p_k; this change in γ is the change that is required to maintain $\dot{k} = 0$ for the given k_0^*. However, since equation (12–7) has a $-n\gamma$ term on the righthand side, the fall in γ that keeps p_k constant will make $\dot{\gamma}$ negative. Therefore, for $\dot{\gamma}$ to be equal to zero, γ has to fall by less than the decrease required to maintain a constant k. This shows that the new $\dot{\gamma} = 0$ schedule lies above the new $\dot{k} = 0$ schedule at k_0^*.

The path that the economy will actually follow between the two steady states is indicated by the heavy arrow in Figure 12–3. The fact that the arrow has a negative slope at E_0 coincides with our conclusion that the impact effect of an increase in the rate of inflation is an increase in the rate of change in the stock of capital and a decrease in the rate of change in the real stock of government debt.

We can explain the rest of the path between E_0 and E_1 as follows. As the stock of capital starts rising and the stock of debt starts falling, the equilibrium price of capital decreases. The increase in k, which lowers output per head in the investment goods sector and increases the level of investment necessary to maintain a constant ratio of capital to labor, and the fall in the price of capital together lower the rate at which the ratio of capital to labor is increasing. On the other hand, as the ratio of capital to labor increases and the price of capital falls, excess supply is created in the consumption goods market. The consumption goods market will clear at a constant rate of inflation π_m, only at a higher deficit. The rise in d causes γ to fall at a lower rate, and there may be a point, like A, at which the real

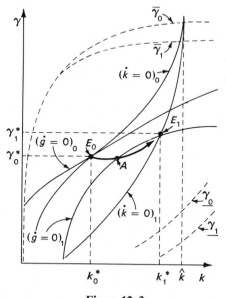

Figure 12–3

π_k, e, x are constant. π_m falls from π_{m_0} to π_{m_1}.

stock of debt may actually start rising. It follows that to maintain a constant rate of inflation, the initial tight fiscal policy may have to revert to an easy fiscal policy, which may in turn result in a higher steady-state stock of real debt. The higher rate of inflation will increase the stock of capital and may increase the stock of real government debt.

Before we conclude this section, we should note the similarity between the effects of a change in the rate of inflation and the effects of an open market operation when a deficit-financed fiscal policy is used to stabilize the price level. x and π_m appear in the same form in both the $\dot{k}$ and $\dot{y}$ equations, and therefore the effects on the real stock of debt and on the stock of capital of a change in the rate of inflation are identical to those of a change in the composition of the government debt when stabilization of the price level is achieved through a deficit-financed fiscal policy. If for some reason, such as the nonexistence of well-developed financial markets in underdeveloped economies, open market operations cannot be conducted the government can achieve the same results insofar as the real changes in the stock of capital are concerned by giving up its price stability goal and using inflation or deflation to achieve the desired path for investment.

There is little that we can say about the behavior of the interest rate. We have already noted in Section 3–6 that a fall in π_m for given stocks of real debt and capital and a given composition of the debt may either raise or lower the equilibrium rate of interest, so the impact effect of an increase in the expected rate of inflation is ambiguous in this model. As the economy moves along the $E_0 A E_1$ path in Figure 12–3, the stocks of capital and real debt vary, and we have concluded in Sections 3–4 and 3–5 that the effects of these changes on the interest rate are ambiguous.

12–4 Stabilization of the Rate of Inflation Through Monetary Policy

In Section 12–3 we analyzed the behavior of the system when inflation is perfectly anticipated and the government continuously adjusts the size of its deficit to maintain a constant rate of inflation over time. We noted that the government has three policy tools: the composition of the debt, the level of government expenditures, and the budget deficit. A long-run steady state requires the composition of the debt and the scale of government expenditures to remain constant over time. In Section 12–3 we fixed them at some constant level and generated the inflationary process, as well as maintained the rate of inflation constant, by varying the deficit.

An alternative to this policy is to have the government fix the rate of expansion in the per-capita stock of debt at some constant level that is consistent with the long-run target rate of inflation and adjust either the composition of the debt or the scale of government expenditures to keep the rate of inflation constant over time. In this case the rate of expansion in the stock of debt will determine the trend of the price level in the long run and either open market purchases and sales or changes in the level of expenditures will assure that the path of the price level does not depart from the long-run trend even in the short run.

Consider first the case in which monetary policy is used to stabilize the rate of inflation. Assume that we start from a steady state with $\theta_0 = (\dot{g}/g)_0 = -\pi_{m_0}$; stocks of capital and real debt, k^* and γ^*; and a steady-state composition of the debt, x^*.

Suppose now that a higher rate of deflation π_{m_1} is announced and that the government adjusts the rate of expansion in its per-capita stock of debt θ to the new level $\theta_1 = -\pi_{m_1}$. Since the rate of expansion in the per-capita nominal stock of debt and the rate of inflation have decreased by the same amount, the deficit was decreased by an amount equal to the decrease in the depreciation of the stock of government debt. This means that disposable income remains unchanged and that the cc schedule does not shift.

On the other hand, the decrease in the expected rate of inflation induces people to shift their portfolios into bonds and money from capital, thus lowering the assets markets equilibrium p_k; the aa line shifts rightward from $a_0 a_0$ to $a_1 a_1$, as shown in Figure 12–4. If a rise in the real stock of debt is to be avoided, because we do not want to allow a jump in p_m, then the government will have to make an open market purchase to shift the aa schedule back to $a_0 a_0$, so that it intersects the cc schedule at the original equilibrium point E. It follows that if monetary policy is used to avoid departures of the price level from its long-run path, the impact effect of an increase in the rate of deflation on the rate of growth is nil. The government deficit and the value of the depreciation of the stock of government debt fall by equal amounts; disposable income is constant; the demand for consumption goods is not affected; and the price of capital has to be kept constant through an open market purchase.

There are, in fact, neither short-run nor long-run effects in this situation. Since the rate of expansion in the stock of debt and the rate of inflation decrease by equal amounts, the rate of change in the real stock of debt remains equal to zero. On the other hand, since the price of capital has not changed, the rate of change in the ratio of capital to labor also remains equal to zero, and no further changes in any of the other variables of the system occur. The economy remains at its original steady state, with stocks of capital and real debt k^* and γ^*, with a lower rate of inflation and a lower

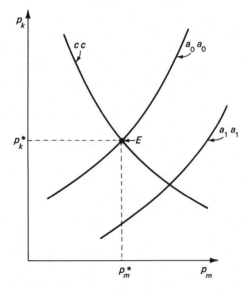

Figure 12–4

g, k, π_k, e are constant. π_m rises from π_{m_0} to π_{m_1} offset by x falling from x_0 to x_2 and d falling from d_0 to d_2.

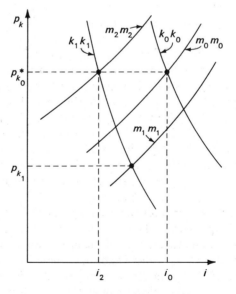

Figure 12–5

g, k, p_m, π_k are constant. π_m rises from π_{m_0} to π_{m_1} offset by x falling from x_0 to x_2.

rate of expansion in the per-capita stock of nominal debt $\theta_1 = -\pi_{m_1}$, and with a lower ratio of debt to money x_1.

The decrease in the expected rate of inflation, other things equal, will decrease the assets markets equilibrium price of capital, and it may raise or lower the equilibrium interest rate. However, if the government stabilizes the rate of inflation by making open market operations, the decrease in p_k has to be avoided by an open market purchase of the proper size, which causes the rate of interest to rise. This is shown in Figure 12–5. The increase in π_m from π_{m_0} to π_{m_1} shifts the kk schedule leftward from $k_0 k_0$ to $k_1 k_1$, and it usually shifts the mm schedule rightward from $m_0 m_0$ to $m_1 m_1$ (under the assumption that the wealth elasticity of the demand for money is not too high; see Proposition 3–2); p_k falls from $p_{k_0}^*$ to p_{k_1}. If p_k is to remain at $p_{k_0}^*$, the government has to make an open market purchase to shift the mm line from $m_1 m_1$ to $m_2 m_2$. The price of capital remains unchanged, but the rate of interest falls. The explanation of this is quite simple. The decrease in the expected rate of inflation lowers the price of capital at which people are willing to hold the existing stock of capital at the given interest rate. If the price of capital is not allowed to change, the interest rate has to fall to induce people to hold the initial stock of capital at the initial price of capital when the rate of inflation is lower.

From the equilibrium condition in the capital goods market, it is easy to see that the interest rate falls by more than the rate of inflation. The leftward shift of the kk line is larger than the increase in π_m, because if the rate of interest decreased by an amount equal to the rise in π_m, the real rate of return on bonds would be unchanged, while the rate of return on money would be higher. There would then be excess supply of capital at the original price of capital. If the capital goods market is to clear at the original p_k, the interest rate has to fall by more than the rise in π_m, so that the higher real rate of return on money is compensated for by a lower real rate of return on bonds. When monetary policy is used to stabilize the rate of inflation, the nominal interest rate, in the short as well as in the long run, decreases by more than the rate of deflation; therefore, while the rate of return on capital remains unchanged, the real rate of interest falls.

12–5 Stabilization of the Rate of Inflation Through a Balanced-Budget Fiscal Policy

Having discussed the short-run and long-run results of a change in the rate of inflation when the rate of inflation is perfectly foreseen and constant over time and either a deficit-financed fiscal policy or monetary policy is used to stabilize the rate of inflation, we are now left with the task of analyzing the behavior of the system when a marginally balanced-budget fiscal policy is used for price stabilization. The government, having fixed the rate of expansion in the nominal per-capita stock of debt at a level equal to the long-run target rate of inflation, varies taxes and expenditures together so as to keep the economy's price level on a path like the one shown in Figure 12–1.

Assume again that we start from a state of steady growth with a given rate of inflation $-\pi_{m_0} = (\dot{g}/g)_0$; stocks of real debt and capital, γ^* and k^*; a composition of the debt x^*, which remains constant; and a scale of expenditures e that will have to change continuously so as to ensure that the rate of inflation will remain constant.

Suppose now that the government increases the rate of expansion in its outstanding debt from $(\dot{g}/g)_0$ to $(\dot{g}/g)_1$ and announces that it will maintain a higher rate of inflation $-\pi_{m_1} = (\dot{g}/g)_1$. Since transfer payments and the real value of the depreciation of the stock of debt increase by the same amount, the cc line does not shift, while the decrease in π_m from π_{m_0} to π_{m_1} does shift the aa schedule to the left, from $a_0 a_0$ to $a_1 a_1$ (Figure 12–6), as people move from money and bonds into capital. This is symmetrical to the case analyzed in Section 12–4, up to this point.

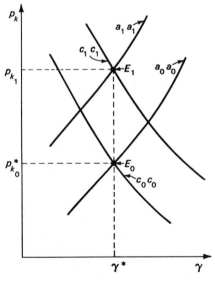

Figure 12–6

g, k, π_k, x are constant. π_m falls from π_{m_0} to π_{m_1} offset by e falling from e_0 to e_1.

If a jump in the price level is to be avoided by using a marginally balanced fiscal policy, taxes and expenditures have to fall to shift the cc schedule leftward until it intersects the $a_1 a_1$ line at E_1. It follows that the result of the higher rate of inflation is an increase in the equilibrium price of capital and an increase in the rate of growth.

Insofar as the rest of the path is concerned, the analysis is straightforward. Since the rate of inflation and the rate of expansion in the stock of debt have risen by equal amounts, the real stock of debt will remain constant over time at its initial level γ^*. With γ constant at γ^*, the equilibrium price of capital will vary only with changes in k. As the capital stock starts increasing, the equilibrium price of capital will fall, thus lowering the economy's rate of growth. Of course, expenditures and taxes will have to vary continuously so as to maintain a constant rate of inflation. As k rises, the assets markets equilibrium p_k has to fall. To soak up the extra output of the consumption goods sector that follows from a higher k and lower p_k, taxes and expenditures will have to rise after their initial fall.

The dynamics of the system can be described by the differential equation

$$(12\text{-}8) \qquad\qquad \dot{k} = q_I(k, p_k) - nk.$$

The equation determining the equilibrium p_k from the assets markets is

$$(12\text{-}9) \qquad\qquad p_k = \Phi(\gamma^*, k, \pi_m^*, x^*).$$

In Figure 12–7, the $\dot{k} = 0$ line shows the combinations (k, p_k) that make $\dot{k} = 0$ in equation (12–8), while the aa line indicates the equilibrium price of capital as a function of the target rate of inflation and the stock of capital. The stock of real debt is constant over time and is not affected when π_m is changed. It follows from Figure 12–7 that the steady-state capital stock k_0^* is stable. At any point to the left of k_0^*, the equilibrium price of capital is higher than the price required to maintain a constant ratio of capital to labor, while at any point to the right of k_0, the opposite holds. Notice that the economy always moves along the aa schedule Figure 12–7 since the assets markets must clear at every instant.

An increase in the target rate of inflation increases the equilibrium price of capital for any given k and shifts the aa line upward, from $a_0 a_0$ to $a_1 a_1$. Since the $\dot{k} = 0$ line is unaffected by the fall in π_m, the result is a higher steady-state stock of capital k_1^* and a higher long-run price of capital $p_{k_1}^*$.

Insofar as the behavior of the rate of interest is concerned, we have already indicated that the impact effect of the increase in the rate of inflation

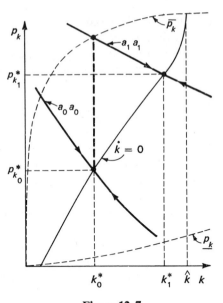

Figure 12–7

γ, π_k, x are constant. π_m falls from π_{m_0} to π_{m_1}.

on the rate of interest is completely described by the analysis of the reaction of the assets markets equilibrium interest rate to changes in π_m when k, γ, and x remain constant. On the other hand, on the rest of the path π_m, γ and x remain constant and only the capital stock changes. The effect of changes in k on the rate of interest are described in Proposition 2–3. As the capital stock rises, the equilibrium rate of interest may move in either direction. The changes in neither π_m nor k have an unambiguous effect on i, and the economy may end up with a higher or lower rate of interest when the rate of inflation rises.

12–6 Summary

The most important effect of a perfectly anticipated change in the rate of inflation is its impact on the price of capital through the assets markets. The income effects are automatically absorbed in general by adjustments in the deficit necessary to avoid a jump in the price level when the change is announced.

If money has a lower rate of return, the price of capital tends to rise, and this promotes capital accumulation. In the cases in which government stabilization policy operates on the consumption market, this effect dominates and produces a higher long-run stock of capital and faster short-run growth. When monetary policy is used to stabilize, this effect is completely offset by open market operations, and nothing happens to the stocks of capital and real debt at all.

13 Imperfectly Anticipated Inflation

13–1 Introduction

So far we have always assumed that the government exercises its policy tools actively to achieve a predetermined path for the aggregate price level. In this chapter we study the situation in which the government fixes all of its policy tools and lets prices and expectations about the price level be determined by the market.

In the long run the rate of inflation cannot be different from the rate of growth of per-capita nominal debt if the real value of the debt is to be constant. A constant value of the per-capita stock of capital is inconsistent with a changing value for the real stock of government debt unless other variables such as the composition of the debt are also changing. In this chapter we study steady states in which the real stocks both of debt and capital are constant, so that the government's debt policy must be to expand the per-capita nominal debt at a constant, predetermined rate. We also require that the composition of the debt and the per-capita real government expenditures remain constant.

Since neither fiscal nor monetary policy is used to stabilize the price level, the value of money at any instant will be determined in the markets by the intersection of the *aa* and *cc* schedules. The actual rate of inflation will be determined by the speeds with which these schedules shift.

203

What, then, determines the expected rate of inflation? We assume that individuals observe the actual rate of inflation and use this as a basis for judging future rates but that they also use other past rates of inflation in forming their expectations. In fact, we assume that they take a weighted average of all past rates of inflation as the expected rate.

13–2   The Adaptive Expectations Model

Since this expectations formation procedure is a new idea in this book, we begin by examining it carefully. A weighted average in continuous time is an integral, just as a weighted average in discrete time is a sum. If the function $g(t)$ is supposed to be a weighted average of all past values of another function $f(t)$, we write

$$(13\text{–}1) \qquad g(t) = \int_{-\infty}^{t} f(\tau)\mu(\tau)\, d\tau,$$

where $\mu(\tau)$ is the weights associated with different times. One of the requirements of a weighted average is that the weights sum to unity:

$$(13\text{–}2) \qquad \int_{-\infty}^{t} \mu(\tau)\, d\tau = 1.$$

A particularly convenient case is when the weights decline exponentially with time. We then want $\mu(\tau)$ to be proportional to $\exp(-\alpha(t-\tau))$ for some positive number α. We need to choose the factor of proportionality β so that if $\mu(\tau) = \beta \exp(-\alpha(t-\tau))$ we will have

$$(13\text{–}3) \qquad \int_{-\infty}^{t} \mu(\tau)\, d\tau = \beta \int_{-\infty}^{t} \exp(-\alpha(t-\tau))\, d\tau = \frac{\beta}{\alpha} = 1$$

or

$$(13\text{–}4) \qquad \mu(\tau) = \alpha \exp(-\alpha(t-\tau)).$$

It is clear that for any choice of α the influence of long past values declines fairly rapidly. The larger is α, the more important are recent values of the $f(t)$ series in determining the $g(t)$ series. As α becomes very small, recent values of $f(t)$ have little influence on $g(t)$. In fact if $\alpha = 0$, $g(t)$ will always be zero, and cannot be affected by the $f(t)$ series at all.

In our case we want to make the expected rate of change in the value of money, π_m, a weighted average of all past actual rates of change:

$$(13\text{--}5) \qquad \pi_m = \alpha \int_{-\infty}^{t} \left(\frac{\dot{p}_m}{p_m}\right)_\tau \exp(-\alpha(t-\tau))d\tau.$$

We can differentiate this to express the model even more simply:

$$(13\text{--}6) \qquad \dot{\pi}_m = \alpha\left(\frac{\dot{p}_m}{p_m} - \pi_m\right).$$

As the actual rate of inflation differs from the expected rate, people begin to change their expectations in the same direction. The larger the discrepancy, the faster they change, but they always change smoothly. Even if $\dot{p}_m/p_m$ suddenly jumps, people will adjust their expectations smoothly. If $\dot{p}_m/p_m$ settles down to some steady value so that the rate of inflation is constant, the expected rate of inflation will also settle down to the same value. This is plausible and an attractive aspect of the theory.

There are other properties of this model of expectation formation that are not so attractive. The expected rate follows the actual rate in a very mechanical way. If the actual rate of change is always increasing, the expected rate will always lag behind; people never become discouraged with the poor performance of their predictions.

When we formulate the theory of expectations in integral form as in equation (13–5), we make an important implicit assumption. This is that sudden jumps in the *price level* have no influence on the expected rate of inflation. A sudden jump means an infinite rate of increase, but this rate continues for only an instant. In the language of integral theory the infinite rate is sustained only on a " set of measure zero " and two functions that are different only on sets of zero measure have the same integral. To put this another way, we can say that the weight on any actual rate of inflation in the weighted average depends on how long that rate held. If it held for a long time, it influences the expected rate more than if it held for a short time. When the price level jumps, the actual rate of inflation is infinite, but this rate lasts no time at all. The expectations model ignores that instant and goes on averaging the continuous part of the inflation process. If prices have always risen at 3 percent per year and expectations are fully adjusted, and suddenly the price level doubles but after its doubling goes on rising at 3 percent, there will be no change in the expected rate.

This property is fairly plausible because price level jumps happen only very infrequently, and it is difficult to know what effect they have on expectations about the more usual process of gradual rises, so it may be reasonable simply to ignore them. On the other hand, sudden jumps in the level of prices should make some difference, and we do not really bring them in any other place.

We have now an admittedly imperfect explanation of how expectations about price changes are formed. This we can use to complete our model.

13-3   The Complete Model

Returning again to the simpler assumption of a proportional consumption function [equation (4–3)], we begin with the same basic five equations that we have used in previous versions of the model:

(13–7) $$\dot{k} = q_I(k, p_k) - nk$$ **(1)**

(13–8) $$\dot{g} = d - ng$$ **(2)**

(13–9) $$p_k = \Phi(gp_m, k, \pi_m, x)$$ **(3')**

(13–10) $$i = \Psi(gp_m, k, \pi_m, x)$$ **(4')**

(13–11) $$q_C(k, p_k) - e = (1 - s)(q(k, p_k) + dp_m + \pi_m gp_m - e).$$ **(5')**

We add two equations specifying that the composition of the debt and per-capita real expenditures remain constant over time:

(13–12) $$x = x^*$$

(13–13) $$e = e^*.$$

As we remarked earlier, the government sets the deficit so that the nominal stock of debt grows at a constant rate θ. This gives us a new equation:

(13–14) $$d = (\theta + n)g.$$

Finally, we append the rule for expectation formation:

(13–15) $$\dot{\pi}_m = \alpha\left(\frac{\dot{p}_m}{p_m} - \pi_m\right).$$

This gives us nine equations in nine variables. What remains is to study the paths determined for different rates of increase in the debt.

13–4 Static Analysis

To begin with we ask what happens in each instant of time. As of any instant k, g and π_m are given by history; and d, e, and x are determined by the rules the government follows. It remains only to determine p_m, p_k, and i. Equations (13–13) and (13–14) allow us to make a very convenient substitution. We can write equation (13–11) as

(13–16) $q_C(k, p_k) - e^* = (1 - s)[q(k, p_k) + (\theta + n + \pi_m)gp_m - e^*].$

We have already observed that p_m affects the *aa* schedule [equation (13–9)] only through its effect on the real value of the outstanding debt, $p_m g = \gamma$. In this particular model it enters the *cc* relationship [equation (13–16)] also only as part of the real value of the debt because $(\theta + n + \pi_m)$ gp_m is just proportional to $p_m g$ for given, θ, n, and π_m. We can redraw the *aa* and *cc* schedules, now plotting $(p_m g, p_k)$ pairs to find the intersection (see Figure 13–1). The *aa* schedule will generally be upward-sloping (see Proposition 3–2), but the slope of the *cc* schedule depends on the sign of $\theta + n + \pi_m$. If this is positive (and in long-run equilibrium it will be if the long-run stock of debt is positive because $\pi_m = \dot{p}_m/p_m = -\theta$ and n is assumed positive), then an increase in $p_m g$ will increase demand, and a lower p_k

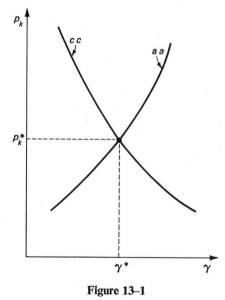

Figure 13–1
k, π_m, π_k, θ, e, x are constant.

will be necessary to clear the consumption market. In this case the cc schedule is downward sloping.

The moral of this is that, given k, π_m, e, θ, and x, in equilibrium p_k, $\gamma = p_m g$, and i are completely determined. At any moment the equilibrium price of money is inversely related to the nominal stock of government debt, since if g rises, p_m must fall to get back to momentary equilibrium. The equilibrium price of capital and the rate of interest are functions only of k, π_m, e, θ, and x. The nominal value of the debt has no effect. This is merely to say that when prices are flexible and the government always adjusts its deficit to maintain a constant rate of expansion of its stock of debt, the government debt is neutral. Doubling g halves p_m because $d = (\theta + n)g$.

The effect of an increase in k is to shift the aa curve down from $a_0 a_0$ to $a_1 a_1$ in Figure 13–2 since, given the supplies of other assets, wealth owners will hold more capital only at a lower price of capital. On the other hand, when the capital stock increases for any given real stock of government debt, under the assumption of a proportional consumption function, the supply of consumption goods rises by more than demand, so that a higher price of capital is necessary to clear the consumption goods market. The cc curve shifts upward from $c_0 c_0$ to $c_1 c_1$.

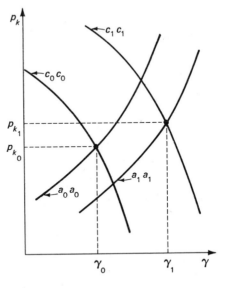

Figure 13–2

π_m, π_k, θ, e, x are constant, k rises from k_0 to k_1.

As we can see from Figure 13–2, the effect of increasing k is always to raise p_m. The effect on p_k can go either way, depending on the relative shifts of the two curves. The increase in the stock of capital requires a fall in the price of capital for wealth owners to be willing to hold the existing stocks of bonds and money; the increase in the real value of these stocks that results from the rise in the price of money necessary to equilibrate the consumption goods market requires an increase in the price of capital for wealth owners to remain in equilibrium. These forces work in opposite directions and make the movement of p_k ambiguous.

When π_m increases (which corresponds to a *fall* in the expected rate of inflation), wealth owners shift out of capital, lowering the assets markets equilibrium price of capital for any given real stock of government debt. The *aa* schedule shifts downward in this case from $a_0 a_0$ to $a_1 a_1$ (see Figure 13–3). The higher π_m in the consumption markets will raise income, because an increase in π_m is equivalent to a fall in the inflation tax; it will, therefore, increase demand when the stock of government debt is positive. In this case a lower price of capital will be needed to stimulate supply and reduce excess demand in the market for consumption goods. The *cc* curve also shifts downward from $c_0 c_0$ to $c_1 c_1$ in Figure 13–3.

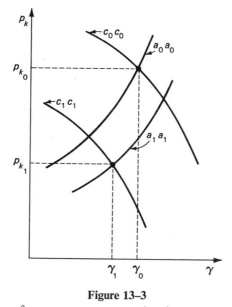

Figure 13–3

k, π_k, θ, e, x are constant. π_m rises from π_{m0} to π_{m1}.

As we can see from Figure 13–3, the effect of a higher π_m is always a decrease in the price of capital, while the real stock of debt may rise or fall since an increase in the expected rate of deflation may force the price level up or down. The increase in the expected rate of deflation requires a fall in the price of capital for wealth owners to be willing to hold the existing stock of government debt; this fall in p_k tends to eliminate the excess demand for commodities that the increase in π_m has created and may be larger or smaller than the change in p_k necessary for the consumption goods market to return to equilibrium with a constant p_m. If the decrease in p_k that equilibrates the assets markets is larger than that necessary to equilibrate the consumption goods market, then p_m will rise and vice versa.

$$(13\text{–}17) \qquad p_k = p_k(k, \pi_m, \theta, e, x)$$

$$(13\text{–}18) \qquad g p_m = \gamma(k, \pi_m, \theta, e, x)$$

or

$$(13\text{–}19) \qquad p_m = (1/g)\gamma(k, \pi_m, \theta, e, x).$$

We see that the experiments we performed give us the following derivatives for these functions, which show the changes in the instantaneous equilibrium solutions for p_k and $p_m g$:

$$(13\text{–}20) \qquad \frac{\partial p_k}{\partial k} \gtreqless 0 \qquad \frac{\partial p_m}{\partial k} > 0,$$

$$(13\text{–}21) \qquad \frac{\partial p_k}{\partial \pi_m} < 0 \qquad \frac{\partial p_m}{\partial \pi_m} \gtreqless 0,$$

$$(13\text{–}22) \qquad \frac{\partial p_k}{\partial g} = 0 \qquad \frac{\partial p_m}{\partial g} = -\frac{p_m}{g}.$$

13–5 Dynamic Analysis

This short-run analysis permits us to reduce the system of equations (13–7) through (13–15) to two differential equations in k and π_m.

First, by differentiating equation (13–19) with respect to time, we can write

$$(13\text{–}23) \qquad \dot{p}_m = \frac{\partial p_m}{\partial k} \dot{k} + \frac{\partial p_m}{\partial \pi_m} \dot{\pi}_m + \frac{\partial p_m}{\partial g} \dot{g}$$

(13–24)
$$\frac{\dot{p}_m}{p_m} = \frac{1}{p_m}\frac{\partial p_m}{\partial k}\dot{k} + \frac{1}{p_m}\frac{\partial p_m}{\partial \pi_m}\dot{\pi}_m - \theta,$$

using (13–22).

This permits us to write (13–15) in a particularly simple form:

(13–25)
$$\dot{\pi}_m = \frac{\alpha[(1/p_m)(\partial p_m/\partial k)\dot{k} - (\theta + \pi_m)]}{1 - \alpha(1/p_m)(\partial p_m/\partial \pi_m)}$$

$$= \frac{\alpha[(1/\gamma)(\partial\gamma/\partial k)\dot{k} - (\theta + \pi_m)]}{1 - \alpha(1/\gamma)(\partial\gamma/\partial \pi_m)}.$$

This expresses π_m as a function of π_m and k, since γ itself is a function only of π_m and k for given θ, e, and x.

The second equation is the familiar dynamics of capital accumulation which is obtained by substituting (13–17) into (13–7):

(13–26)
$$\dot{k} = q_I(k, p_k(k, \pi_m, \theta, e, x)) - nk.$$

The system turns out not to be as easy to study as previous systems. We might start by studying the $\dot{k} = 0$ schedule. Suppose that for the pair of values (π_m^*, k^*) the rate of change in the ratio of capital to labor is equal to zero. Assume now that we increase π_m. According to equation (13–21) the equilibrium price of capital falls, and $\dot{k}$ will become negative. A smaller ratio of capital to labor means a higher rate of change in k by increasing the per-capita output of investment goods q_I and by reducing nk, the amount of investment necessary to maintain a constant k over time. If the smaller ratio of capital to labor also unambiguously raised the price of capital, that is, if $\partial p_k/\partial k < 0$, we would then know that the $\dot{k} = 0$ line was downward-sloping and that the system always tended to move toward it. As we have seen, a lower stock of capital may actually decrease the equilibrium price of capital because of its inflationary impact on the consumption goods market, and this effect may outweigh the others. We cannot definitely say whether an increase in the capital stock lowers its own rate of change or whether the $\dot{k} = 0$ line is upward or downward-sloping. We show in Section 13–10, however, that if at any steady-state pair (π_m^*, k^*) the slope of the $\dot{k} = 0$ line is positive, the steady state is unstable. If a steady state is to be stable in this model, the rate of capital accumulation should be a decreasing function of the stock of capital.

The slope of the $\dot{k} = 0$ schedule is obtained by setting equation (13–26) equal to zero and by differentiating partially with respect to k and π_m.

$$(13\text{–}27) \qquad \left.\frac{\partial k}{\partial \pi_m}\right|_{\dot{k}=0} = - \frac{(\partial q_I/\partial p_k)(\partial p_k/\partial \pi_m)}{\partial q_I/\partial k + (\partial q_I/\partial p_k)(\partial p_k/\partial k) - n}.$$

If $\partial \dot{k}/\partial k < 0$, $(\partial k/\partial \pi_m)_{\dot{k}=0} < 0$ by (13–21), and the $\dot{k} = 0$ line has a negative slope.

What of the $\dot{\pi}_m = 0$ schedule? According to equation (13–25), $\dot{\pi}_m$ is equal to zero when

$$(13\text{–}28) \qquad (1/p_m)(\partial p_m/\partial k)\dot{k} - (\theta + \pi_m) = 0.$$

If π_m rises from an initial $\dot{\pi}_m = 0$ situation, the expression (13–28) becomes negative for two reasons. First, the term $\theta + \pi_m$ becomes larger; second, an increase in π_m lowers p_k and reduces $\dot{k}$. Whether these effects force $\dot{\pi}_m$ to become positive or negative depends on the sign of the denominator in equation (13–25):

$$(13\text{–}29) \qquad 1 - \alpha(1/p_m)(\partial p_m/\partial \pi_m),$$

which may be positive or negative. It will certainly be positive if $\partial p_m/\partial \pi_m < 0$, and even if $\partial p_m/\partial \pi_m > 0$, a small α will ensure that it is positive. If this coefficient is positive, the increase in $\dot{\pi}_m$ makes $\dot{\pi}_m$ negative.

According to the expectations hypothesis, given the actual rate of change in the price of money, an increase in its expected rate lowers the rate at which the expected rate is changing, and this has a stabilizing effect on expectations. In addition, an increase in the expected rate lowers the equilibrium price of capital and the rate of capital accumulation. Since a fall in the capital stock is inflationary and lowers the price of money, a decrease in the rate of capital accumulation reduces the rate of deflation (or increases the rate of inflation). The decrease in the rate of deflation, again according to the expectations hypothesis, reduces the rate of change in its expected rate, and this effect is also stabilizing. On both of these accounts, an increase in π_m lowers $\dot{\pi}_m$.

This is not the end of the story, however. As the rate of change in the expected rate of deflation changes, this in turn affects the actual rate of change in the price of money. If the price of money is a decreasing function of its expected rate of change, this will add to the stabilizing effect of a fall in π_m. However, if the equilibrium price of money is an increasing function of its expected rate of change, and in particular if expectations adjust rapidly, that is, if α is large, a fall in the rate of change of the expected rate of deflation lowers the actual rate of change, which in turn lowers the rate of change in the expected rate: we have an unstable price mechanism. This is the case when the coefficient $\alpha/[1 - (\alpha/\gamma)(\partial\gamma/\partial\pi_m)]$ is negative.

As in the case of the $\dot{k} = 0$ schedule, we cannot be sure that $\dot{\pi}_m$ is a decreasing function of π_m. In Section 13–10 we show that $\partial\dot{\pi}_m/\partial\pi_m < 0$ is actually a necessary condition for the stability of the steady state. Stability requires that the coefficient be positive in expression (13–29).

Since another stability condition requires that $\partial k/\partial k$ be negative, it follows that in the neighborhood of a stable steady state, as the ratio of capital to labor increases, the rate of growth falls; and given the rate of expansion in the government debt, this leads to an increase in the rate of inflation, which, if expression (13–29) is positive, leads to a rise in the rate of change in the expected rate of inflation, that is, to a fall in $\dot{\pi}_m$. If a steady state is stable, around that steady state $\partial\dot{\pi}_m/\partial\pi_m < 0$ and $\partial\dot{\pi}_m/\partial k < 0$.

The slope of the $\dot{\pi}_m = 0$ line is obtained by setting equation (13–25) equal to zero and differentiating partially with respect to k and π_m at $\pi_m = \pi_m^*$ and $k = k^*$, that is, at pairs (k, π_m) for which $\dot{k} = 0$:

$$(13\text{–}30) \qquad \frac{\partial k}{\partial \pi_m}\bigg|_{\dot{\pi}_m = 0} = -\frac{(1/\gamma)(\partial\gamma/\partial k)(\partial k/\partial \pi_m) - 1}{(1/\gamma)(\partial\gamma/\partial k)(\partial k/\partial k)} < 0,$$

because $\partial\gamma/\partial k > 0$ by (13–20); $\partial k/\partial\pi_m = (\partial q_1/\partial p_k)(\partial p_k/\partial\pi_m) < 0$ by (13–21); and $\partial k/\partial k < 0$ in the neighborhood of a stable steady state.

Under the assumption that (13–29) is positive, at any point to the right of the $\dot{\pi}_m = 0$ line, $\dot{\pi}_m$ is falling, and at any point to the left, it is rising, as is indicated by the arrows pointing east and west in Figure 13–4.

Since $\partial k/\partial k$ and $\partial\dot{\pi}_m/\partial\pi_m$ may be positive, the stability of the model is not guaranteed. Unstable steady states may exist even though the consumption goods sector is more capital-intensive than the investment goods sector and even though expectations lag. In contrast to the one-sector growth model, however, a lag is not necessary for the system to have a stable solution. While in the one-sector model an increase in the expected rate of inflation necessarily raises the price level, fueling destabilizing assets speculation, in the two-sector model the increase in the expected rate of inflation may actually lower the equilibrium price level, which probably lowers the expected rate of inflation and discourages destabilizing speculation.

We exhibit the $\dot{k} = 0$ and $\dot{\pi}_m = 0$ schedules in Figure 13–4. Notice that we have drawn both schedules downward-sloping and that the arrows indicate the fact that the system tends to move toward both schedules. We

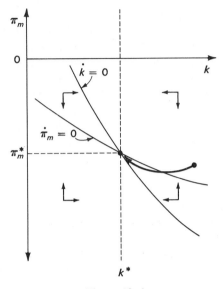

Figure 13–4

π_k, θ, e, x are constant.

have also drawn the $\dot{\pi}_m = 0$ schedule with a higher absolute slope than the $\dot{k} = 0$ schedule. To show that this must be true in the stable case, imagine that starting from the intersection (π_m^*, k^*) in Figure 13–4, we increase π_m. This makes both $\dot{\pi}_m$ and $\dot{k}$ negative. If we decrease k exactly enough so that $\dot{k}$ returns to zero, $\dot{\pi}_m$ will still be negative. Why? Because when $\dot{k} = 0$, we have

$$(13\text{--}31) \qquad\qquad \dot{\pi}_m = -(\theta + \pi_m)$$

and at (π_m^*, k^*) we must have had

$$(13\text{--}32) \qquad\qquad \theta = -\pi_m^*.$$

θ has not changed, but π_m has increased, so that even when $\dot{k}$ returns to zero, $\theta + \pi_m$ will be positive and $\dot{\pi}_m$ will be negative. To get to the $\dot{\pi}_m = 0$ schedule, k must fall even farther, so that the assertion about the relative slopes is proved. The $\dot{\pi}_m = 0$ schedule is steeper than the $\dot{k} = 0$ schedule near a stable intersection.

That the $\dot{\pi}_m = 0$ line is steeper than the $\dot{k} = 0$ line can also be shown by comparing their slopes at a steady-state intersection, as given by equations

(13–30) and (13–27). The condition is

$$\frac{(1/\gamma)(\partial\gamma/\partial k)(\partial \dot{k}/\partial \pi_m) - 1}{(1/\gamma)(\partial\gamma/\partial k)(\partial \dot{k}/\partial k)} < -\frac{\partial \dot{k}/\partial \pi_m}{\partial \dot{k}/\partial k}$$

or, alternatively,

$$-\frac{\partial \dot{k}/\partial \pi_m}{\partial \dot{k}/\partial k} + \frac{1}{(1/\gamma)(\partial\gamma/\partial k)(\partial \dot{k}/\partial k)} < -\frac{\partial \dot{k}/\partial \pi_m}{\partial \dot{k}/\partial k}.$$

Since in the neighborhood of a stable steady state $\partial \dot{k}/\partial k < 0$, the inequality holds there.

From Figure 13–4, we can see that if the government maintains a constant composition of its debt, constant real per-capita expenditures, and a constant rate of expansion of its debt, the economy, if it has a stable long-run growth path, will approach it without oscillations. Given, then, any initial stock of capital, k_0, and any initial expected rate of change in prices, π_{m_0}, in the neighborhood of (π_m^*, k^*), the economy will approach π_m^* and k^* without cyclical movements of these variables.

13–6   Effects of Changes in the Deficit

Now that we have characterized the dynamic behavior of the economy near a stable steady state, we can perform the experiment of raising θ, the rate of expansion of the government debt. We want to study how the economy achieves the new, higher, long-run rate of inflation and what effect this has on the steady-state stock of capital.

Given per-capita expenditures, an increase in the rate at which the government increases its nominal per-capita debt is equivalent to a decrease in the net taxes, that is, taxes less transfers, levied on the private sector. As one would expect, the decrease in taxes increases private disposable income and the demand for consumption goods. This increase in demand, as already indicated in Section 5–2, lowers both the price of money and the price of capital goods. As the price of capital goods falls, so does the rate at which capital is accumulating. It follows that given any combination (π_m, k) for which the rate of capital accumulation was initially equal to zero, $\dot{k}$ will now be negative. To get the rate of capital accumulation back up to zero, the price of capital must rise and the only thing that will accomplish this for a given stock of capital is a higher expected rate of inflation. Thus for any k, the π_m that makes $\dot{k} = 0$ will now be lower, remembering that π_m is the expected rate of deflation. The

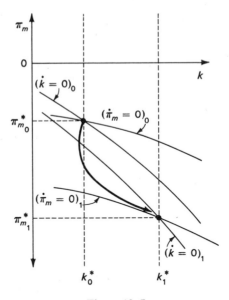

Figure 13–5

π_k, e, x are constant. θ rises from θ_0 to θ_1.

$\dot{k} = 0$ schedule has shifted leftward (see Figure 13–5) as a result of the more rapid increase in the nominal stock of debt.

This can be proved by setting equation (13–26) equal to zero and partially differentiating with respect to π_m and θ:

$$(13\text{–}33) \qquad \left.\frac{\partial \pi_m}{\partial \theta}\right|_{k=0} = -\frac{(\partial q_I/\partial p_k)(\partial p_k/\partial \theta)}{(\partial q_I/\partial p_k)(\partial p_k/\partial \pi_m)} < 0.$$

The increase in θ also affects the $\dot{\pi}_m = 0$ schedule. For a given stock of capital, the increase in the rate of expansion in the stock of government debt has two effects. First, it lowers $\dot{k}$ for any (π_m, k) pair, as shown in the preceding two paragraphs, and this, according to equation (13–25), also reduces $\dot{\pi}_m$. Second, it raises the $\theta + \pi_m$ term in equation (13–25), which reduces $\dot{\pi}_m$. To get $\dot{\pi}_m$ back up to zero for the given k, π_m itself must fall.

Setting equation (13–25) equal to zero and differentiating with respect to π_m and θ, we obtain the leftward shift of the $\dot{\pi}_m = 0$ schedule:

$$(13\text{–}34) \qquad \left.\frac{\partial \pi_m}{\partial \theta}\right|_{\dot{\pi}_m=0} = -\frac{(1/\gamma)(\partial \gamma/\partial k)(\partial q_I/\partial p_k)(\partial p_k/\partial \theta) - 1}{(1/\gamma)(\partial \gamma/\partial k)(\partial q_I/\partial p_k)(\partial p_k/\partial \pi_m) - 1} < 0.$$

This can be explained in conventional economic terms. The increase in the rate of change in the government debt, besides increasing the flow supply of government debt in the assets markets, also reduces the rate at which the private sector desires to add to its holdings of government debt; that is, the increase in θ by lowering the rate of capital accumulation reduces the rate at which wealth owners desire to accumulate alternative assets to real capital. Both the increase in the flow supply and the decrease in the flow demand increase the actual rate of changes in prices. Given the expected rate π_m, as $\dot{p}_m/p_m$ falls, the rate of change in π_m becomes negative. For π_m again to equal zero, the expected rate of deflation would have to fall.

Which schedule shifts farther? The $\dot{\pi}_m = 0$ schedule will, so that the new long-run k_1^* will actually be higher. To see this, imagine that k remains at k_0^* and that the rate of debt expansion increases. If the expected rate of inflation rises so that $\pi_m + \theta$ remains zero, there will be no effect on the cc schedule. The lower π_m shifts the aa schedule upward, leading to a higher equilibrium price of capital and a positive rate of capital accumulation for the original k_0^*. The new steady state must involve a higher steady-state capital stock than the old one to soak up this extra investment.

We see that an increase in the government deficit financed by a higher rate of expansion in the government debt results in a lower short-run rate of growth but increases the economy's steady-state stock of capital.

How do we explain the fact that while in the short run a higher rate of expansion in the nominal stock of government debt leads to a lower rate of capital accumulation, in the longer run the result will be a higher capital stock? As indicated earlier, the higher rate of expansion in the stock of government debt results from an initial tax cut that has increased the government deficit. The tax cut in turn raises private income and consumption and lowers the equilibrium price of capital, thereby decreasing the rate of capital accumulation. As time passes, the increase in the rate of expansion of the nominal stock of debt and the lower rate of growth induce an increase in the actual rate of inflation. As the actual rate goes up, the expected rate of inflation begins to increase. People adjust the expected rate in accordance with the behavior of the actual rate, but with a lag. The increase in the expected rate of inflation induces wealth owners to shift the composition of their portfolios toward real capital and away from government debt. In addition, the increase in the expected rate of inflation increases the rate of depreciation on government debt, lowering private disposable income and reducing private consumption. Both the increase in the demand for real capital and the decline in the demand for consumption goods raise the equilibrium price of capital and increase the rate of capital accumulation. The decrease in the stock of capital, on the other hand, is partially self-correcting. As k falls, if the system is stable, the rate of growth of the capital stock rises. Sooner or later, there is going to be a stock of capital low enough and an expected rate of inflation high enough to make the rate of capital accumulation positive.

After this point the capital stock will continue to rise to its new higher value, and the expected rate of deflation will approach $-\theta$ smoothly. We cannot say what will happen to the real value of per-capita debt. If π_m were not changing, a higher p_k and k would be compatible in the assets markets only with a higher $p_m g$, but the fall in π_m tends to offset this. In the long run, $p_m g$ may rise or fall.

The path of the interest rate is usually ambiguous as the economy moves toward the new long-run equilibrium. Different forces push the interest rate in different directions, and we can say nothing definite about it.

13–7   Effects of an Open Market Purchase

In Chapters 8 and 9, we analyzed the short-run and long-run effects of a change in the composition of the outstanding stock of debt through an open market operation when fiscal policy, either marginally balanced budget or deficit-financed, is used to stabilize the price of consumer goods. In both cases we concluded that this results in an acceleration of the short-run rate of growth as well as in a higher long-run stock of capital.

In this section we analyze the effects of an open market operation when the government does not follow a policy of maintaining a constant price level or a constant rate of inflation through time. The government now sets government expenditures and the rate of expansion in its outstanding debt at some constant levels e^* and θ^* and lets the market determine the equilibrium values of the prices of money, capital, and the rate of interest.

In this case again the long-run rate of inflation is determined only by the rate of expansion in the per-capita stock of debt. Changes in the composition of the government debt, however, affect the short-run rate of change in prices, in particular by affecting the economy's growth rate.

Suppose, then, that we start our analysis with an economy in a state of steady growth, with a capital stock k^* and a rate of inflation $-\pi_m^* = \theta^*$. The government then carries out an open market purchase, reducing the ratio of debt to money x, and maintains the composition of the debt constant at this new level thereafter.

We have shown in Section 5–4 that an open market purchase increases the price of capital at which wealth owners are willing to hold the existing stock of capital, thus shifting the aa schedule to the left. On the other hand, the cc schedule is unaffected by an open market operation, so that the immediate effect of the open market purchase is to produce a discrete increase in the price of capital and a discrete fall in the price of money.

In the analysis of the long-run equilibrium of the model that follows, we consider only the case of a stable equilibrium, that is, when both the $\dot{\pi}_m = 0$ and $\dot{k} = 0$ loci are downward-sloping and when the $\dot{\pi}_m = 0$ locus is steeper.

The decrease in the proportion of bonds in the debt, that is, the fall in x, increases the price of capital for any pair (π_m, k), as we have shown above, and this causes the output of investment goods to rise. We see from equation (13-26) that, for given π_m, a fall in x requires a higher capital stock to make $\dot{k} = 0$.

(13-35)
$$\left.\frac{\partial k}{\partial x}\right|_{\dot{k}=0} = -\frac{(\partial q_I/\partial p_k)(\partial p_k/\partial x)}{\partial \dot{k}/\partial k} < 0.$$

Capital will have to accumulate until the economy reaches a new steady state where the capital stock is high enough to absorb the increased output of investment goods resulting from a higher price of capital. Accordingly, the $\dot{k} = 0$ schedule shifts upward from $(\dot{k} = 0)_0$ to $(\dot{k} = 0)_1$.

The increased rate of growth as of any (π_m, k) reduces the expected rate of inflation by lowering the actual rate. Thus where $\dot{\pi}_m$ was previously zero, it is now positive; to restore $\dot{\pi}_m$ to zero, a higher π_m (lower expected rate of inflation) is needed. One of the conditions for stability is that an increase in the expected rate of inflation reduces the rate of change of the expected rate. Accordingly, the $(\dot{\pi}_m = 0)_0$ locus shifts up to $(\dot{\pi}_m = 0)_1$.

(13-36)
$$\left.\frac{\partial \pi_m}{\partial x}\right|_{\dot{\pi}_m=0} = -\frac{\alpha}{1 - \alpha(1/\gamma)(\partial\gamma/\partial\pi_m)}\left[\frac{(1/\gamma)(\partial\gamma/\partial k)(\partial q_I/\partial p_k)(\partial p_k/\partial x)}{\partial\dot{\pi}_m/\partial\pi_m}\right] < 0.$$

$(\pi_m = 0)_1$ intersects the $(\dot{k} = 0)_1$ locus at the original rate of inflation, $-\pi_m^*$, and a higher capital stock, k_1^*. It should be no surprise that the steady-state rate of inflation is unchanged since we know that this depends only on the rate of expansion of the per-capita debt θ, which is unchanged. More formally, π_m^*, since it can be obtained by solving equation (13-25) when $\dot{k} = 0$ and $\dot{\pi}_m = 0$, is clearly independent of x.

The arrows drawn in Figure 13-6 are those that are relevant to the $(\dot{\pi}_m = 0)_1$ and $(\dot{k} = 0)_1$ loci. We see that the capital stock increases

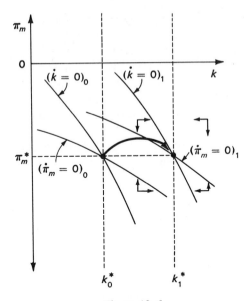

Figure 13–6

π_k, θ, e are constant. x falls from x_0 to x_1.

continually to its new equilibrium level k_1^*, while the expected rate of inflation first falls and then eventually begins to rise again. The reason the capital stock grows is that the price of capital has risen, while the expected rate of inflation $-\pi_m$ falls since k enters equation (13–25) with a positive sign. Ultimately, as $\dot{k}$ becomes small and π_m itself rises, $\dot{\pi}_m$ turns negative and the expected rate of inflation $-\pi_m$ begins to rise back to π_m^*. While the capital stock is rising, the growth rate of the economy is higher than it is in the steady state.

The effects of the fall in x on the real value of the steady-state stock of government debt are ambiguous. On the one hand, the increase in the capital stock tends to increase the value of the debt [equation (13–20)]; on the other hand, the decrease in the ratio of debt to money tends to reduce the value of the debt. We cannot be sure which effect predominates.

Similarly, the long-run effects of the change in the composition of the debt on the interest rate are ambiguous. The fall in x tends to reduce the interest rate, but a change in the capital stock may either increase or lower the interest rate, so that on this score alone we cannot be sure of the change in the interest rate. Any changes in the real value of the debt (and we do not know in which direction this changes) will also exert an (ambiguous) influence on the interest rate.

13–8   Effects of an Increase in the Scale of Expenditures

What are the effects on the steady-state capital stock and expected (and actual) rates of inflation when the government increases its expenditures without altering the rate of debt expansion or the composition of the debt? We already know that the long-run rate of inflation depends on the rate of debt expansion, θ, so that the expected rate of inflation will be unchanged when θ is unchanged. Changes in the rate of government expenditure, e, will affect the cc schedule and result in changes in the price of capital, so that we would expect the steady-state capital stock to be affected.

An increase in the level of government expenditures has the net effect of creating excess demand in the consumption goods market (see Section 4–7) so that, as of any p_m, the price of capital that clears that market has to fall. The cc schedule shifts downward and to the left so that the short-run effect of an increase in the level of government expenditures is a reduction of both the price of money and the price of capital.

Once again we consider only a stable steady state of the system in Figure 13–7. The fall in the price of capital reduces the rate of production of investment goods as of any pair (π_m, k) so that $\dot{k}$ is now lower than it originally was at any (π_m, k). To restore $\dot{k}$ to zero as of any π_m, k itself should be

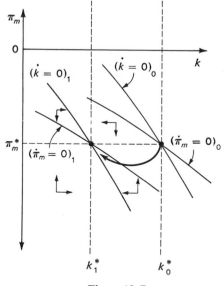

Figure 13–7

π_k, θ, x are constant. e rises from e_0 to e_1.

lower so that the $\dot{k} = 0$ schedule shifts leftward from $(\dot{k} = 0)_0$ to $(\dot{k} = 0)_1$. Remembering again that $\partial \dot{k}/\partial k < 0$, formally, from equation (13–26), we have

$$(13\text{--}37) \qquad \frac{\partial k}{\partial e}\bigg|_{\dot{k}=0} = -\frac{(\partial q_I/\partial p_k)(\partial p_k/\partial e)}{\partial \dot{k}/\partial k} < 0.$$

The capital stock will have to fall until a new equilibrium is reached where the lower capital stock can be maintained, with the lower rate of production of investment goods arising from the fall in p_k. The fact that $\dot{k}$ is now negative as of any pair (π_m, k) for which it was previously zero means that $\dot{\pi}_m$ is now negative for any pair for which it was previously zero [equation (13–25);] that is, the lower rate of growth increases the expected rate of inflation by increasing the actual rate of inflation. To make the actual rate equal to the expected rate for any given level of capital stock, the expected rate of inflation $-\pi_m$ has to rise, since this tends to reduce the rate of change of the expected rate. This means that the $\dot{\pi}_m = 0$ line shifts downward from $(\dot{\pi}_m = 0)_0$ to $(\dot{\pi}_m = 0)_1$:

$$(13\text{--}38)$$

$$\frac{\partial \pi_m}{\partial e}\bigg|_{\dot{\pi}_m=0} = -\frac{\alpha}{1 - \alpha(1/\gamma)(\partial \gamma/\partial \pi_m)}\left[\frac{(1/\gamma)(\partial \gamma/\partial k)(\partial q_I/\partial p_k)(\partial p_k/\partial e)}{\partial \dot{\pi}_m/\partial \pi_m}\right] < 0.$$

That the intersection is at $-\pi_m^*$ is seen by setting k and π_m at zero in equation (13–25). The solution is clearly independent of e.

The arrows drawn in Figure 13–7 are those appropriate to the new equilibrium (π_m^*, k_1^*). The capital stock falls continually to its new equilibrium level k_1^*, so that the rate of growth is lower than in the steady state. The expected rate of inflation initially rises, owing to the fall in the rate of growth, but eventually falls back to the old level as the rate of growth begins to return to the equilibrium level and the expected rate of inflation rises.

The results of this section are just the opposite of those of Section 13–7, so that by the same arguments the effects of the change in government expenditures on the value of the debt and the interest rate are ambiguous.

13–9 Summary

In this chapter we have studied a model of imperfectly anticipated inflation. The government sets the rate of expansion of its nominal debt and lets the actual rate of inflation and the expected rate converge to this. We found that the stability and uniqueness of steady-state solutions were not guaranteed but that by assuming stability we could derive many other properties of the system.

In particular, we examined the consequences of a sudden unannounced increase in the rate of expansion of the nominal debt. This leads to a change in the rate of price change from the new higher level of prices. The initial impact of the higher rate of debt expansion is a decrease in the growth rate and a reduction of capital accumulation, but in the long run the stock of capital will rise.

We may contrast this with the anticipated inflation studied in Chapter 12. There, the higher rate of inflation increased growth and the steady-state capital stock. Here the steady-state effect is the same, but the short-run effect is reversed. This need not be the case if the government also exercises its other policy tools. For instance, it can prevent the initial fall in p_k by making an open market purchase at the same time it increases the rate of expansion of the debt. The new x could remain constant for the rest of the path, but if the purchase were large enough at the beginning, the short-run capital decumulation would not occur.

We also considered the effects of changes in the composition of the debt and the level of government expenditures. An increase in the proportion of debt that consists of bonds—an increase in x—or an increase in the level of government expenditures have the same effect of reducing the short-run growth rate and long-run capital stock while temporarily increasing the expected rate of inflation. Ultimately, the expected rate of inflation returns to its original level.

13-10   Addendum on Dynamic Stability

We can summarize our dynamic model by writing the two basic differential equations of our system:

$$(13\text{-}39) \qquad \dot{k} = q_I(k, p_k(k, \pi_m, \theta, e, x)) - nk$$

$$(13\text{-}40) \qquad \dot{\pi}_m = \frac{\alpha[(1/\gamma)(\partial\gamma/\partial k)\dot{k} - (\theta + \pi_m)]}{1 - \alpha(1/\gamma)(\partial\gamma/\partial\pi_m)}.$$

The steady-state solution of these differential equations (if it exists) will give us a pair (π_m^*, k^*) for each triplet of policy variables θ, e, and x. Our analysis will be concerned only with the local stability of this steady-state growth path. For this purpose we take the Taylor approximation of the system of differential Equations (13–39) and (13–40) about the steady-state values (π_m^*, k^*), and we obtain the following system:

(13–41)

$$\begin{bmatrix} \dot{k} \\ \dot{\pi}_m \end{bmatrix} = \begin{bmatrix} \partial \dot{k}/\partial k & \partial \dot{k}/\partial \pi_m \\ \dfrac{\alpha(1/\gamma)(\partial \gamma/\partial k)(\partial \dot{k}/\partial k)}{1 - \alpha(1/\gamma)(\partial \gamma/\partial \pi_m)} & \dfrac{\alpha[(1/\gamma)(\partial \gamma/\partial k)(\partial \dot{k}/\partial \pi_m) - 1]}{1 - \alpha(1/\gamma)(\partial \gamma/\partial \pi_m)} \end{bmatrix} \begin{bmatrix} k - k^* \\ \pi_m - \pi_m^* \end{bmatrix},$$

where the expressions in the two-by-two matrix are valued at (π_m^*, k^*). If λ is a characteristic root of the system (13–41), then

(13–42)

$$\lambda^2 - \lambda \left\{ \frac{\partial \dot{k}}{\partial k} + \frac{\alpha[(1/\gamma)(\partial \gamma/\partial k)(\partial \dot{k}/\partial \pi_m) - 1]}{1 - \alpha(1/\gamma)(\partial \gamma/\partial \pi_m)} \right\} - \frac{\alpha(\partial \dot{k}/\partial k)}{1 - \alpha(1/\gamma)(\partial \gamma/\partial \pi_m)} = 0.$$

Stability requires the roots of the characteristic equation, if real, to be negative, and if complex, to have negative real parts. This in turn requires, first, the coefficient of λ in (13–42), that is, the trace of the matrix in (13–41), to be negative; and, second, the third term in (13–42), that is, the determinant of the matrix in (13–41), to be positive. We can write the stability conditions as

(13–43) $$\frac{\partial \dot{k}}{\partial k} + \frac{\alpha[(1/\gamma)(\partial \gamma/\partial k)(\partial \dot{k}/\partial \pi_m) - 1]}{1 - \alpha(1/\gamma)(\partial \gamma/\partial \pi_m)} < 0$$

(13–44) $$-\frac{\alpha(\partial \dot{k}/\partial k)}{1 - \alpha(1/\gamma)(\partial \gamma/\partial \pi_m)} > 0.$$

We have already proved that an increase in the stock of capital raises the equilibrium price of money and that a decrease in the expected rate of inflation lowers the price of capital, which produces a lower rate of capital accumulation; that is, we proved that $\partial \gamma/\partial k > 0$ and $\partial \dot{k}/\partial \pi_m < 0$. It follows that $[(\partial \gamma/\partial k)(1/\gamma)(\partial \dot{k}/\partial \pi_m) - 1]$ in expression (13–43) is negative. From this we conclude that expressions (13–43) and (13–44) can be satisfied if and only if $\partial \dot{k}/\partial k < 0$ and $\alpha/[1 - \alpha(\partial \gamma/\partial \pi_m)(1/\gamma)] > 0$, which proves our statements in the text concerning the necessary conditions for the local stability of a steady state.

Expected Changes in the Price of Capital

14–1 Introduction

In this chapter we relax our previous assumption that the expected change in p_k is always zero. Expected changes in the price of capital influence both the assets and consumption goods markets. A nonzero π_k affects the demand for capital because π_k is an additional component in the return on capital, and the demand for consumption because expected capital gains on capital must now be included in disposable income. In the long run, if the economy converges to a state of steady growth, the price of capital moves toward some constant value, and the expected rate of change of p_k, if it bears any relation to the actual rate of change, will go to zero. The chief purposes in investigating the model with expected changes in the price of capital not fixed at zero are to understand its short-run behavior and to see whether additional problems of stability arise. Since we have not been able in past chapters to reach firm conclusions about stability, the discussion on the second point will be somewhat sketchy.

We concentrate our attention on the effects of expected changes in the price of capital and maintain the discussion at a level that can be treated geometrically. Therefore, we revert in this chapter to the assumption that the government holds the consumer price level constant, either through monetary policy or through a balanced-budget fiscal policy. We use the adaptive expectations hypothesis to describe the formation and correction of people's ideas about the rate of change in p_k. Everything we said in Chapter 13 about the properties, both attractive and unattractive, of this model hold here.

14–2 Static Analysis

Our first task is to understand clearly how the assumption of a nonzero π_k affects the assets and consumption goods markets separately. The assets markets equilibrium schedule in (p_m, p_k) space may be shifted in position because of expected capital gains or losses on the capital stock, but its slope will remain positive. The relationship between p_k and the rate of return to capital is not changed by $\pi_k \neq 0$, and so an increase in p_m is still necessary to restore equilibrium when p_k rises. (See Proposition 3–2.)

The situation in the consumption goods market is more complicated. Disposable income now contains the term $\pi_k p_k k$. If $\pi_k > 0$, then an increase in p_k still increases disposable income and, indeed, is reinforced by an additional effect. A rise in p_k in this case will require a fall in the equilibrium p_m, and the cc schedule will be downward-sloped. If $\pi_k < 0$, however, it is possible that the net effect of a rise in the price of capital is a fall in disposable income and, therefore, demand. In that case a rise in p_m (fall in prices) would be necessary to restore equilibrium in the consumption goods market when p_k rose; the cc schedule would be upward-sloped. This situation is exactly analogous to that of expected inflation ($\pi_m < 0$) discussed at length above. In the long run we expect the economy to converge to a constant price of capital and π_k to go to zero. In the near vicinity of a point of long-run equilibrium, the cc schedule will be downward-sloped for the usual reasons, which will come to dominate as π_k approaches zero. We confine our attention to such neighborhoods of long-run equilibria, even though away from such points the cc schedule may have a positive slope.

We now turn to examining the effects on static equilibrium when π_k changes. In Figure 14–1, we show the assets markets kk and mm schedules in (i, p_k) space for a given p_m, g, k, x, and π_m. An increase in π_k raises the rate of return to capital for any p_k and creates excess demand for capital at any point on the original kk schedule. The new equilibrium requires a higher p_k for each i, and so the kk schedule shifts upward to $k_1 k_1$. In the money market an increase in p_k reduces the demand for money by increasing the rate of return on capital so that an increase in p_k is needed

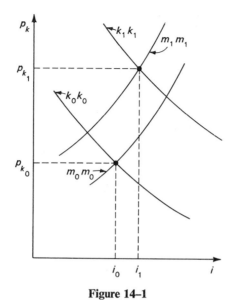

Figure 14–1

g, k, p_m, π_m, x are constant. π_k rises from π_{k_0} to π_{k_1}.

for any interest rate to restore the market to equilibrium. The mm schedule also shifts upward to m_1m_1. The price of capital definitely rises, while the interest rate may rise or fall.

Checking these signs algebraically, by differentiating equations (3–8) and (3–10), we obtain

$$(14\text{--}1) \qquad \frac{\partial p_k}{\partial \pi_k} = \frac{1}{\Delta}\left(\frac{\partial J}{\partial \rho_k}\frac{\partial L}{\partial \rho_b} - \frac{\partial J}{\partial \rho_b}\frac{\partial L}{\partial \rho_k}\right) > 0$$

$$(14\text{--}2) \qquad \frac{\partial i}{\partial \pi_k} = \frac{1}{\Delta}\left[-\frac{\partial J}{\partial \rho_k}\frac{\partial L}{p_k} + \left(\frac{\partial J}{\partial p_k} - k\right)\frac{\partial L}{\partial \rho_k}\right] \gtreqless 0,$$

where Δ is given by equation (3–14).

Subject to the invertibility of the system (3–8) through (3–10), we can use equations (3–23) and (3–24) which give p_k and i as a function of g, p_m, k, x, π_m, and π_k, in the form:

$$(14\text{--}3) \qquad\qquad p_k = \Phi(gp_m, k, \pi_m, \pi_k, x)$$

$$(14\text{--}4) \qquad\qquad i = \Psi(gp_m, k, \pi_m, \pi_k, x),$$

with $\partial p_k/\partial \pi_k > 0$ and $\partial i/\partial \pi_k \gtreqless 0$.

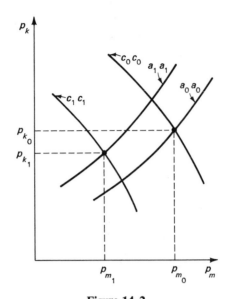

Figure 14–2

g, k, π_m, d, e, x are constant. π_k rises from π_{k0} to π_{k1}.

An increase in π_k clearly raises the assets markets equilibrium p_k for any p_m. In other words, the aa schedule in Figure 14–2 shifts upward to $a_1 a_1$, as the result of a rise in π_k.

The consumption market clearing condition now is:

$$(14\text{–}5) \quad q_C - e = c(kp_k + gp_m, q_C + p_k q_I + (d + \pi_m g)p_m + \pi_k kp_k - e).$$

An increase in π_k raises disposable income and the demand for consumption goods, since k and p_k are always positive. To clear the consumption goods market, p_k itself must fall, increasing the supply of consumption goods and lowering wealth and income. For a given p_m, then, the p_k that clears the consumption market is lower after an increase in π_k, so that the cc schedule shifts down to $c_1 c_1$ in Figure 14–2.

We can see that the results of a higher π_k on the instantaneous equilibrium are a lower p_m and an uncertain change in p_k. That fact that an increase in π_k might lower p_k would be important for the stability of an uncontrolled economy, as the corresponding possibility for π_m and p_m was in Chapter 13. In this chapter we assumed that the government uses either monetary policy or expenditures to prevent any changes in p_m. These two different policy alternatives give different outcomes for the final change in p_k arising from an increase in π_k.

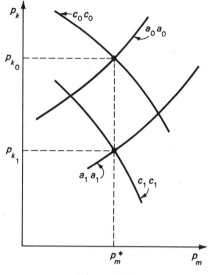

Figure 14–3

g, k, π_m, d, e are constant. π_k rises from π_{k_0} to π_{k_1} offset by x rising from x_0 to x_1.

First, suppose that the government uses monetary policy to peg the price level at p_m^*. As shown in Figure 14–3, the rise in π_k still forces down the cc schedule. But now the shift in the aa schedule will be the sum of the original movement arising from the rise in π_k and the government's open market sale designed to prevent p_m from falling. The $a_1 a_1$ schedule must intersect the $c_1 c_1$ schedule at p_m^* itself, and this clearly implies a lower equilibrium p_{k_1}.

In this case p_k is determined not in the assets markets but in the consumption goods market; and it is useful to have an expression such as (14–3) for the cc curve. Solving the consumption goods market equilibrium condition (14–5) for p_k, we obtain

$$(14\text{–}6) \quad p_k = \zeta(k, \pi_k, g^* p_m^*, e) \quad \frac{\partial \zeta}{\partial k} \gtreqless 0, \frac{\partial \zeta}{\partial \pi_k} < 0, \frac{\partial \zeta}{\partial \gamma} < 0, \frac{\partial \zeta}{\partial e} < 0.$$

We have just shown that an increase in π_k lowers p_k. An increase in e has the same effect since it creates excess demand, and a rise in $p_m g$ will also require a lower equilibrium p_k when π_m is zero because of the wealth effect. Changes in the capital stock are ambiguous because they move supply and demand in the same direction, and it is not certain which effect will predominate.

Now let us turn to the situation in which the government manipulates e (with d unchanged) to maintain a constant p_m. In Figure 14–4 we show that the aa schedule moves upward to a_1a_1 as a result of the rise in π_k. This time, however, the final position of the cc schedule includes government changes in e to make the c_1c_1 schedule intersect the a_1a_1 schedule at p_m^*. The result is obviously an unambiguously higher p_{k_1} as the result of the higher π_{k_1}, exactly the opposite of the monetary policy result. The government must lower expenditures and taxes to clear the consumption goods market at a higher p_k.

The fact that the two policies create opposite movements in p_k shows that we must study them separately. In all cases, however, we assume that the deficit exactly maintains the existing stock of debt,

$$(14\text{–}7) \qquad\qquad d^* = ng^*,$$

and that the price of money remains constant so that π_m is zero:

$$(14\text{–}8) \qquad\qquad p_m = p_m^*$$

$$(14\text{–}9) \qquad\qquad \pi_m = 0.$$

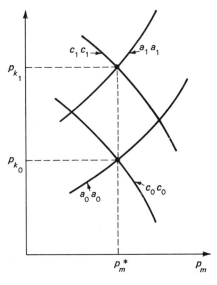

Figure 14–4

g, k, π_m, d, x are constant. π_k rises from π_{k_0} to π_{k_1} offset by e falling from e_0 to e_1.

14–3   Price Stabilization Through a Balanced-Budget Fiscal Policy

In this case the government fixes the composition of the debt at some level:

$$(14\text{–}10) \qquad\qquad x = x^*.$$

The price of capital is always determined in the assets markets, so that equation (14–3) applies:

$$(14\text{–}11) \qquad\qquad p_k = \Phi(\gamma^*, k, \pi_k, x^*).$$

From equation (14–5) we obtain at each instant the level of expenditures, e, necessary to clear the consumption goods market. The two differential equations of the system are the laws of capital accumulation and expectation formation:

$$(14\text{–}12) \qquad\qquad \dot{k} = q_I(k, p_k) - nk$$

$$(14\text{–}13) \qquad\qquad \pi_k = \beta\left(\frac{\dot{p}_k}{p_k} - \pi_k\right).$$

We can eliminate p_k from the system since it is a function only of k and π_k. By differentiating (14–11), we can rewrite (14–13):

$$(14\text{–}14) \qquad\qquad \dot{\pi}_k = \frac{\beta[(1/p_k)(\partial\Phi/\partial k)\dot{k} - \pi_k]}{1 - \beta(1/p_k)(\partial\Phi/\partial\pi_k)}.$$

To write the system solely in terms of π_k and k, we must use (14–11) in (14–12) and (14–12) itself in (14–14):

$$(14\text{–}15) \qquad\qquad \dot{k} = q_I(k, \Phi(\gamma^*, k, \pi_k, x^*)) - nk$$

$$(14\text{–}16) \quad \dot{\pi}_k = \frac{\beta[(1/p_k)(\partial\Phi/\partial k)(q_I(k, \Phi(\gamma^*, k, \pi_k, x^*)) - nk) - \pi_k]}{1 - \beta(1/p_k)(\partial\Phi/\partial\pi_k)}$$

The $\dot{k} = 0$ and $\dot{\pi}_k = 0$ loci in Figures 14–5 and 14–6 indicate the pairs (k, π_k) that make $\dot{k}$ and $\dot{\pi}_k$, respectively, equal to zero. Consider first the $\dot{k} = 0$ locus. An increase in the capital stock unambiguously reduces its own rate of change: first, directly, by reducing the output of investment goods; second, indirectly, by reducing the price of capital and so further

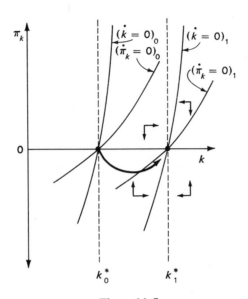

Figure 14–5

g, p_m, π_m, d are constant. x falls from x_0 to x_1.

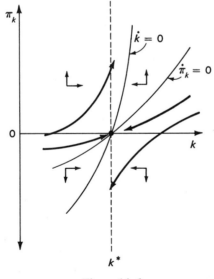

Figure 14–6

g, p_m, π_m, d, x are constant.

reducing the output of investment goods; and, third, by requiring a higher output of investment goods for its own maintenance. An increase in the expected rate of change in the price of capital raises the price of capital and increases the output of investment goods.

These two facts show that as k increases, π_k must also increase to keep $\dot{k} = 0$. The $\dot{k} = 0$ schedule slopes upward.

The $\dot{\pi}_k = 0$ schedule also must slope upward. When the denominator of equation (14–16) is positive, an increase in k raises $\dot{\pi}_k$. Since $\partial \Phi / \partial k$ is negative, the increase in k lowers p_k. To offset this, π_k itself must rise, both to raise $\dot{k}$ by raising p_k and to increase the $-\pi_k$ term in (14–16). Thus, to keep $\dot{\pi}_k = 0$ as k increases, π_k must also increase, and the $\dot{\pi}_k = 0$ schedule slopes upward. When the denominator of (14–16) is negative, an increase in k lowers $\dot{\pi}_k$ and an increase in π_k raises it, so that the two still work in opposite directions and the $\dot{\pi}_k = 0$ still slopes upward. Figure 14–5 corresponds to the case where the denominator in (14–16)is positive, and an increase in π_k reduces $\dot{\pi}_k$. Figure 14–6 corresponds to the case where the denominator in (14–16) is negative; an increase in π_k increases $\dot{\pi}_k$. The directions of the vertical arrows are dependent on this.

Notice that the two loci intersect at $\pi_k = 0$. The value of π_k at the intersection of the loci is obtained by setting $\dot{\pi}_k = 0$ in equation (14–14) and solving for π_k, where $\dot{k} = 0$. Clearly, π_k must also be zero. Further, the $\dot{k} = 0$ schedule always has a steeper slope than the $\dot{\pi}_k = 0$ schedule. We can demonstrate this by inspection of equation (14–15) and (14–16). Suppose that we are at the intersection of the two schedules, so that $\dot{k} = 0$ and $\dot{\pi}_k = 0$. If k increases in equation (14–15), some increase in π_k is needed to restore $\dot{k}$ to zero. But if we raise π_k just enough to do this, we can see from (14–16) that $\dot{\pi}_k$ will be negative because of the extra $-\pi_k$ term. We need a smaller increase in π_k to balance the increase in k along the $\dot{\pi}_k = 0$ schedule than along the $\dot{k} = 0$ schedule.

Figures 14–5 and 14–6 also show that the case in which $[1 - \beta(\partial \Phi / \partial \pi_k)(1/p_k)]$ is negative is unstable (Figure 14–6), while the other case (Figure 14–5) is stable. Since as β increases, the expression $[1 - \beta(\partial \Phi / \partial \pi_k)(1/p_k)]$ gets smaller, it is clear that the stability of the system depends on β not being too large, so that expectations do not adjust too rapidly. Because an increase in π_k raises p_k in this version, explosive speculation is possible, and can be damped only by sluggish adaptation of expectations to reality.

We conclude this section by using the model to study the effects of an open market purchase, that is, a permanent fall in x.

We examine only the stable case shown in Figure 14–5. An open market purchase that produces a fall in x leads to an increase in the price of capital that clears the assets markets. In terms of the diagrams, this shifts both the $\dot{k} = 0$ and $\dot{\pi}_k = 0$ schedules to the right since the output of investment goods will now be higher as of any pair (k, π_k), and a higher capital stock will be needed to absorb the additional output of investment goods in the steady state. The capital stock increases continually to its new higher level so that the overall rate of growth will be higher in the period of disequilibrium than in the steady state. The expected rate of increase in the price of capital initially falls below zero as the accumulation of capital forces p_k down after its first upward jump. The fall in π_k depresses p_k even farther for a while, but the depressing effect on p_k of the rise in k diminishes as k approaches its steady-state value, and $\dot{k}$ approaches zero. In the end, π_k, following the actual rate of change in p_k, moves back to zero.

What is required of fiscal policy is order to stabilize the price level following the rise in the price of capital and the subsequent accumulation of capital? An increase in the price of capital has an inflationary effect in the consumption goods market. To offset the effects of the initial rise in the price of capital, then, fiscal policy has to be tightened—the level of government expenditures and taxes has to be reduced. Then as capital accumulates over time, the price of capital in the assets markets begins to fall from its new level so that fiscal policy can be eased on this account. However, the accumulation of capital also affects the equilibrium of the consumption goods market, although the effects are ambiguous since an increase in the capital stock increases supply and increases demand through wealth and income effects. After the initial tightening, the direction of fiscal policy is uncertain.

14-4   Price Stabilization Through Monetary Policy

In this version of the model the government fixes the size of its expenditures:

$$(14\text{--}17) \qquad\qquad e = e^*.$$

This implies that the price of capital is determined by the equilibrium condition in the consumption goods market, so we use equation (14–6) instead of (14–3):

$$(14\text{--}18) \qquad\qquad p_k = \zeta(k, \pi_k, \gamma^*, e^*), \frac{\partial \zeta}{\partial \pi_k} < 0.$$

At each instant the government must choose the composition of the debt so that this p_k clears the assets markets at the given p_m^*.

As in Section 14–3, the two basic differential equations are the laws of capital accumulation and of expectation formation:

$$(14\text{–}19) \qquad \dot{k} = q_I(k, p_k) - nk$$

$$(14\text{–}20) \qquad \dot{\pi}_k = \beta\left(\frac{\dot{p}_k}{p_k} - \pi_k\right).$$

This time we use equation (14–18) to eliminate p_k, and we obtain the following two equations in π_k and k:

$$(14\text{–}21) \quad \dot{k} = q_I(k, \zeta(k, \pi_k, \gamma^*, e^*)) - nk$$

$$(14\text{–}22) \quad \dot{\pi}_k = \frac{\beta[(1/p_k)(\partial\zeta/\partial k)(q_I(k, \zeta(k, \pi_k, \gamma^*, e^*)) - nk) - \pi_k]}{1 - \beta(1/p_k)(\partial\zeta/\partial\pi_k)}.$$

The denominator of equation (14–22) is always positive because $\partial\zeta/\partial\pi_k < 0$ in this version of the model. This does not, however, make things much easier for us because the sign of $\partial\zeta/\partial k$ is ambiguous.

We begin by merely stating without proof that whenever $\partial\dot{k}/\partial k > 0$, the system is unstable. The reader can work this case out diagrammatically. (Notice that $\partial\dot{k}/\partial k > 0$ can hold only if $\partial\zeta/\partial k > 0$.)

In what follows we assume that $\partial\dot{k}/\partial k < 0$ and consider possible stable configurations. The $\dot{k} = 0$ schedule must slope downward because an increase in k lowers $\dot{k}$ and an increase in π_k, by lowering p_k, also lowers $\dot{k}$. Thus, if $\dot{k}$ is to be kept at zero while k rises, π_k must fall. In Figures 14–7, 14–8, and 14–9, the $\dot{k} = 0$ schedule is downward-sloped.

The slope of the $\dot{\pi}_k = 0$ schedule depends on the sign of $\partial\zeta/\partial k$. When this is negative (which is the case where increases in k create excess demand in the consumption markets), the $\dot{\pi}_k = 0$ schedule may slope either way. An increase in k, by lowering $\dot{k}$, raises $\dot{\pi}_k$ [as long as $\partial\zeta/\partial k > 0$ in equation (14–21)]. But an increase in π_k has two contradictory effects. First, by reducing p_k, it lowers $\dot{k}$ and tends to make $\dot{\pi}_k$ larger. But through the $-\pi_k$ term, an increase in π_k tends to lower $\dot{\pi}_k$. Figure 14–7 shows the case of $\partial\dot{\pi}_k/\partial\pi_k < 0$, where the $\dot{\pi}_k = 0$ schedules slopes upward; the system is stable and cannot produce cyclical movements. In the event that $\partial\dot{\pi}_k/\partial\pi_k > 0$, Figure 14–8 applies. The equilibrium may or may not be stable and, in either event, can exhibit cyclical movements. We have indicated the stable case.

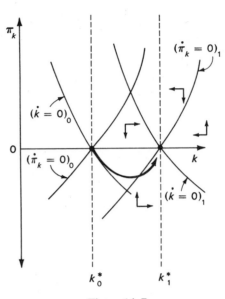

Figure 14–7

g, p_m, π_m, d are constant. e falls from e_0 to e_1.

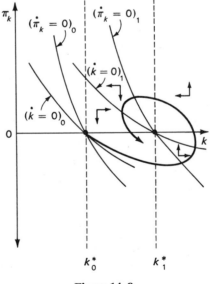

Figure 14–8

g, p_m, π_m, d are constant. e falls from e_0 to e_1.

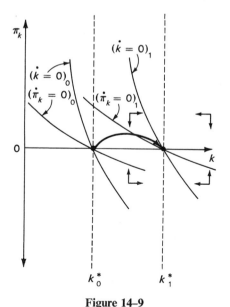

Figure 14–9

g, p_m, π_m, d are constant. e falls from e_0 to e_1.

The same arguments we used in Section 14–3 still prove that the inter-section will be at $\pi_k = 0$ and that the $\dot\pi_k = 0$ schedule has an algebraically smaller (more negative) slope than the $\dot k = 0$ in Figure 14–8.

In Figure 14–9, we show the remaining stable possibility, where $\partial \zeta / \partial k > 0$, but $\partial k / \partial k < 0$. In this case the $\dot\pi_k = 0$ schedule also slopes downward, because an increase in k reduces $\dot\pi_k$ and must be offset by a fall in π_k, which raises $\dot\pi_k$ both by lowering p_k and k, and through the $-\pi_k$ term in equation (14–22). Again it is easy to show that the $\dot k = 0$ has the algebraic-ally smaller (more negative) slope. If we increase k and compensate by reducing π_k enough to keep $\dot k = 0$ near the intersection, we can see from (14–22) that $\dot\pi_k$ will be negative. We need a smaller movement of π_k to keep $\dot\pi_k = 0$.

We use this version of the model to perform one experiment: a tightening of fiscal policy through a reduction of expenditures and taxes that keeps the deficit constant.

A decrease in the level of government expenditures with a constant deficit is deflationary in the consumption goods market so that the price of capital that clears the consumption goods market rises as of any pair (k, π_k). Around a position of stable equilibrium this will shift the $\dot k = 0$ and $\dot\pi = 0$ schedules to the right, increasing the equilibrium stock of capital since a higher capital stock is now needed to absorb the higher output of investment goods in the steady state. If the economy were initially at a stable steady state, the capital stock would increase to its new steady state level. As can be seen from the diagrams, the movement to the new equilibrium capital stock may involve cycles, in the case illustrated in Figure 14–8.

The long-run effect of the tighter fiscal policy is a higher stock of capital, just as the long-run effect of easier money in our previous example was a higher stock of capital. At first the accompanying monetary policy must be easy to prevent changes in the price level, but the continuing changes necessary in monetary policy depend on the effect of the growing capital stock on the consumption goods market. If, as the capital stock increases, it raises the consumption goods market equilibrium p_k, monetary policy must always be getting easier, to achieve the necessary p_k with the larger capital stock. If a rise in the capital stock lowers the consumption goods market equilibrium p_k, x may have to move in different directions at different times.

14–5   Summary

The main purpose of these exercises is to convince the reader that the inclusion of expected capital gains on capital complicates the analysis without changing the basic ideas. They also illustrate ways of using the relatively elementary techniques we have already developed to study the model with adaptive expectations in the price of capital. In this place perhaps more than anywhere else we should emphasize our inability to prove stability. The economy may be unstable because of speculation.

Finally, this example also points up a limitation of the graphical analysis we have used so far. If we had tried to study deficit stabilization, we would have developed a model with three differential equations, one for the capital stock, one for the stock of debt, and one for expected capital gains. The graphical methods we use, except in special cases, are effective only in studying two-equation systems.

 Optimal Fiscal and Monetary Policy*

15-1 Introduction

Most analyses of economic growth fall into one of two classes. The first is typified by Frank Ramsey's famous paper in which the economist tries to answer the question, What is the best path of capital accumulation for the economy to follow, supposing that full planning is possible? The second is well represented by R. M. Solow's work, which attempts to explain how an unplanned but full employment economy will grow given its technology and the market behavior of consumers. (See Bibliography for exact references.)

Our model so far fits neither of these paradigms. On the one hand, the economy we describe is not fully planned and consumer market behavior is very important; on the other hand, there is government intervention and control exercised by manipulating the deficit, expenditures, and the

* This chapter is the result of work done with Karl Shell. A similar analysis is contained in D. Foley, K. Shell, and M. Sidrauski, "Optimal Fiscal and Monetary Policy and Economic Growth," *Journal of Political Economy*, Vol. 77, No. 4, Pt. II, July-August 1969, pp. 698–719 (published by the University of Chicago Press). © 1969 by the University of Chicago. This paper studies the problem where the marginal utility of private consumption diminishes, and there is no utility to public consumption.

composition of the debt. This model attempts to capture the central policy problems of a modern "mixed" economy in which the government can influence investment and saving, but only indirectly, through fiscal and monetary policy.

In this chapter we make the government's growth goal more explicit and try to find the relationship between an optimal investment strategy and the policy variables the government has at its disposal. We continue to assume that the government maintains a stable price level. We add to this goal the aim of maximizing a welfare functional that depends on the path of per-capita consumption over time.

The simplest form of an intertemporal welfare function is the integral of a utility function of per-capital consumption at each instant. The utility function does not change over time, but the government discounts future utility at a rate δ, called the social rate of time preference. In this scheme the government cares about the per-capita consumption of future generations but attaches less weight to utility gained further in the future. We also assume that the government cares about all future generations, so that its horizon is infinite. A dilemma suggests this choice of horizon, for if the government were to choose any finite period over which to plan, it would then have to decide what capital stock it wanted to leave at the end of the period. The only reason for preferring one stock to another would be the effects in the postplan period, so that one way or another the government must concern itself with the postplan period. Since there is no natural stopping place, we choose an infinite horizon.

This model has a number of features that we should mention at the outset. First, the utility measure is cardinal in the sense that a monotonic transformation of the measure will generally imply a different optimal path for consumption. This is because the shape of the utility determines the relative weight given to increasing the consumption of rich and poor generations in the government's planning. The functional represents government preferences over whole paths of consumption. Second, the number δ can be interpreted in two ways. Each generation will have a utility measure for its per-capita consumption, and this will be discounted at the government's rate of time preference to find the total value of a path. But should the utility of large generations be weighted more heavily than that of small generations? If population grows exponentially, the functional for weighted utilities is formally similar to that for unweighted utilities, but the discount rate is reduced by the rate of population growth in the weighted case. In what follows we assume $\delta > 0$, and the reader can choose whether to interpret it as including weight for population size or not.

It is not at all clear where the preferences of the government come from, or if governments do have consistent preferences of the kind we discuss, but a constant theme of policy literature is that government intervention in the economy is effective and can be judged as good or bad for the economy without direct reference to consumer preferences. This is particularly true of prescriptions for policies to influence economic growth. It seems to us that postulating a social welfare function for the government is the best way to make rigorous the prescription of government control in the mixed economy. At the same time, the preferences of consumers in the model are reflected in the demand functions for assets and consumption goods. The government manipulates the policy variables in such a way as to maximize the social welfare function, taking these demand functions as given. Also given to the government at the time at which planning begins (time zero) are the technology of the economy and the initial stocks of capital, labor, and government debt. We also retain the goal of price stabilization in this chapter. This goal partially fills the gap created in our model by failure to include unemployment and the social costs (if any) of inflation.

15–2   The Optimal Growth Path

In this section we study the paths that the capital stock and the price of capital, and therefore consumption and investment, have to follow to maximize the integral of discounted utility of per-capita consumption. We assume here, to simplify our analysis, that there is no production of public consumption goods. In Section 15–5, we allow for the production of such goods by assuming that both private and public consumption goods enter the government's utility function and analyze optimal paths for the production of both types of goods. If public consumption goods produce utility, it is not desirable for government expenditure to vary for stabilization purposes, since expenditure should be determined on the basis of its contribution to social welfare. The government can use monetary and deficit policy to achieve its two goals. In Section 15–3 we discuss the way in which the government must vary its policy instruments to ensure that the optimal path is followed, subject to the price level remaining constant.

We can write the government's social welfare function as

$$(15–1) \qquad W = \int_0^\infty U(c(\tau)) \exp(-\delta\tau) \, d\tau.$$

Until Section 15–5 we assume that marginal utility is positive and constant, so that $U'' = 0$ and $U(c(t)) = \beta c(t) + \alpha$ for arbitrary constants α and β. This substantially simplifies the mathematical difficulties of determining the optimal path. We treat a more general case in Section 15–5. We assume that δ, the social rate of time preference, is strictly positive. (Recall that δ may include population weights.)

At any instant the rate of change of the per-capita capital stock is

$$(15\text{–}2) \qquad\qquad \dot{k} = q_I(k,\, p_k) - nk.$$

The initial capital stock is given as

$$(15\text{–}3) \qquad\qquad k(0) = k_0.$$

Although the initial stock of capital is fixed, the initial price of capital is not. In fact, the path of the price of capital, as is evident from equation (15–2), will completely determine the path of the capital stock and consumption through time. We shall try to find which path for p_k maximizes the integral in equation (15–1).

Imagine that we have chosen some path and that we perform the experiment of reducing consumption by one unit at some time t and increase investment. The future capital stock will be larger so that future consumption can be permanently higher. If the new path has higher welfare, the old path obviously was not optimal.

The loss of utility from giving up one unit of consumption is proportional to $U'(q_C(k(t),\, p_k(t)))$, and we can increase investment by an amount proportional to $1/p_k$ units when the economy is not specialized.

What is the increase in consumption at each future instant when the capital stock is increased at each future instant by $1/p_k$ units? At all times, factor payments are equal to the value of output:

$$(15\text{–}4) \qquad w(p_k) + r(p_k)k = q_C(k,\, p_k) + p_k q_I(k,\, p_k),$$

where w is the wage rate and r the rental rate of capital in consumption good units. We can rewrite the above expression as

$$(15\text{–}5) \qquad q_C(k,\, p_k) = w(p_k) + r(p_k)k - p_k q_I(k,\, p_k).$$

The increase in the capital stock requires a permanent rise in q_I to maintain the new higher k in the face of population growth. This increase in q_I will be n times the increase in k. Differentiating equation (15–5) and holding the path of p_k constant, we obtain

$$(15\text{–}6) \qquad \frac{\partial q_C}{\partial k} = r - np_k.$$

This is the net extra consumption we can obtain permanently in the future for a small increase in k. The total increase in welfare from increasing the capital stock by $1/p_k$ unit at time t is therefore

$$(15\text{–}7) \qquad \frac{1}{p_k} \int_t^\infty [r(\tau) - np_k(\tau))U'(q_C(\tau)) \exp(-\delta(\tau - t))\, d\tau.$$

This is the integral of the increase in the per-capita output of consumption goods at each instant multiplied by its marginal utility and discounted at the rate δ from period t to ∞.

For the path to be optimal, we require that the gain of utility from increased future consumption not be greater than the loss of utility from lower current consumption. But if the economy is unspecialized along the whole path from t on, we can also do exactly the opposite experiment: increase current consumption a little and decrease the future capital stock and future consumption. In this case the gain from current consumption will be smaller than the whole future loss discounted if we are on the optimal path. If both these changes fail to increase the integral of utility the following condition must hold.

$$(15\text{–}8) \quad U'(q_C(t)) = \frac{1}{p_k} \int_t^\infty (r(\tau) - np_k(\tau))U'(q_C(\tau)) \exp(-\delta(\tau - t))\, d\tau.$$

This relationship is true at all times along an unspecialized optimal path. It follows that the rates of change of both sides of equation (15–8) are equal at each instant of time. Differentiating both sides with respect to time, we have

$$(15\text{–}9)$$

$$0 = -\frac{1}{p_k}\Bigg[(r(t) - np_k(t))U'(q_C(t))$$

$$-\left(\delta - \frac{\dot{p}_k}{p_k}\right) \int_t^\infty (r(\tau) - np_k(\tau))U'(q_C(\tau)) \exp(-\delta(\tau - t))\, d\tau\Bigg].$$

Using equation (15–8) to substitute for the integral in the two places where it appears on the right-hand side of equation (15–9) and dividing through by $p_k U'[q_C(t)]$, we obtain

$$(15\text{--}10) \qquad\qquad \frac{\dot{p}_k}{p_k} = n + \delta - \frac{r(p_k)}{p_k}.$$

Along an unspecialized optimal path, the rate of return to capital—the rental rate plus the rate of capital gains net of population growth—must equal the rate of time preference when the economy is not specialized.

The two differential equations (15–2) and (15–10) constitute a system in two unknowns, k and p_k. Any unspecialized optimal path has to satisfy these and, in addition, has to begin with the initial capital stock given by equation (15–3). The initial price of capital is not given: as we remarked above, it has to be chosen and then to be changed in accordance with equation (15–10). Of course, these are only necessary conditions, and there will be many nonoptimal paths satisfying them.

We plot the loci of points that make $\dot{k}$ and $\dot{p}_k$, respectively, equal to zero in the $\dot{k} = 0$ and $\dot{p}_k = 0$ loci of Figure 15–1. These curves are derived from equations (15–2) and (15–10) and the $\dot{k} = 0$ locus is the same as that studied earlier, for example in Figure 2–7. The capital stock is falling

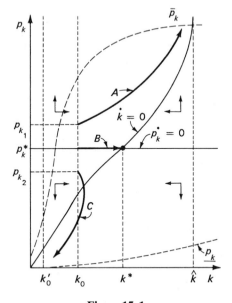

Figure 15–1
δ is constant.

anywhere to the right of the $\dot{k} = 0$ locus and rising to the left of the locus; this is shown by the horizontal arrows.

For $\dot{p}_k$ to be zero, we need

$$(15\text{–}11) \qquad \frac{r(p_k^*)}{p_k^*} = n + \delta.$$

From the fact that $r(p_k)/p_k$ falls as p_k rises, we see that there is a unique p_k^* that satisfies equation (15–11). The $\dot{p}_k = 0$ schedule is a horizontal line at height p_k^* since there is only one price of capital for which the rental on capital net of population growth is equal to the discount rate. Anywhere above that line, $r(p_k)/p_k$ is lower than $r(p_k^*)/p_k^*$, and by equation (15–10) p_k is rising. Anywhere below the $\dot{p}_k = 0$ line the price of capital is falling. This accounts for the vertical arrows.

Each of the three paths we show starting from the initial capital stock, k_0, obeys the necessary conditions (15–2), (15–3), and (15–10). Now we show that only Path B of the three paths indicated can be optimal. (The reader can work out the reasons why only a path on which the price of capital is constant can be optimal for $k_0 > k^*$ using much the same arguments as those that follow.) On Path A, the price of capital is always rising so that

$$(15\text{–}12) \qquad \frac{\dot{p}_k}{p_k} = n + \delta - \frac{r(p_k)}{p_k} > 0$$

or

$$(15\text{–}13) \qquad \frac{r(p_k)}{p_k} < n + \delta.$$

From this condition, we can show that it is possible to improve on Path A by increasing current consumption by one unit and reducing future consumption. The gain in welfare from increasing current consumption at time t evaluated at that time is $U'(q_C(k(t), p_k(t)))$. The loss in welfare from future losses in consumption is

$$(15\text{–}14) \qquad \frac{1}{p_k(t)} \int_t^\infty (r(\tau) - n p_k(\tau)) U'(q_C(\tau)) \exp(-\delta(\tau - t))\, d\tau.$$

Notice that since the price of capital is always rising on Path A,

$$(15\text{–}15) \qquad \left. \begin{array}{c} p_k(t) < p_k(\tau) \\ r(p_k(t)) > r(p_k(\tau)) \end{array} \right\} \quad \text{for all } \tau > t.$$

Therefore the total loss in welfare is certainly less than

$$(15\text{--}16) \quad \varepsilon = \frac{1}{p_k(t)} \int_t^\infty (r(t) - np_k(t))U'(q_C(t)) \exp(-\delta(\tau - t)) \, d\tau$$

$$= \frac{1}{p_k(t)} \frac{r(t) - np_k(t)}{\delta} U'(q_C(t)),$$

since U' is a constant. We now have a gain in welfare of $U'(q_C(t))$ with a loss less than ε, but we can show that the gain outweighs even ε, so that the gain in utility outweighs the loss in utility from lower future consumption. If

$$(15\text{--}17) \qquad U'(q_C(t)) > \frac{1}{p_k(t)} \frac{r(t) - np_k(t)}{\delta} U'(q_C(t)),$$

then the gain in utility will be greater than ε. This can be rewritten as

$$\delta + n > \frac{r}{p_k},$$

which is the condition (15–13) that prevails when p_k is rising.

By similar reasoning we can show that Path C is not optimal. On Path C the price of capital is always falling so that

$$(15\text{--}18) \qquad \delta + n < \frac{r}{p_k}.$$

Path C can be improved by giving up one unit of current consumption to increase future consumption by an argument symmetric to the one just given.

Under our assumptions we are assured of the existence of an optimal path (although we do not prove this). We can eliminate all paths that do not obey conditions (15–2), (15–3), and (15–1). We have just shown that paths such as Path A and Path C are nonoptimal; thus we are left with Path B, which is the optimal path. If at the initial capital stock, k_0, p_k^* is not a specialization price, the policy is to set the price of capital at p_k^* and to keep it there forever. Capital will accumulate (if $k_0 < k^*$), approaching k^*, the optimal long-run ratio of capital to labor.

There is no guarantee that the economy will not be specialized at (k_0, p_k^*). In Figure 15–1, k_0' represents an initial capital stock that has this property. Any path can then be divided into two parts, a beginning where no consumption is produced and capital accumulates as rapidly as possible and an ending in which both investment and consumption are produced. The beginning adds nothing to welfare. The ending must satisfy the optimal condition we just derived, so it should enter the nonspecialization region at p_k^*. During specialization, capital accumulates at the same rate whatever the price of capital. Thus the planners cannot do better than to set the initial price of capital at p_k^*, even where this means an initial period of specialization. Now our rule is: set p_k at p_k^* whatever the initial ratio of capital to labor happens to be. This rule depends on our choice of a linear utility function.

In practice, the labor force could not survive if there were no consumption during an initial period. One might want to impose additional constraints that rule out specialization to investment goods. Where the utility function is not linear, the assumption $U'(0) = \infty$ will rule out specialization. This approach is used in Section 15–5.

The linear utility function is somewhat peculiar because it counts an increase in c when c is very low the same as an increase in c when it is very high. Early poor generations may starve, but on this social welfare assumption the very high consumption of later richer generations more than makes up for it.

Some other features of the optimal path require comment. First, on the optimal path the own rental to capital is equal to the rate of population growth plus the discount rate [from equation (15–11)]. At lower discount rates, the optimal rental rate is closer to the rate of growth of population. The lower is δ, the closer the long-run ratio of capital to labor approaches its Golden Rule value. Second, if k_0 is less than k^*, k increases through time on the optimal path and vice versa. Third, if k_0 is less than k^*, consumption is nondecreasing along the optimal path. It is possible, if the initial capital stock is very low, that there will be no consumption during some initial period but consumption will become positive once the $\bar{p}_k$ schedule is reached. This conclusion follows from the fact that

$$(15\text{–}19) \qquad\qquad q_c = q_c(k, p_k) \qquad \frac{\partial q_c}{\partial k} \geq 0,$$

and we know p_k should be constant at p_k^*, so that where there is no specialization, consumption will increase as capital accumulates. (The reader can easily work out for himself the equivalent results for $k_0 > k^*$.)

15–3   Optimal Fiscal and Monetary Policy

We have shown that with a linear utility function the optimal growth strategy is to fix p_k at the appropriate p_k^* forever. In this section we study the deficit and monetary policies necessary to achieve this in the model. We are adding to our original government goal of maintaining p_m at a given p_m^* the goal of maintaining p_k at a given p_k^*. In this version of the model it is very plausible to require $\pi_m = 0$ and $\pi_k = 0$, since both p_m and p_k will, in fact, be constant. We also use the proportional consumption function without wealth because it is simpler.

Consumption is a constant fraction $(1 - s)$ of disposable income:

$$(15\text{–}20) \qquad c^d = (1 - s)(q_C(k, p_k) + p_k q_I(k, p_k) + dp_m).$$

Along the optimal path, p_k is fixed at p_k^* and p_m at p_m^*, the level chosen by the government. For the consumption goods market to clear at each instant (at which k is also given), the government must manipulate transfer payments so that the deficit satisfies

$$(15\text{–}21) \qquad q_C(k, p_k^*) = (1 - s)(q_C(k, p_k^*) + p_k^* q_I(k, p_k^*) + dp_m^*).$$

From (15–21) we can write

$$(15\text{–}22) \qquad d = \frac{s q_C(k, p_k^*) - (1 - s)p_k^* q_I(k, p_k^*)}{(1 - s)p_m^*}.$$

This gives the level of the deficit that ensures consumption goods market equilibrium. As k increases along the optimal path (if $k_0 < k^*$), excess supply tends to develop in the consumption goods market, so that the government has to increase the deficit to offset this:

$$(15\text{–}23) \qquad \frac{\partial d}{\partial k} = \frac{s(\partial q_C/\partial k) - (1 - s)p_k^*(\partial q_I/\partial k)}{(1 - s)p_m^*} > 0.$$

The debt then changes according to the law

$$(15\text{–}24) \qquad \dot{g} = d(k, p_m^*, p_k^*) - ng.$$

Together with equation (15–2) this gives a system of two equations in two unknowns, g and k (taking p_k^* and p_m^* as given). We plot the $\dot{g} = 0$ and $\dot{k} = 0$ loci in Figure 15–2.

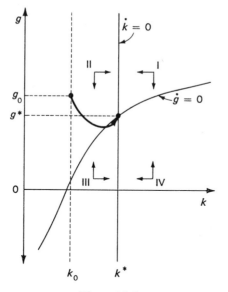

Figure 15–2

p_m, p_k, π_m, π_k are constant.

Since p_k is fixed at p_k^*, there will be only one k^* that will satisfy

(15–25) $q_1(k^*, p_k^*) - nk^* = 0$.

The $\dot{k} = 0$ schedule is a vertical line. Anywhere to the right of this line, k is falling, as indicated by the horizontal arrows.

The $\dot{g} = 0$ schedule is upward-sloping because for a higher k, a higher d is necessary [from (15–23)] and a higher g is necessary to absorb the larger additions to the debt while maintaining a constant per-capital debt. Above this line the debt is larger than can be maintained by the deficit, so that g is falling, as shown by the vertical arrows.

The system shown in Figure 15–2 is stable and the economy always settles down in the long run to the unique equilibrium k^* and g^*. The optimal stocks of capital and debt, k^* and g^*, are independent of the initial stocks, k_0 and g_0.

We can see from Figure 15–2 that it is possible for the stock of government debt to fall for some time and then to rise along the optimal path. This is what happens along the path we have shown. The $\dot{k} = 0$ and $\dot{g} = 0$ loci divide the space of the diagram into four zones, indicated by roman numerals. If the initial position is in Region I or Region III, the debt and capital stock will both either decrease together (I) or increase together

(III) until (k^*, g^*) is reached. If the initial position is in either II or IV, then although k will steadily increase (II) or decrease (IV) to k^*, g may first decrease and then increase (II) to g^* or first increase and then fall (IV) to g^*. There may also be initial positions in Regions II and IV from which g will change monotonically. If both the capital stock and debt are initially low relative to the optimal stocks, it is likely that both will increase along the optimal path. (The reader can easily work out the equivalent statement for high k_0 and g_0.)

One other important point should be noted: we have shown g^* as positive in Figure 15-2. Nothing in the analysis requires that this be the case, and the optimal steady-state debt may be negative, zero, or positive. The optimal steady-state debt is given by the intersection of the $\dot{k} = 0$ and $\dot{g} = 0$ loci in Figure 15-2, that is, by the solution to equation (15-24), where $\dot{g} = 0$ and $k = k^*$:

$$(15\text{-}26) \qquad g^* = \frac{s q_c(k^*, p_k^*) - (1 - s) p_k^* q_I(k^*, p_k^*)}{n(1 - s) p_m^*}.$$

Equation (15-24) is derived from the consumption market clearing equation, so that whether the debt is positive or negative in the steady state depends on whether there tends to be excess supply or demand in the consumption goods market at the triple (k^*, p_m^*, p_k^*) when the deficit is zero. If at the long-run equilibrium (k^*, p_m^*, p_k^*) with a zero deficit, there is excess supply in the consumption goods market, the government will have to increase transfer payments to increase demand and clear the consumption goods market. This makes for a positive deficit and a positive stock of debt in the long-run; but there could be excess demand at (k^*, p_m^*, p_k^*) with a zero deficit so that the government has to run a surplus and the economy ends up with a negative debt.

What of equilibrium in the assets markets? It is the task of monetary policy to ensure that at each instant the optimal p_k^*, together with the chosen p_m^* and the given g and k, clears those markets. This is achieved by varying the ratio of debt to money x. In our earlier analysis we obtained equation (3-23), which expresses the assets markets equilibrium price of capital p_k as a function of $g p_m$, k, π_m, π_k, and x.

$$(15\text{-}27) \quad p_k = \Phi(g p_m, k, \pi_m, \pi_k, x) \qquad \frac{\partial \Phi}{\partial (g p_m)} > 0, \frac{\partial \Phi}{\partial k} < 0, \frac{\partial \Phi}{\partial x} < 0.$$

Along the optimal path, p_k and p_m are constant, and $\pi_m = \pi_k = 0$; at any time t the stock of debt g and the capital stock k are given. Then x has to be varied to satisfy

$$(15\text{--}28) \qquad p_k^* = \Phi(g(t)p_m^*, k(t), \pi_m, \pi_k, x),$$

when $\pi_m = \pi_k = 0$.

On those optimal paths on which g and k increase or decrease together, we cannot say how x will change to ensure that p_k^* clears the assets markets because an increasing g tends to increase p_k, while an increasing k tends to reduce p_k. If the effects through k dominate so that p_k tends to fall, x must be reduced (the money supply increased by open market operations) to offset this. On those paths, or portions of paths, on which g falls while k increases, both effects will tend to reduce p_k. x definitely has to be reduced when the debt is falling and the capital stock rising, so that the proportion of money in the debt would increase over time, while (k^*, g^*) is approached from $g_0 > g^*$ and $k_0 < k^*$.

15-4   Effects of Changes in the Rate of Time Preference

In a sense, the magnitude of δ, the rate of time preference, is a measure of the impatience of the government. The higher is δ, the less weight does the government attach to the utility enjoyed by future generations and the more relative weight is attached to the consumption of the present generation. One might then expect that a higher rate of time preference would lead to a lower steady-state capital stock; this expectation is correct.

To see this, we need only examine Figure 15-1. The position of the $k = 0$ schedule is independent of δ. An increase in δ does affect the position of the $\dot{p}_k = 0$ schedule by reducing the price of capital for which $r(p_k)/p_k = \delta + n$. This moves the $\dot{p}_k = 0$ schedule downward, and it then intersects $k = 0$ at a lower capital stock. (This result is independent of the special assumption that marginal utility is constant, as we show in Section 15-5.)

One might also expect that a higher δ leads to a lower long-run stock of debt. This expectation is not necessarily correct. In Figure 15-2 the $k = 0$ schedule shifts to the left when δ increases because the long-run equilibrium stock of capital is lower, but the $\dot{g} = 0$ schedule moves upward at the same time because the optimal price of capital is lower. This means that for any given k and p_m^*, d will have to be higher than it previously was to equilibrate the consumption goods market, because the fall in p_k tends to produce excess supply in that market, but then the level of g that makes $\dot{g} = 0$ in equation (15-24) is higher for any given k. Accordingly, the $\dot{g} = 0$ schedule shifts upward, and its intersection with the new $\dot{k} = 0$ locus may be at a higher or lower g.

An increase in the social rate of time preference may actually lead to a lower stock of debt in the long run. This fact provides an additional illustration of the point we made in Chapter 11 that the stock of government debt alone is not a reliable guide to the long-run welfare of an economy. The pertinent variable is the capital stock, and there is no one-to-one relationship between the stocks of capital and debt. Policy is best judged by its effect on investment, not on the stock of debt.

15–5 Addendum on More General Welfare Functionals

(A) THE OPTIMAL GROWTH PATH

The analysis to this point has been kept as simple mathematically as possible. In particular, we excluded public consumption goods from the utility function and assumed that the marginal utility of private consumption was constant. In this section we work with a more general, concave utility function that includes public consumption.

The consumption function used in Sections 5–2 through 5–4 took consumption to be a constant fraction of disposable income. We shall not complicate the analysis of this appendix by using a more sophisticated consumption function, since it will be seen that the results are not clear-cut even when a simple consumption function is used.

The welfare function now becomes

$$(15\text{–}29) \qquad W = \int_0^\infty U(c_\tau, e_\tau) \exp(-\delta\tau)\, d\tau,$$

where the utility function has continuous first and second derivatives and is concave, that is, $U_c > 0$, $U_e > 0$, $U_{cc} < 0$, $U_{cc} U_{ee} - U_{ce}^2 \geq 0$. We also assume that the marginal utility of each of private and public consumption goods is infinite where the consumption of such goods is zero: $U_c(0, e) = \infty$ and $U_e(c, 0) = \infty$. These assumptions ensure that there will not be specialization to investment goods and that positive amounts of each good will be produced along the optimal path.

As always, we have

$$(15\text{–}30) \qquad \dot{k} = q_I(k, p_k) - nk.$$

It is clear that at each moment of time on any optimal path and for any level of production of consumption goods, the marginal utility of private consumption goods should be equal to the marginal utility of public consumption goods. To see this, suppose that the marginal utility of private consumption exceeds that of public consumption: then utility as of that instant, and therefore welfare, would be increased by increasing the production of private consumption goods by one unit and reducing the production of public consumption goods by one unit. Thus, at each instant along the optimal path,

$$(15\text{--}31) \qquad U_c(c_t, e_t) = U_e(c_t, e_t).$$

Along the optimal path it must still be true that giving up one unit of consumption goods now to increase future consumption leads to no increase in welfare. In particular, assume that the one unit of consumption goods now given up to increase the capital stock is withdrawn from private and public consumption in such a way as to maintain the equality of current marginal utilities and that the future consumption is added in such a way as to keep marginal utilities equal. The loss of current utility is $\alpha U_c + (1 - \alpha)U_e$, where α is the proportion of private consumption goods in the total production of consumption goods. Since $U_c = U_e$, the loss of utility is just U_c. The reduction of consumption by one unit increases the capital stock by $1/p_k$ units.

By the same argument as used earlier in this chapter, the increase in welfare is

$$\frac{1}{p_k} \int_t^\infty (r(\tau) - np_k(\tau))U_c(c_\tau, e_\tau) \exp(-\delta(\tau - t)) \, d\tau$$

so that on any optimal path

$$(15\text{--}32) \qquad U_c(c_t, e_t) = \frac{1}{p_k} \int_t^\infty (r(\tau) - np_k(\tau))U_c(c_\tau, e_\tau) \exp(-\delta(\tau - t)) \, d\tau.$$

Since this relation holds at each instant of time, the rates of change on both sides must be equal: differentiating both sides with respect to time yields

$$(15\text{--}33) \quad U_{cc}\dot{c} + U_{ce}\dot{e} = -\frac{1}{p_k}\left[(r(\tau) - np_k(\tau))U_c(c_t, e_t) \right.$$

$$\left. - \left(\delta - \frac{\dot{p}_k}{p_k} \right) \int_t^\infty (r(\tau) - np_k(\tau))U_c(c_\tau, e_\tau) \exp(-\delta(\tau - t)) \, d\tau \right].$$

Using equation (15–32) to substitute for the integral in the right-hand side of expression (15–33), we obtain

$$(15\text{–}34) \qquad U_{cc}\dot{c} + U_{ce}\dot{e} = U_c\left[n + \delta - \left(\frac{r(p_k)}{p_k} + \frac{\dot{p}_k}{p_k}\right)\right].$$

This gives us a condition on the rates of change of public and private consumption and the rate of change of prices that must hold along an optimal path. A clearer understanding of the nature of the optimal path is obtained from conditions on the rate of change of the prices of capital and the capital stock since the levels of these variables determine the production of investment goods and total consumption goods at each instant. Given the production of consumption goods, the rule given by equation (15–31) of equalizing marginal utilities dictates the proportions in which public and private consumption goods should be produced.

To express equation (15–33) in terms of the rates of change of the capital stock and the price of capital, we first differentiate (15–31) with respect to time,

$$U_{cc}\dot{c} + U_{ce}\dot{e} = U_{ec}\dot{c} + U_{ee}\dot{e},$$

and obtain a relationship between the rates of change of public and private consumption goods that holds on the optimal path:

$$(15\text{–}35) \qquad (U_{cc} - U_{ec})\dot{c} = (U_{ee} - U_{ce})\dot{e}.$$

An alternative way of reaching equation (15–35) may be helpful: the discussion of a necessary condition for optimality which resulted in equation (15–32) was conducted in terms of private consumption goods. If, instead, we used public consumption goods and therefore wrote U_e in (15–32), where U_c now appears, and then differentiated with respect to time, we would obtain an equation like (15–34), with $U_{ec}\dot{c} + U_{ee}\dot{e}$ on the left-hand side and U_e instead of U_c on the right-hand side. Since $U_e = U_c$, equating left-hand sides would give us (15–35).

Another relationship that holds at each instant of time is the supply function of consumption goods:

$$q_C(k, p_k) = c + e.$$

Differentiating both sides of this with respect to time, we obtain

$$(15\text{–}36) \qquad \frac{\partial q_C}{\partial k}k + \frac{\partial q_C}{\partial p_k}\dot{p}_k = \dot{c} + \dot{e}.$$

Now use equation (15–35) to substitute for $\dot{e}$ in equations (15–34) and (15–36); then use the expression for $\dot{c}$ in terms of $\dot{p}_k$ and k that results from the substitution of (15–35) in (15–36) to substitute for $\dot{c}$ in the expression resulting from the substitution for $\dot{e}$ in (15–34) and simplify, to obtain

(15–37)

$$\left(\frac{U_{cc}U_{ee} - U_{ce}^2}{U_{cc} - U_{ee} - 2U_{ce}}\right)\left(\frac{\partial q_c}{\partial k}k + \frac{\partial q_c}{\partial p_k}\dot{p}_k\right) = U_c\left[n + \delta - \left(\frac{r(p_k)}{p_k} + \frac{\dot{p}_k}{p_k}\right)\right].$$

(We require $U_{ee} - U_{ce} \neq 0$, so that we can divide through by $U_{ee} - U_{ce}$ in (15–35).)

Note that if $U_{ce}U_{ee} = U_{ce}^2$, equation (15–37) reduces to the same equation for $\dot{p}_k/p_k$ as equation (15–10). One condition on the utility function that ensures $U_{cc}U_{ee} = U_{ce}^2$ is homogeneity of first degree in public and private consumption (though the converse is not true). This is the case in which an increase in the consumption of each of private and public consumption goods by a given proportion, say λ, increases utility by the same percentage, λ. One among the many such utility functions would be of Cobb–Douglas form:

$$U = c^\nu e^{1-\nu}.$$

If we were dealing with a utility function in only one good which was homogeneous of first degree, then marginal utility would be constant—this was the case analyzed in Sections 15–2 through 15–4.

Where $U_{cc}U_{ee} = U_{ce}^2$, the optimal paths for the price of capital and the stock of capital goods are the same as those described earlier in this chapter. We now proceed to discuss optimal paths where $U_{cc}U_{ee} > U_{ec}^2$, that is, where the utility function is strictly concave. The analysis in terms of p_k and k from now on is very similar to that obtained where only the private consumption good enters the utility function but marginal utility is diminishing.

Given the condition $U_{cc}U_{ee} > U_{ce}^2$, it can be proved that $U_{cc} + U_{ee} - 2U_{ce}$ is, in fact, negative, whatever the sign of U_{ce}. If U_{ce} is positive, this is true by inspection because U_{cc} and U_{ee} are negative. If U_{ce} is negative, and $U_{ce} + U_{ee} > 2U_{ce}$, then $U_{cc}^2 + U_{ee}^2 < 4U_{ce}^2 - 2U_{cc}U_{ee} < 2U_{cc}U_{ee}$ (because $U_{ce}^2 < U_{cc}U_{ee}$). This implies that $U_{cc}^2 - 2U_{cc}U_{ee} + U_{ee}^2 = (U_{cc} - U_{ee})^2 < 0$, which is impossible. Thus the bracketed coefficient on the lefthand side of (15–37) is always negative. To simplify discussion, we define the variable κ where

(15–38) $$\kappa(c, e) = \frac{U_{cc}U_{ee} - U_{ce}^2}{U_{cc} + U_{ee} - 2U_{ce}} < 0.$$

Notice that κ is a function of the levels of private and public consumption; it must not be thought of as a constant. It is always negative.

Equations (15–30) and (15–37) are a system of two differential equations for k and $\dot{p}_k$ and indicate conditions that must be fulfilled along the optimal path. We plot the curves that maintain the capital stock and the price of capital, respectively, equal to zero in the $\dot{k} = 0$ and $\dot{p}_k = 0$ loci of Figure 15–3. The $\dot{k} = 0$ schedule is, once more, the same as that obtained from the analysis of Section 2–7, and horizontal arrows are accounted for in the same ways as previously.

We can rewrite equation (15–37) as

(15–39)

$$\left(\frac{\kappa(c, e)}{U_c}\frac{\partial q_c}{\partial p_k} + \frac{1}{p_k}\right)\dot{p}_k = n + \delta - \frac{r(p_k)}{p_k} - \frac{\kappa(c, e)}{U_c}\frac{\partial q_c}{\partial k}k.$$

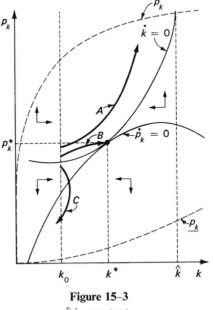

Figure 15–3

δ is constant.

Where the $\dot{p}_k = 0$ locus intersects the $\dot{k} = 0$ locus, both $\dot{p}_k$ and $\dot{k}$ are zero, so that from equation (15–39) we can find p_k at the point of intersection of the two curves by setting $\dot{p}_k$ and $\dot{k}$ equal to zero:

$$(15\text{–}40) \qquad \frac{r(p_k^*)}{p_k^*} = n + \delta.$$

That is, for a given rate of time preference, the two curves intersect in this case at precisely the same price of capital and capital stock as in our earlier analysis. We call these levels p_k^* and k^*. Notice in particular that there is only one level of the price of capital at which both $\dot{p}_k$ and $\dot{k}$ are zero, so that the intersection point is unique.

To the left of the intersection point, the $\dot{p}_k = 0$ curve lies above the $\dot{k} = 0$ locus. This is seen by observing from equation (15–40) that where $\dot{p}_k = 0$ and $\dot{k} = 0$, the $\dot{p}_k = 0$ locus is horizontal (as was the $\dot{p}_k = 0$ locus earlier), while the $\dot{k} = 0$ locus has a positive slope [from (15–30)]. Since the $\dot{p}_k = 0$ locus is horizontal where it cuts the $\dot{k} = 0$ curve, it is almost horizontal just to the left of the $\dot{k} = 0$ curve and, therefore, must lie above it. By the same argument, the $\dot{p}_k = 0$ curve lies below $\dot{k} = 0$ to the right of their intersection. We now know that the two loci intersect only once and that the $\dot{p}_k = 0$ locus lies above $\dot{k} = 0$, to the left of the intersection point and below it to the right

We can also establish that the $\dot{p}_k = 0$ locus lies below the p_k^* line, to the left of the intersection point and above it to the right. Setting $\dot{p}_k = 0$ in (15–39), we have, along the $\dot{p}_k = 0$ locus,

$$(15\text{–}41) \qquad \frac{r(p_k)}{p_k} = n + \delta - \frac{\kappa(c, e)}{U_c} \frac{\partial q_c}{\partial k} k.$$

To the left of the intersection point and above $\dot{k} = 0$, $\dot{k}$ is positive, as indicated by the horizontal arrows. Accordingly, the third term on the right-hand side of equation (15–41),

$$(\kappa(c, e)/U_c)(\partial q_c/\partial k)\dot{k},$$

is negative to the left of (k^*, p_k^*). Since $\kappa(c, e)$ is negative and the other terms positive, this means that $r(p_k)/p_k$ should be higher to the left of the intersection point than it is at (k^*, p_k^*) and, similarly, lower to the right of (k^*, p_k^*) than at p_k^*. We know that $r(p_k)/p_k$ rises as p_k falls, so that anywhere to the left of (k^*, p_k^*), the $\dot{p}_k = 0$ locus lies below the p_k^* line and is above it to the right. Because we do not know how $\kappa(c, e)/U_c$ varies as k

varies, we cannot ascertain whether the slope of $\dot{p}_k = 0$ is monotonic. Accordingly, we have drawn the $\dot{p}_k = 0$ locus obeying only two restrictions: to the left of the intersection point, it lies below the p_k^* line; above the $k = 0$ curve and to the right, it is above the p_k^* line and below $k = 0$.

Anywhere above the $\dot{p}_k = 0$ locus, the price of capital is higher than the price that, at that capital stock, makes the price of capital constant, which implies that $r(p_k)/p_k$ is lower than it would be if $\dot{p}_k$ were at zero, and k higher than it would be at $\dot{p}_k = 0$. Since the coefficient of k is positive, the right-hand side of equation (15–39) is positive on both accounts, and this makes $\dot{p}_k$ positive above the $\dot{p}_k = 0$ locus. The price of capital falls below the $\dot{p}_k = 0$ curve. We have indicated this by the vertical arrows.

To analyze the optimal path, we use an argument similar to that used earlier in this chapter. First, we observe that (starting at any given initial capital stock, k_0) only one path leads to (k^*, p_k^*). We confine ourselves to paths that begin with $k_0 < k^*$. (The reader can use similar arguments where $k_0 > k^*$.) If the initial price of capital is set greater than p_k^*, then the vertical arrows assure us that the price of capital can never fall below its original level, so that p_k^* can never be reached. Next consider a path starting just below p_k^*; the price of capital will always be rising on such a path, and if p_k^* is reached before the capital stock k^* is reached, p_k will continue rising beyond p_k^*. However, the initial p_k can be chosen such that the price of capital rises along the entire path and yet p_k^* is reached at precisely the instant that k^* is reached. To show that there is such a path, we appeal to the principle of continuity: we see that if the initial price of capital is below the $k = 0$ line, the price of capital will always fall thereafter so that p_k^* is never reached. Similarly, if $p_k(0)$ is just above the $k = 0$ locus, the path will cross the $k = 0$ locus and the price of capital will fall thereafter. What we have shown is that there are paths in the region bounded by the p_k^* and $k = 0$ loci on which the price of capital will eventually rise continually and other paths on which the price of capital ultimately falls continually. Because nothing in the system can change discontinuously, there will be at least one path (under the conditions assumed there will be only one path, though we do not prove this) where these two tendencies are exactly balanced and the price of capital goes to p_k^* while the capital stock goes to k^*. This is Path B in Figure 15–3. Notice that the path is not necessarily monotonic in terms of p_k.

After it has been shown that there is only one path on which the pair (k^*, p_k^*) is reached and that on other paths the price of capital eventually rises continually (Path A) or the price of capital eventually falls continually (Path C), it follows by the same arguments as used earlier that only Path B can be optimal.

Many of the definite results we obtained where the marginal utility of consumption was constant no longer hold. This is not due to the fact that there are two goods in the utility function (since with $U_{cc} U_{ee} = U_{ce}^2$, the earlier analysis is applicable), for the different results occur in the one-good case where the marginal utility of consumption is diminishing.

The initial price of capital, $p_k(0)$, will now depend on the initial capital stock. It is still true that if $k_0 < k^*$, the capital stock will be increasing along the optimal path, while the capital stock will fall on the optimal path if $k_0 > k^*$.

Also, on the optimal path where $k_0 < k^*$, the rental to capital exceeds the rate of population growth plus the discount rate, except at the steady-state capital stock, k^*. If $k_0 > k^*$, the rental to capital falls short of $\delta + n$, again except at the steady-state capital stock. As the rate of discount falls, the optimal steady-state rate approaches the rate of growth of population and the long-run ratio of capital to labor approaches its Golden Rule value.

Note that there is now no part of the path on which the economy is specialized to investment goods since an infinite increase in utility could then be obtained by allowing the production of one unit of consumption goods. As in the case of constant marginal utility of consumption, the production of consumption goods (the sum of private and public consumption) is increasing along the optimal path if $k_0 < k^*$ and decreasing if $k_0 > k^*$. We now prove this assertion. The rate of change of the production of consumption goods is obtained by differentiating the supply function of consumption goods:

$$\dot{q}_c = \frac{\partial q_c}{\partial k} \dot{k} + \frac{\partial q_c}{\partial p_k} \dot{p}_k.$$

Use equation (15–39) to substitute for $\dot{p}_k$ in the above expression:

$$\dot{q}_c = \frac{\partial q_c}{\partial k} \dot{k} + \frac{\partial q_c}{\partial p_k} \left(\frac{1}{\dfrac{\kappa(c, e)}{U_c} \dfrac{\partial q_c}{\partial p_k} + \dfrac{1}{p_k}} \right) \left(n + \delta - \frac{r(p_k)}{p_k} - \frac{\kappa(c, e)}{U_c} \frac{\partial q_c}{\partial k} \dot{k} \right).$$

and rewrite

(15–42)

$$\dot{q}_c = \frac{1}{(\kappa/U_c)(\partial q_c/\partial p_k) + (1/p_k)} \left[\frac{\partial q_c}{\partial k} \frac{\dot{k}}{p_k} + \frac{\partial q_c}{\partial p_k} \left(n + \delta - \frac{r(p_k)}{p_k} \right) \right].$$

The right-hand side of equation (15–42) is positive on the optimal path if $k_0 < k^*$ since $\dot{k}$ is positive on such a path and $\delta + n < r(p_k)/p_k$ for $p_k < p_k^*$, while the coefficient of k is positive and that of $\{\delta + n - [r(p_k)/p_k]\}$ is negative. It follows that the production of consumption goods increases on the optimal path ($\dot{q}_C > 0$) where the initial capital stock is below k^*, and $\dot{q}_C < 0$ on the optimal path where $k_0 > k^*$.

(B) OPTIMAL FISCAL AND MONETARY POLICY

The simplicity of our earlier results on the relations between the optimal stock of debt and the optimal capital stock is now lost. At each instant where the capital stock k is given to the economy, the price of capital, p_k, and the production of public consumption goods, e, should be set at the levels appropriate to the optimal path. In addition, the price of money is at the desired level p_m^*.

Fiscal policy then consists of varying the deficit to ensure that

(15–43)

$$q_C(k, p_k) - e = (1 - s)(q_C(k, p_k) + p_k q_I(k, p_k) + d p_m^* - e).$$

Note that we neglect expected capital gains on the stock of capital; this produces no essential change in the results. We also assume $\pi_m = 0$, as previously.

From equation (15–43) we see that the deficit is a function of the capital stock, the price of capital, and the level of government consumption:

(15–44) $d = \dfrac{s q_C - s e - (1 - s) p_k q_I}{(1 - s) p_m^*}$ $\dfrac{\partial d}{\partial k} > 0, \dfrac{\partial d}{\partial p_k} < 0, \dfrac{\partial d}{\partial e} < 0.$

The signs of the partial derivatives can be obtained by total differentiation of equation (15–43); in economic terms, the derivatives indicate that an increase in the capital stock is deflationary so that increases in the capital stock require an offsetting increase in the deficit, while increases in the price of capital or government consumption are inflationary, requiring decreases in the deficit.

We still have

$$\dot{g} = d - ng$$

or

(15–45) $$\dot{g} = d(k, p_k, e) - ng.$$

Consider an optimal path where $k < k^*$. We have seen that on such a path the capital stock will be increasing, as will the production of consumption goods. If we make the reasonable assumption that neither private nor public consumption is an inferior good so that the consumption of both types of goods will increase or decrease together, then e will be increasing on those paths where $k_0 < k^*$. The price of capital need not change monotonically on an optimal path, but for $k_0 < k^*$, the long-run price of capital exceeds $p_k(0)$. The fact that k increases on optimal paths where $k_0 < k^*$ and e also increases on such paths means that on these grounds alone we cannot tell whether the deficit is increasing or decreasing on the optimal path. Further ambiguity results from the required changes in p_k on the optimal path.

Plotting the curves that make $\dot{k}$ and $\dot{g}$ respectively equal to zero, we obtain Figure 15–4. From equation (15–30) we have a vertical $\dot{k} = 0$ line where $k = k^*$; the capital stock falls for higher k and rises for lower k, explaining the horizontal arrows. The slope of the $\dot{g} = 0$ line as ambiguous, for the reasons described in the previous paragraph. Anywhere above this line $\dot{g}$ is negative since g exceeds the level of the stock of debt for which $\dot{g} = 0$, hence the vertical arrows. The equilibrium (k^*, g^*) is unique and stable, but the level of the debt may alternately rise and fall on the optimal path. Such a path is indicated in Figure 15–4.

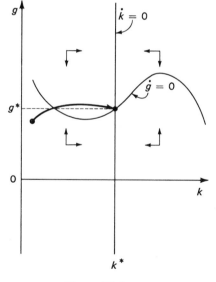

Figure 15–4

p_m, π_m, π_k are constant.

Note once more that there is no reason for the optimal stock of government debt to be positive.

Insofar as monetary policy is concerned, the composition of the debt should be varied, so that at each instant

$$(15\text{--}46) \qquad\qquad p_k = \Phi(g p_m^*, k, \pi_m, \pi_k, x).$$

Since we do not know whether p_k and g change monotonically along the optimal path, we cannot say how x should change over time to ensure that the appropriate assets-markets price of capital obtains, when $\pi_m = \pi_k = 0$.

(C) EFFECTS OF CHANGES IN THE RATE OF TIME PREFERENCE

As before, an increase in the rate of time preference, δ, will reduce the long-run capital stock, since at the new equilibrium capital stock $r(p_k)/p_k$ will be higher than for a lower δ. Then the intersection of the $\dot{p}_k = 0$ and $\dot{k} = 0$ loci in Figure 15–3 will be at a lower k^*.

Finally, it is again the case that an increase in the rate of time preference may lead to either an increase, decrease, or no change in the steady-state stock of government debt. In Figure 15–4, the $\dot{k} = 0$ locus shifts to the left while the shift in the $\dot{g} = 0$ locus is ambiguous.

16 A Model of International Capital Markets

16–1 Introduction

In this chapter we study an extension of our model to a world with two governments. The basic ideas of this model are similar to the ones already studied. The people of each country have their own saving propensity and their own assets preferences. Likewise, each government has its own debt and its own fiscal and monetary policy. Bonds issued by one government can be held in the other country.

That each government is free to follow its own policy is very important because the characteristic behavior of this model depends crucially on the interaction of the government's policies. Each government, by its open market policies, can cause reserve flows between the two countries. But even where monetary policies are coordinated and the balance of payments is in equilibrium in the sense that no reserve flows are taking place, serious conflicts of interest can arise: there are many consistent paths for the fiscal and monetary policies of the two countries that give very different distributions of income and welfare between their citizens.

The production model we use is fairly restrictive in that the same consumption and investment goods are produced in both countries with the same production function; it is, however, no more restrictive than models commonly used in trade theory. On the other hand, the model does allow for many of the typical features of international finance. Reserves move, foreign investment occurs, and foreign liabilities can accumulate.

16–2   The Model

We call the "countries" Europe (E) and America (A) for convenience. Superscripts indicate ownership of an asset; subscripts indicate issuance.

(A) PRODUCTION AND GROWTH

We assume that the two countries have the same sized population and that their populations grow at the same rate, n. Furthermore, we assume that the production functions of the two are identical two-sector technologies of the type that we discussed in Chapter 2. In fact, we suppose that factor price equalization occurs, so that capital earns a rental, r, and labor a wage, w, depending only on p_k, regardless of its geographical position. (The assumption of factor price equalization implicitly restricts our analysis to paths of p_k that keep both countries nonspecialized.) Then there is a world price of capital, and the supply of investment and consumption per capita in the world are, for nonspecialized cases, functions exactly like the supply functions of the early part of the book:

$$(16\text{–}1) \qquad q_I(k, p_k) \quad \frac{\partial q_I}{\partial k} < 0, \frac{\partial q_I}{\partial p_k} > 0$$

$$(16\text{–}2) \qquad q_C(k, p_k) \quad \frac{\partial q_C}{\partial k} > 0, \frac{\partial q_C}{\partial p_k} < 0,$$

where k and other per-capital variables now represent world stocks divided by *world population*. We can resurrect unchanged the law of capital growth per capita:

$$(16\text{–}3) \qquad\qquad k = q_I(k, p_k) - nk.$$

(B) THE CONSUMPTION GOODS MARKET

Both Europeans and Americans consume a constant fraction of their disposable income. Income has four components: wages, rentals on capital owned, interest received or paid on net holdings of bonds, and transfers less taxes paid or collected by the government. In what follows, per-capita quantities will always have *world* population as the denominator.

y_A is total American income divided by world population, so that it is exactly half per-capita American income, and so on:

$$(16\text{–}4) \qquad y_A = w(p_k) + r(p_k)k^A + ib^A p_m + v^A p_m$$

$$(16\text{–}5) \qquad y_E = w(p_k) + r(p_k)k^E + ib^E p_m + v^E p_m)$$

where k^A and b^A are, respectively, American-owned capital and bonds divided by world population and v^A is net nominal American transfers divided by world population. The $w(p_k)$ term in the expression for disposable income is the wage rate divided by world population: it is exactly one half the usual $w(p_k)$ term. We shall not permit the exchange rate between the currencies of the two countries to vary (which is very convenient, since we can ignore the denomination of bonds and consider bonds of the two countries as perfect substitutes), so we need only one p_m.

The clearing of the consumption market requires

$$(16\text{–}6) \qquad q_C(k, p_k) = (1 - s_A)y_A + (1 - s_E)y_E.$$

We are assuming that there is no government expenditure on public consumption goods. The assumption is made for the sake of simplicity and is not a serious omission, since we discuss changes in fiscal policy that affect net transfers minus taxes.

Notice also that we assume that no capital gains on either the debt or the capital stock are expected in either country. This is a further assumption that is not a necessary consequence of either factor price equalization or a fixed exchange rate; instead, we assume that both governments agree on a relative price of capital, p_k, and a price level, p_m, and take appropriate policy measures to enforce them. This assumption is discussed again in Section 16–4.

(C) THE ASSETS MARKETS

There are six assets in the economy: capital located in America, capital located in Europe, bonds issued in America, bonds issued in Europe, American money (dollars), and European money (marks). Since factor price equalization takes place, capital yields the same rate of return—exclusive of capital gains—in each country. We have already stated that we shall later assume that the relative price of capital is fixed and that no capital gains are expected so that there will be no reason for investors to differentiate between capital in the two countries.

The exchange rate is fixed and there is no risk of capital loss or gain on bonds, so there is no reason for investors to prefer the bonds of one country to those of the other. Investors in each country may hold bonds issued by the other, and there is a single international bond market. On the other hand, we assume that currency is held only by the citizens of the issuing country; this seems reasonable because there is no point in holding the currency of the other country as a speculation when the exchange rate is absolutely fixed.

These assumptions about assets are very strong and are useful chiefly in making the model comprehensible. They also permit us to use some of the analysis of the earlier parts of the book.

The demand functions for assets have forms similar to those outlined in Chapter 3. Both Americans and Europeans have demand functions for assets that depend on national wealth, national income measured in consumption goods (this is the counterpart of the transactions demand for money represented by national income in Chapter 3), and rates of return to capital and bonds. Our assumptions ensure that rates of return to capital and bonds held by nationals of either country are the same: $\rho_k(p_k) = r(p_k)/p_k$ and i, respectively. Then,

$$(16\text{-}7) \quad p_k k^A = J^A(a^A, q^A, i, \rho_k(p_k)) \left.\begin{array}{l} \\ \\ \end{array}\right\} \quad 1 > \frac{\partial J^j}{\partial a^j} > 0, \frac{\partial J^j}{\partial q^j} < 0,$$

$$(16\text{-}8) \quad p_k k^E = J^E(a^E, q^E, i, \rho_k(p_k)) \qquad\qquad \frac{\partial J^j}{\partial i} < 0, \frac{\partial J^j}{\partial r} > 0$$

$$(16\text{-}9) \quad p_m b^A = H^A(a^A, q^A, i, \rho_k(p_k)) \left.\begin{array}{l} \\ \\ \end{array}\right\} \quad \frac{\partial H^j}{\partial a^j} \gtrless 0, \frac{\partial H^j}{\partial q^j} < 0,$$

$$(16\text{-}10) \quad p_m b^E = H^E(a^E, q^E, i, \rho_k(p_k)) \qquad\qquad \frac{\partial H^j}{\partial i} > 0, \frac{\partial H^j}{\partial r} < 0$$

$$(16\text{-}11) \quad p_m m^A = L^A(a^A, q^A, i, \rho_k(p_k)) \left.\begin{array}{l} \\ \\ \end{array}\right\} \quad \frac{\partial L^j}{\partial a^j} > 0, \frac{\partial L^j}{\partial q^j} > 0,$$

$$(16\text{-}12) \quad p_m m^E = L^E(a^E, q^E, i, \rho_k(p_k)) \qquad\qquad \frac{\partial L^j}{\partial i} < 0, \frac{\partial L^j}{\partial r} < 0$$

where $q^j = w + r(p_k)k^j$ and $j = A, E$.

At each instant, the total value of demands for wealth in each country must be equal to actual national wealth: in their portfolio decisions, investors plan to distribute all their wealth between money, bonds, and capital. We have

$$(16\text{–}13) \qquad a^j = p_k \hat{k}^j + p_m \hat{b}^j + p_m \hat{m}^j = p_k k^j + p_m b^j + p_m m^j,$$

where the caret over a letter represents initial holdings of the particular asset, and the noncareted letters represent the amounts of assets demanded.

When the history of this economy begins, we can imagine the holdings of bonds, capital, and money of each country to be given; these are the variables with a caret above them. We can think of an auctioneer calling out some triple (p_m, p_k, i) and the individuals valuing their initial holdings of capital, bonds, and money to calculate their wealth and then announcing their demands according to equations (16–7) through (16–12). As the auctioneer varies p_k and i, holding p_m constant (this is merely one way he might seek an equilibrium position), the value of initial holdings will also change until the system comes to equilibrium in the capital and bond markets. The equilibrium reached will in general depend on the initial distribution of assets, and there will be a unique distribution of assets between the two countries in the new equilibrium. Then, at the next instant, equilibrium holdings of the last instant become the initial holdings. In the situations we are studying prices will usually change in a continuous fashion, so that neither wealth nor holdings of individual assets will jump and there will usually be no need to distinguish wealth as initial holdings in an instant from wealth as final holdings in the same instant. But in principle instantaneous jumps are possible. The path the economy follows through time will depend not only on the total supplies of assets at time zero but also on their distribution.

In what follows, we generally ignore the distinction between initial holdings at an instant and final holdings in an instant. Demand schedules will be drawn on the assumption of given initial holdings and will determine equilibrium prices. The final holdings will be different from the initial holdings whenever some other variable has made a discrete jump at the instant in question. For example, if a government makes a discrete open market operation in an instant, it changes the initial holdings of money and bonds, which shift the demand curves and force interest rates and the prices of capital and money to jump. At the "end" of the instant, exchange will have taken place and final holdings will be different from the initial holdings implied by the open market operation. The more usual case will be a continuous variation of policy parameters, prices, and portfolio holdings. In this case there is no mathematical or conceptual reason to distinguish initial and final holdings.

For the capital and bond markets to clear at each instant, the total demands for each asset have to be equal to the total supply:

(16–14)

$$J^A(a^A, q^A, i, \rho_k(p_k)) + J^E(a^E, q^E, i, \rho_k(p_k)) = p_k k = p_k \hat{k}^A + p_k \hat{k}^E$$

(16–15)

$$H^A(a^A, q^A, i, \rho_k(p_k)) + H^E(a^E, q^E, i, \rho_k(p_k)) = p_m b = p_m \hat{b}^A + p_m \hat{b}^E.$$

The total supply of capital is given at each instant; it is determined by past investment, as is the supply of bonds from the viewpoint of the private sectors.

It is not necessarily the case that both money markets will be in equilibrium whenever capital and bond markets clear. The clearing of bond and capital markets implies by Walras' Law only that the total demand for money in the two countries is equal to the total supply. There is no guarantee when bond and capital markets clear that Americans will want to hold the current supply of dollars or Europeans the current supply of marks. By Walras' Law we know that the excess supply for money in one country must be equal to the excess demand in the other.

Suppose, then, that at some triple (p_m, p_k, i) the bond and capital markets are in equilibrium but there is an excess supply of money in one country (and, therefore, excess demand in the other country). In what way can the money markets come into equilibrium?

To meet this problem we introduce a reserve asset, such as gold, held only by the governments. The governments are committed to exchange their own currency for the reserve asset at a fixed rate. Under this regime the supply of money in each country is an endogenous variable. When the assets markets have come into equilibrium, reserves must also have shifted to make the supply of marks and dollars equal to the demand, on the assumption that inflows and outflows of reserves are immediately monetized by the authorities of each country.

The equilibrium conditions in the money markets are

(16–16) $$p_m m_A = L^A[a^A, q^A, i, \rho_k(p_k)] = \frac{p_m g_A}{x_A} + z_m^A$$

(16–17) $$p_m m_E = L^E[a^E, q^E, i, \rho_k(p_k)] = \frac{p_m g_E}{x_E} + z_m^E,$$

where z_m stands for monetized reserves, which may be positive or negative. Total reserves in each country are the sum of initial reserves and monetized reserves. The initial reserves are exogenous while the positive or negative monetized reserves are the result of international transactions:

$$(16\text{--}18) \qquad z^A_{\text{total}} = z^A_{\text{initial}} + z^A_m$$

$$(16\text{--}19) \qquad z^E_{\text{total}} = z^E_{\text{initial}} + z^E_m .$$

We assume a law of conservation of reserves stating that the total of all reserves is a constant or that

$$(16\text{--}20) \qquad z^A_m = -z^E_m .$$

It is clear that reserves could be exhausted if one country ran a persistent balance of payments deficit. This problem does not, however, arise in our model because we shall be discussing situations in which the governments coordinate policies to control reserve flows.

If there were no reserves, the money markets could be cleared by appreciation or depreciation of the currencies of the countries relative to consumption goods. This involves a variable exchange rate and raises the awkward problem of the denomination of bonds. If the bonds are consumption goods bonds, then everything will go through without much trouble except that a loss of reserves will turn into a depreciation of currency for a country. If the bonds are denominated in local currency, it would be necessary to differentiate them in the assets demands and allow them to have different interest rates.

In the analysis of Chapter 3 we were able to describe assets markets equilibrium in terms of the aa schedule. We now repeat the graphical analysis of Chapter 3 to see whether any of our conclusions there are affected by the fact that there are now two separate demand functions in each of the bond and capital markets and two distinct money markets.

In Figure 16–1 we plot combinations of p_k and i that equilibrate each of the four markets in the model as of a given price of money, p_m. The position of each schedule depends on the distribution of each asset as of that instant. The kk schedule indicates pairs of p_k and i that clear the capital goods market. Any increase in the price of capital increases wealth in each country but increases the value of the capital stock held in each country by the same amount; since we assume that the marginal propensity to demand capital out of wealth is less than one, this produces excess supply. Excess supply is also produced by the two other effects of an

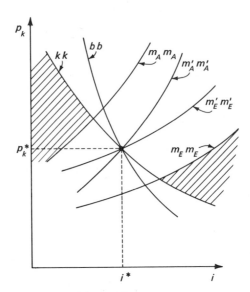

Figure 16–1

$\hat{m}^A$, $\hat{m}^E$, $\hat{b}^A$, $\hat{b}^E$, $\hat{k}^A$, $\hat{k}^E$, p_m, π_m, π_k are constant.

increase in p_k: the level of national income in each country rises and the rate of return on capital falls. This excess supply has to be offset by a fall in the interest rate, which, by itself, tends to create an excess demand for capital; hence the downward slope of the kk schedule.

The $m_A m_A$ and $m_E m_E$ schedules slope upward for precisely the same reasons that the mm schedule in Figure 3–5 slopes upward. An increase in p_k creates excess demand in each market through wealth, transactions, and substitution effects, and this increase in demand has to be offset by a rise in the interest rate, which would, by itself, tend to create excess supply. There is no necessary relationship between the slopes and positions of the mm schedules for the two countries.

As in Chapter 3, we cannot be sure of the slope of the bb schedule. We can tell, however, that it cannot enter either of the shaded areas in Figure 16–1. Anywhere to the northeast of the kk schedule there is an excess supply of capital since the price of capital is higher than it need be to equilibrate the capital market. Anywhere below both money market equilibrium curves there is an excess supply of money in both markets since the price of capital is lower than it need be to equilibrate each money market. Thus in the shaded area to the right of the kk curve and below $m_E m_E$, there is excess supply in three markets: it follows—for the same reasons as outlined in Chapter 3—that the bb curve cannot enter that region. For symmetric reasons, the bb curve cannot enter the shaded area to the left of the kk curve. This means that the bb locus must intersect the kk locus between the intersections of the mm curves with kk.

The intersection of the kk and bb curves fixes an interest rate and price of capital that clear the capital and bond markets as of the fixed price of money, p_m. But as we have drawn the $m_A m_A$ and $m_E m_E$ curves, the two money markets are not in equilibrium at that triple (p_k, p_m, i). Specifically, at the equilibrium interest rate, a higher p_k would be needed to equilibrate the American money market and a lower p_k would equilibrate the European money market; there is excess supply in the American money market and an equal excess demand in the European money market. To equilibrate the two markets, reserves flow from America to Europe, reducing the American supply of money and increasing the European supply. As reserves flow, the two money market curves shift to the primed positions indicated and intersect at the (i, p_k) pair that equilibrates the other two markets. Once again, there is no necessary relation between the slopes of the two mm curves. The intersection of the curves also fixes the final distribution of assets between the two countries.

Now consider the effects of an increase in p_m. An increase in p_m increases wealth and so produces excess demand in the capital market; a higher p_k is needed to equilibrate the capital market as of any interest rate, so that the kk curve in Figure 16–2 shifts up to $k_1 k_1$. An increase in p_m will produce excess supply in each money market. (This depends on the assumption made in Chapter 3 about the wealth elasticity of the demand for money, which must hold in both countries. Notice also that the shifts of the curves will depend on the initial distribution of assets.) Therefore, the price of capital that clears each market as of a given interest rate will have to rise. The mm curves move up to $m_{A_1} m_{A_1}$ and $m_{E_1} m_{E_1}$, respectively. Whatever the slope of the bb schedule, it will have to shift in such a way that it intersects the $k_1 k_1$ schedule between the intersections of the two money market curves, $m_{A_1} m_{A_1}$ and $m_{E_1} m_{E_1}$ with $k_1 k_1$. It is clear that the price of capital will rise and that the interest rate may either rise or fall. The aa schedule is again upward-sloping.

In this world a single country finds that its monetary policy has somewhat different effects from the case of an isolated country. We can, for example, follow the results of an American open market purchase, which initially increases the supply of dollars and reduces the supply of bonds. In terms of Figure 16–3, the immediate effect of the open market purchase is a shift of the $m_A m_A$ schedule upward to $m_{A_1} m_{A_1}$ because a higher p_k is needed to absorb the increased supply of money in America. The $m_A m_A$ and $m_E m_E$ schedules then move toward each other as Americans try to

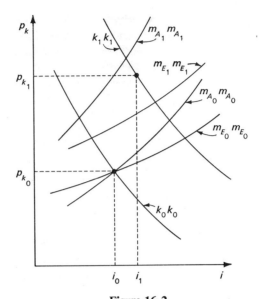

Figure 16–2

$\hat{m}^A$, $\hat{m}^E$, $\hat{b}^A$, $\hat{b}^E$, $\hat{k}^A$, $\hat{k}^E$, π_m, π_k are constant. p_m rises from p_{m0} to p_{m1}.

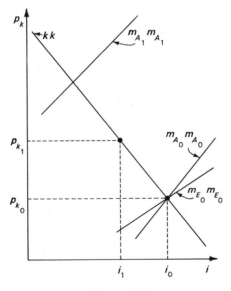

Figure 16–3

$\hat{b}^A$, $\hat{k}^E$, $\hat{k}^A$, p_m, π_m, π_k are constant. $\hat{m}^A$ rises from $\hat{m}_0^A$ to $\hat{m}_1^A$ while $\hat{b}^A$ falls from $\hat{b}_0^A$ to $\hat{b}_1^A$.

balance their portfolios by buying bonds and capital from Europeans and so cause a reserve loss for Americans and a corresponding reserve gain for Europeans. This increases the supply of marks and leads Europeans to bid for bonds and capital, so that in the end the interest rate will fall and the price of capital will rise; the new equilibrium will be between the intersection of the $m_{E_0}m_{E_0}$ and $m_{A_1}m_{A_1}$ loci with kk. The world aa schedule has shifted up just as before. America has lost reserves; Europe has gained them. We emphasize again that the extent of changes in variables, though not the directions of the changes, depends on the initial distribution of assets. Thus the kk schedule actually pivots through the *new* equilibrium position following the open market purchase since there is now a different distribution of assets.

The upward shift of the aa schedule will normally lead to inflationary pressure. The price of money will fall unless some government takes appropriate steps. Either Europe or America or both may tighten fiscal policy, or Europe may make an open market sale. (As in our earlier analysis, a reduction of the deficit of either country would constitute a tightening of fiscal policy.) If either country tightens fiscal policy, the price of capital will be permanently higher. If Europe tightens monetary policy, the effect will be to offset the American action, although America still will lose reserves since a European open market sale sets in motion a series of events symmetric to those we saw after the American open market purchase.

The two-country world is basically similar to the model we have studied so far. Everything we have shown about the price of capital and the importance of fiscal-monetary mix holds true. The path of the world economy is determined jointly by the fiscal and monetary policies of the two countries. When either country makes an open market transaction uncoordinated with the other, there will generally be a movement of reserves as well as the usual effects. Only by simultaneously buying or selling in the open market can the two governments alter monetary policy without reserve movements.

(D) TRADE AND THE BALANCE OF PAYMENTS

It may seem odd that so far we have not said anything about trade. Trade will take place in our model whenever one country's demand for consumption goods exceeds its production of consumption goods. Because of the factor price equalization, it does not matter whether investment goods are actually physically shipped or not (as long as p_k and the amounts of capital physically located in the two countries do not imply specialization). It only matters who gets title. If America's holdings of capital increase by more than American output of investment goods, capital must be aquired by Americans in Europe, whether this capital is physically moved to America or not.

The balance of payments, as always, adds up to zero as an accounting identity. The balance consists of net consumption exports, net capital exports, net decrease in holdings of bonds, net rentals from capital owned abroad, net interest on bonds, and reserve changes:

$$(16\text{--}21) \quad [q_C^A(k, p_k) - (1 - s_A)y_A] + p_k[q_I^A(k, p_k) - (\dot{k}^A + nk^A)]$$
$$+ p_m[\dot{b}_A + nb_A - (\dot{b}^A + nb^A)] + r(k^A - k_A) + i(b^A - b_A)p_m + \dot{z}_m.$$

But $q_C^A + p_k q_I^A = w + rk_A$ is just factor income from domestic factors, and the change in reserves is the difference between increases in the monetized debt and actual holdings of money:

$$(16\text{--}22) \qquad \dot{z}_m^A = \frac{1}{x}(\dot{g}_A + ng_A)p_m - (\dot{m}^A + nm^A)p_m.$$

We can write income as

$(16\text{--}23)$

$$y_A = w + rk_A + r(k^A - k_A) + i(b^A - b_A)p_m + ib_A p_m + v_A p_m,$$

where

$$(16\text{--}24) \quad ib_A + v_A = \dot{g}_A + ng_A = \dot{b}_A + nb_A + \frac{1}{x}(\dot{g}_A + ng_A).$$

By substituting, we obtain for (16–21)

$(16\text{--}25)$

$$y_A - (1 - s_A)y_A - p_k(\dot{k}^A + nk^A) - p_m(\dot{b}^A + nb^A) - p_m(\dot{m}^A + nm^A)$$
$$= y_A - (1 - s_A)y_A - s_A y_A = 0;$$

that is, the balance of payments adds up to zero when reserve movements are taken into account.

Reserve movements in this model are the sign of disequilibrium in the balance of payments, and we define balance of payments equilibrium as existing when no reserve movements take place. There are, however, many paths of the policy variables that avoid reserve movements, so that balance of payments equilibrium by itself is not a sufficiently strong requirement to determine fully the governments' policies. This is not surprising, since each government has more than one policy parameter at its disposal, but what is surprising is that even *given the goals of stable prices, no reserve movements, and a predetermined path for the price of capital, an additional degree of freedom still remains.* This turns out to involve the distribution of the necessary fiscal ease or restraint between the two countries. Reserve movements in this model arise only from a lack of coordination of monetary policy in the two countries, which may be the result of a deeper conflict about the desired world price of capital. Even if monetary policies are coordinated so that reserves do not shift, there remains a profound policy problem, which we study in Section 16–3.

There is one other phenomenon that is very important in the real world that we neglect. Since there is only one consumption good, the price level in the two countries must be the same; it is impossible for one country to have a rate of inflation different from the other's because of arbitrage between goods and currency. In the real world there are differences in the goods produced in different countries, so price level differentials have a meaning and produce another degree of freedom in the balance of payments equation. To take account of this phenomenon would require a substantial complication of the model.

16–3   Dynamic Analysis

We have indicated in Section 16–2 that a serious policy problem may arise in this model, even given agreement on the coordination of the monetary policies of the two countries. In this section we analyze that problem carefully.

There are four policy variables in the model: monetary and fiscal policy for each of the two countries. One policy goal we ascribe to the two governments is that of price level stability; this is a goal we think most governments do have in mind, and we have usually ascribed it to the single government in the model of the rest of the book. For dynamic analysis, though, we have to specify three more rules before the model is complete, and we can study its solution paths.

We are interested in cases where there are no reserve movements. We have seen that reserve movements can be avoided only when the two countries coordinate their monetary policy. This means that they must agree on a common monetary policy goal. We choose to define this goal as a certain world price of capital for each instant. We make the heroic assumption that the countries have decided on a world investment policy that can be described as a path for p_k and have agreed to coordinate their monetary policies to enforce this path without reserve movements. Because it substantially simplifies matters, we further assume that the two countries have agreed on a *stable* price of capital, p_k^*, to hold for all time. This p_k^* might have been chosen on the basis of an optimizing analysis such as that of Chapter 15 using a linear utility functional. The two countries would choose the same p_k, given the linear utility functional, only if each had the same rate of time preference.

We are, therefore, assuming a substantial degree of agreement on a basic social issue—the time path of investment—between the two countries. Only one price of capital can exist at any time because titles to capital are freely traded in an international market. If one country tried to change the price of capital, it would alter the price of capital in both countries; agreement on the price of capital is needed to prevent competitive attempts by the two countries to change that price.

The aggregate outcome of the fiscal and monetary policies of the two countries, by our assumptions, will always be to maintain the same p_m and p_k through time, but there will be many combinations of national fiscal and monetary policies that will achieve these goals. We must further specify how the control burden is to be divided.

For example, the requirement of a stable (p_m^*, p_k^*) pair will determine at any moment the supply of bonds necessary to achieve the target p_k^* and the interest rate. To see this graphically, examine Figure 16–4. The position of the kk schedule is fixed at any instant, given the stocks of capital and debt and the chosen price level. To ensure that the chosen price of capital p_k^* clears the assets markets, the authorities have to ensure that the bb locus and the mm loci intersect kk at p_k^*; this also determines the interest rate. The authorities can affect the position of the bb and mm loci by open market operations, that is, by changing the quantity of bonds and money. Whatever the slope of the bb schedule, the authorities have to carry out open market operations until the supply of bonds is such that the bb locus intersects kk at p_k^*. This supply of bonds can come through many combinations of the two nations' open market policies. America might keep its x_A constant and force European central bankers to do all the open market dealings, or both countries might adjust their open market policy. We know that every combination but one will result in reserve movements. We can, therefore, add a restriction that the nations cooperate to avoid any reserve movements.

The division of the monetary policy burden is important because it determines the distribution of reserves. The division of the fiscal policy burden is important because it determines the distribution of wealth. This is an

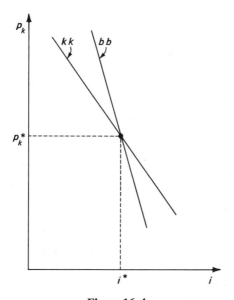

Figure 16–4

$\hat{k}^A$, $\hat{k}^E$, p_m, π_m, π_k are constant. $\hat{b}^A$ and $\hat{b}^E$ adjust to give p^*.

important result derived from our model, and to justify it, we have to consider the dynamics of the model.

The dynamic model can actually be reduced to three basic equations in k, a^A, and a^E. Remember that, as always,

$$(16\text{–}26) \qquad k = q_I(k, p_k) - nk.$$

This equation by itself determines the growth of the capital stock to its steady-state value; the steady-state value of the capital stock is obtained by solving equation (16–26) for k, given $k = 0$.

We also have

$$(16\text{–}27) \qquad \dot{a}^A = s_A y_A - na^A$$

and

$$(16\text{–}28) \qquad \dot{a}^E = s_E y_E - na^E .$$

Equations (16–27) and (16–28) state that the rate of growth of the value of per-capita assets in each country is equal to savings per capita minus the amount of savings needed to maintain the per-capita stock of assets constant as population grows.

The levels of income, y_A and y_E, are related by the necessity of clearing the consumption goods market at each instant at the chosen (p_m^*, p_k^*) pair. The supply of consumption goods is given at each instant, since the price of capital, p_k^*, and the capital stock are given. Demand has to be made just equal to this supply at (p_m^*, p_k^*). There are two sources of demand, Europeans and Americans; and each demand is proportional to national disposable income. Given any level of disposable income in America at (p_m^*, p_k^*) there is a unique level of disposable income in Europe consistent with the clearing of the consumption goods market.

$$(16\text{--}29) \quad q_C(k, p_k^*) = (1 - s_A)y_A + (1 - s_E)y_E$$

$$= (1 - s_A)(w(p_k^*) + r(p_k^*)k^A + ib^A p_m + v^A p_m^*)$$

$$+ (1 - s_E)(w(p_k^*) + r(p_k^*)k^E + ib^E p_m + v^E p_m^*).$$

Of the variables appearing in equation (16–29), k, p_k^*, and p_m^* are given at any instant, and k^A, k^E, b^A, b^E, and i are determined by the clearing of the assets markets at the pair (p_m^*, p_k^*). The fact that assets markets equilibrium also implies a particular distribution of assets was discussed above. That particular distribution is, in general, dependent on the distribution of assets at time zero and on the timing of any subsequent jumps of stock variables caused for whatever reasons, for example, noncontinuous open market operations.

Thus the only variables that can be adjusted by the two governments to ensure consumption goods market clearing are their respective transfer payments, v^A and v^E.

We can rewrite equation (16–29) as

$$(16\text{--}30) \quad (1 - s_A)v^A + (1 - s_E)v^E$$

$$= (1/p_m^*)[q_C(k, p_k^*) - (1 - s_A)(w(p_k^*) + r(p_k^*)k^A + ib^A p_m^*)$$

$$- (1 - s_E)(w(p_k^*) - r(p_k^*)k^E + ib^E p_m^*)] = \sigma.$$

This puts one restriction on the policy variables v^A and v^E but is not sufficient to determine both v^A and v^E at each instant. We define a variable μ, which is the fraction of the necessary ease or restraint on aggregate demand contributed by America:

$$(16\text{--}31) \qquad\qquad (1 - s_A)v^A = \mu\sigma$$

$$(16\text{--}32) \qquad\qquad (1 - s_E)v^E = (1 - \mu)\sigma.$$

We can now substitute for v^A and v^E in the expressions for y^A and y^E and use equation (16–30) to obtain

(16–33) $(1 - s_A)y_A = \mu q_c - \mu(1 - s_E)(w + rk^E + ib^E p_m^*)$

$$+ (1 - \mu)(1 - s_A)(w + rk^A + ib^A p_m^*)$$

(16–34) $(1 - s_E)y_E = (1 - \mu)q_c - (1 - \mu)(1 - s_A)(w + rk^A + ib^A p_m^*)$

$$+ \mu(1 - s_E)(w + rk^E + ib^E p_m^*).$$

For the sake of notational compactness we write

(16–35) $$(1 - s_A)y_A = \mu q_c + P$$

(16–36) $$(1 - s_E)y_E = (1 - \mu)q_c - P$$

where

(16–37)

$$P = (1 - \mu)(1 - s_A)(w + rk^A + ib^A p_m^*) - \mu(1 - s_E)(w + rk^E + ib^E p_m^*)$$

and P is a function of k, a^A, and a^E along a continuous path, since i, k^A, k^E, b^A, and b^E are determined in the assets markets after k, a^A, a^E, p_m^*, and p_k^* are given.

The dynamic system (16–26) through (16–28) may now be rewritten as

(16–38) $$\dot{k} = q_I(k, p_k^*) - nk$$

(16–39) $$\dot{a}^A = \frac{s_A}{1 - s_A} [\mu q_c(k, p_k^*) + P] - na^A$$

(16–40) $$\dot{a}^E = \frac{s_E}{1 - s_E} [(1 - \mu)q_c(k, p_k^*) - P] - na^E.$$

16–4   Comparative Dynamics

Some properties of the solution are immediately apparent. First notice that the equation that determines the growth of the capital stock [equation (16–38)] is independent of the rest of the system. The steady-state capital stock is fully determined by the choice of the price of capital p_k^*. If the system ever reaches a steady state and one of the parameters of the system other than p_k^* is changed, the capital stock will remain at its steady-state

level, and the supplies of investment and consumption goods (both functions only of k and p_k) will remain constant. We make use of this later in
this section.

Second, there is a direct trade off between the national wealths of the two
countries in the steady state; there is a linear wealth distribution frontier
such as the one shown in Figure 16–5. To see this, set $\dot{a}^A$ and $\dot{a}^E$ in equations
(16–39) and (16–40) equal to zero, solve (16–39) for P, substitute that
expression for P into (16–40), and rearrange to obtain

$$(16\text{–}41) \qquad q_C(k^*, p_k^*) = n\left(\frac{1 - s_A}{s_A} a^A + \frac{1 - s_E}{s_E} a^E\right).$$

In the steady state, q_C is determined by p_k^* and k^* (defined as the steady-
state value of k) and is constant. Any increase in a^A implies a decrease in
a^E if the consumption goods market is to clear. The slope of the wealth
distribution frontier in Figure 16–5 is obtained from equation (16–41).

The distribution of wealth determines the distribution of consumption,
for steady-state wealth is proportional to disposable income and consumption in turn is proportional to disposable income. We show this for

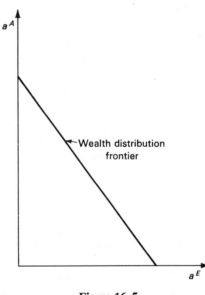

Figure 16–5

p_m, p_k, π_m, π_k are constant.

America. Set $\dot{a}^A$ equal to zero in equation (16–27) and solve for y_A:

$$(16\text{–}42) \qquad\qquad y_A = \frac{na^A}{s_A}.$$

Also,

$$(16\text{–}43) \qquad\qquad c_A = (1 - s_A)y_A = \frac{1 - s_A}{s_A}\,na^A.$$

Similarly, European consumption is proportional to European wealth.

What determines the position actually attained on the wealth distribution frontier? Given the other parameters of the system, this depends on μ, the share of the necessary ease or restraint maintained by America. Specifically, what happens when μ increases? If σ is positive so that there is excess supply in the consumption goods market in the absence of transfer payments, then an increase in μ implies an increase in American transfer payments and a decrease in European transfer payments. American disposable income rises and European disposable income falls, and so in the new steady state American wealth is higher and European lower. If σ is negative, an increase in μ leads to a decrease in American transfer payments and lower steady-state wealth.

To prove this, differentiate equation (16–39), with $\dot{a}^A = 0$, with respect to μ:

$$(16\text{–}44) \qquad\qquad \frac{\partial a^A}{\partial \mu} = \frac{s_A}{n(1 - s_A)}\left(q_C(k^*, p_k^*) + \frac{\partial P}{\partial \mu}\right).$$

Now obtain $\partial P / \partial \mu$ from (16–37) and substitute it in equation (16–44):

$$(16\text{–}45) \quad \frac{\partial a^A}{\partial \mu} = \frac{s_A}{n(1 - s_A)}\,[q_C(k^*, p_k^*)$$

$$- (1 - s_A)(w + rk^A + ib^A p_m^*) - (1 - s_E)(w + rk^E + ib^E p_m^*)]$$

and, using the definition of σ from equation (16–30),

$$(16\text{–}46) \qquad\qquad \frac{\partial a^A}{\partial \mu} = \frac{s_A}{n(1 - s_A)}\,p_m^*\,\sigma \lesseqgtr 0 \quad \text{as } \sigma \gtreqless 0.$$

Notice that μ does not necessarily lie between zero and one. If the range of possible values for μ were limited, then not all positions on the wealth distribution frontier would be attainable.

We have now considered one comparative dynamic exercise: a change in μ. A second such exercise we want to discuss is that of an increase in the savings rate of one country, say America, holding μ constant.

When the American savings rate rises, American consumption demand falls. To prevent excess supply emerging in the consumption goods market, each government has to increase transfer payments (assuming μ to lie between zero and one) and so the disposable income of each country will rise immediately following the increase in the American savings rate. This makes it seem likely that European wealth will be higher in the new steady state since wealth is proportional to disposable income; one would also expect American wealth to rise since the savings rate rises, as does disposable income. In fact, both levels of wealth *may* rise, but it is not necessary that they do so; we can, however, show that the wealth of at least one country *must* rise, although we cannot specify which country that is. This has an interesting implication: an increase in the American savings rate may increase *European* wealth and reduce *American* wealth.

In the first place, the total of world consumption must remain unaffected by the change in the savings rate since the steady-state supply of consumption goods is determined by k^*, a function of p_k^*, and p_k^*, which has not changed. Consumption is proportional to wealth, and we see from equation (16–43) that American consumption as a proportion of wealth falls as the savings rate rises. If both levels of wealth remained unchanged or fell after the increase in the American savings rate, consumption demand would fall below supply; this cannot happen, so the wealth of at least one country must rise.

The reason that either wealth may actually fall has to do with the redistribution of earning assets as Americans save more. It is true that disposable income rises as a result of increased transfer payments immediately following the rise in the American savings rate. In both countries, savings will rise. As savings rise, holdings of earning assets will rise, and transfer payments can be reduced. What we cannot rule out is a large increase in earning assets in one country with a relatively higher propensity to consume, thus adding demand to the consumption goods market, which requires a large reduction in transfer payments, which could actually lead to a fall in disposable income in the other country. As an example, suppose that the American propensity to consume is much higher than the European, even after the rise in the American savings rate. As Americans add to their assets, each government will have to reduce transfer payments. European income from earning assets may also be rising, but we assume this adds relatively little to consumption demand; suppose further that assets demand functions are such that Americans add comparatively more to their holdings of capital and bonds than Europeans. Then as transfer payments are reduced, European disposable income may actually fall; European wealth, being proportional to European disposable income, will then also fall. The argument can be applied, *mutatis mutandis*, to explain a possible fall in American wealth.

The fact that an increase in the American savings rate could increase European wealth and reduce American wealth is a somewhat surprising result of our strong assumptions about the governments' fiscal and monetary policies.

16–5   Summary

We have presented a complete model of international value transactions in a two-nation world. We excluded one degree of freedom and one policy variable by making consumption goods of the two countries perfect substitutes and requiring fixed exchange rates, but we allowed for monetary and fiscal policy in the two countries.

In this model reserve flows can be prevented through coordination of the monetary policies of the two governments, and inflation can be controlled by joint fiscal policy. World growth is the joint outcome of the policies of the two governments.

This model exhibits clearly two crucial problems in international finance. First is the well-known requirement that in a fixed-exchange-rate system the countries must coordinate monetary policies. We have seen that this also requires agreement on a world price of capital, or, in other words, on a world investment policy. Failure to reach agreement on this point will be reflected in persistent reserve flows. If America, for example, prefers a high p_k and Europe a low one, and America attempts to enforce the high p_k by an easy monetary policy while Europe tries to hold it down by a tight money policy, the result will be a flow of reserves from America to Europe.

The second critical issue on which our analysis focuses attention is the division of the fiscal policy burden between the two countries, even given an agreement about p_k that prevents systematic reserve movements. This is a direct political conflict of major proportions since there is a constant trade off between the two countries' long-run welfare and is a subject that has been less well studied than the problem of monetary coordination.

When America gains, Europe loses. The characteristic mark of this conflict is the fact that the country that runs the larger proportion of the collective deficit both consumes more and saves more.

The spirit of our analysis runs against the concepts of balance of payments equilibrium and overvalued currency. There are many equilibria and the choice among them makes a very substantial difference to the distribution of welfare, not only between generations but also among members of the same generation. It appears to us from this perspective that disequilibrium is a symptom of political disagreement between the countries as to which equilibrium is desirable. The sources of disagreement lie not only in conflicts over the amount of investment that is desirable for the world, but also in conflicting national interests at a very basic level.

Bibliography

This is meant to be a working, not an exhaustive, selection of references. We have emphasized work which will help the reader in understanding the model, which bears directly on our conclusions concerning policy, or which will serve as an introduction to more extensive literature on some subjects we only touch on.

CHAPTER 2

The reader who is unfamiliar with the growth literature and models may find it helpful first to examine one-sector models of economic growth. The two fundamental, and by now classic, papers in which one-sector models are set forth are R. M. Solow, "A Contribution to the Theory of Economic Growth," *Quarterly Journal of Economics* (February 1956, pp. 65–94), and T. W. Swan, "Economic Growth and Capital Accumulation," *Economic Record* (November 1956, pp. 334–61). For a review of much of the growth literature extending well beyond simple one-sector models, the reader is referred to F. Hahn and R. C. O. Matthews, "Theory of Economic Growth: A Survey," *Economic Journal* (December 1964, pp. 779–902).

285

The particular characteristics of two-sector models are treated in several sources. The exposition we use follows T. M. Rybczynski, "Factor Endowment and Relative Commodity Prices," *Economica* (November 1955, pp. 336–41). A two-sector model was analyzed by James E. Meade in *A Neo-Classical Theory of Economic Growth* (London: George Allen & Unwin, 1961). Other two-sector models are that of H. Uzawa, "On a Two-Sector Model of Economic Growth," *Review of Economic Studies* (Part I, October 1961, pp. 40–47; Part II, June 1963, pp. 105–18), commented on by R. M. Solow in the same publication (August 1961, pp. 225–50), and that of Harry G. Johnson, developed in Chapter I of his *International Trade and Economic Growth* (Cambridge: Harvard University Press, 1961).

Finally, we note the clear expositions by Emanuel M. Drandakis, "Factor Substitution in the Two-Sector Growth Model," *Review of Economic Studies* (October 1963, pp. 217–28), and Ken-Ichi Inada, "On a Two-Sector Model of Economic Growth: Comments and a Generalization," *Review of Economic Studies* (June, 1963, pp. 119–27).

CHAPTER 3

Our treatment of assets markets draws heavily on the ideas of James Tobin concerning portfolio selection. Very close in spirit to our treatment are James Tobin and William C. Brainard, "Financial Intermediaries and the Effectiveness of Monetary Controls" (Cowles Mimeograph); William C. Brainard, "Financial Intermediaries and a Theory of Monetary Control," pp. 94–141, in *Financial Markets and Economic Activity*, Donald D. Hester and James Tobin, eds. (Cowles Foundation for Research in Economics at Yale University, Monograph 21, 1967); James Tobin, "An Essay on Principles of Debt Management," in *Fiscal and Debt Management Policies* (Supporting Papers for the Commission on Money and Credit, Englewood Cliffs, N.J.: Prentice-Hall, 1963), and "Money, Capital, and Other Stores of Value," *American Economic Review Papers and Proceedings* (May 1961, pp. 26–37).

The idea of portfolio balance leads naturally to the problem of explaining assets demands from more fundamental considerations. This tradition begins with J. R. Hicks, "A Suggestion for Simplifying the Theory of Money," *Economica* (February 1935, pp. 1–19). The modern quantity theory of money approach is outlined by M. Friedman, "A Restatement of the Quantity Theory of Money," in *Studies in the Quantity Theory of Money*, M. Friedman, ed. (Chicago: University of Chicago Press, 1956).

Both James Tobin and W. J. Baumol analyze the demand for money for transactions purposes from an inventory point of view, the former in "The Interest-Elasticity of Transactions Demand for Cash," *Review of Economics and Statistics* (August 1956, pp. 241–47), and the latter in "The Transactions Demand for Cash: An Inventory Theoretic Approach," *Quarterly Journal of Economics* (November 1952, pp. 545–56).

The idea that part, at least, of the demand for money arises from its "liquid" quality was put forth by J. M. Keynes in *The General Theory of Employment, Interest, and Money* (New York: Harcourt, Brace, 1936, especially chs. 13 and 15) and further examined by James Tobin in "Liquidity Preference as Behavior towards Risk," *Review of Economic Studies* (February 1958, pp. 68–86), and in "The Theory of Portfolio Selection," *The Theory of Interest Rates*, F. Hahn and F. P. R. Brechling, eds. (London: St. Martin's Press, 1965), and by H. M. Markowitz in "Portfolio Selection," *Journal of Finance* (March 1952, pp. 77–91). In addition, James Duesenberry uses this approach in "The Portfolio Approach to the Demand for Money and Other Assets," *Review of Economics and Statistics* (February 1963, pp. 9–24), as does Don Patinkin in the context of an entire macromodel in *Money, Interest, and Prices* (New York: Harper & Row, 1965).

This work leads to a large literature on risk bearing. We mention only two: John Lintner, "The Valuation of Risk Assets and the Selection of Risky Investments in Stock Portfolios and Capital Budgets," *Review of Economics and Statistics* (February 1965, pp. 13–37), and Kenneth J. Arrow, *Aspects of the Theory of Risk-Bearing* (Helsinki: Vrjö Jahnssonin Säätiö, 1965).

CHAPTER 4

The idea of an aggregate, macroeconomic consumption function was put forth as one of the key economic variables in a macroeconomic system by J. M. Keynes in *The General Theory of Employment, Interest, and Money* (New York: Harcourt, Brace, 1936, especially chs. 8–10). Three formulations and estimations of such a function are of prime importance: A. K. Ando and F. Modigliani, "The Life Cycle Hypothesis of Saving: Aggregate Implications and Tests," *American Economic Review* (March 1963, pp. 55–84); M. Friedman, *A Theory of the Consumption Function* (Princeton: Princeton University Press, 1957); and J. Duesenberry, *Income, Saving, and the Theory of Consumer Behavior* (Cambridge: Harvard University Press, 1959).

CHAPTER 5

The fitting together of assets markets and consumption markets is characteristic of many models. In static analysis we mention two classics: J. R. Hicks, "Mr. Keynes and the Classics," *Econometrica* (April 1937, pp. 147–59), and Don Patinkin, *Money, Interest and Prices* (New York: Harper & Row, 1965, chs. X and XI).

CHAPTER 6

The closest general dynamic models to our analysis are one-sector monetary growth models. We mention James Tobin, "Money and Economic Growth," *Econometrica* (October 1965, pp. 671–84); H. G. Johnson, "The Neo-Classical One-Sector Growth Model: A Geometrical Exposition and Extension to a Monetary Economy," *Economica* (August 1966, pp. 265–87), and "Correction," *Economica* (June 1967, pp. 73–74); and Miguel Sidrauski, "Inflation and Economic Growth," *Journal of Political Economy* (December 1967, pp. 796–810).

T. Haavelmo, *A Study in the Theory of Investment* (Chicago: University of Chicago Press, 1960), shows that the firm's demand for investment cannot be derived from its demand for capital. The traditional literature depends on the assumption of a lag in adjustment or of increasing cost to investing to breach the gap. A summary of the theoretical and empirical work done in such investment models can be found in E. Kuh, "Theory and Institutions in the Study of Investment Behavior," *American Economic Review Papers and Proceedings* (May 1963, pp. 260–68). Examples of models built on the assumption of lagged adjustment are R. Eisner, "A Distributed Investment Function," *Econometrica* (January 1960, pp. 1–29), and D. W. Jorgenson, "Capital Theory and Investment Policy," *American Economic Review* (May 1963, pp. 247–59). The alternative assumption of increasing costs to investing is made by R. Eisner and R. H. Strotz, "Determinants of Business Investment," in *Impacts of Monetary Policy* (Supporting Papers for the Commission on Money and Credit, Englewood Cliffs, N.J.: Prentice-Hall, 1963), and by J. P. Gould in "Market Value and the Theory of Investment of the Firm," *American Economic Review* (September 1967, pp. 910–13).

An approach very similar to ours is taken by J. G. Witte in his stimulating article, "The Microfoundations of the Social Investment Function," *Journal of Political Economy* (October 1963, pp. 441–56).

Let us also tip our hat to the Sirinesque figure of Axel Leijonhufvud whose *On Keynesian Economics and the Economics of Keynes* (London: Oxford University Press, 1968) touches on many topics we cover and contains among other excellences a prescient review of our work (cf. p. 400, fn. 12).

For the reader who is unfamiliar with dynamic techniques in economics we suggest first a very general treatment by P. A. Samuelson, "Dynamic Process Analysis," *The Collected Scientific Papers of Paul A. Samuelson* (Cambridge: M.I.T. Press, 1966, vol. 1, pp. 590–625). For the particular technique of differential equations and phase diagrams, of which we make extensive use, we recommend W. Hurwicz, *Lectures on Ordinary Differential Equations* (New York: Wiley, 1958), especially chs. 3 and 4. The same material is covered on a more advanced level by L. S. Pontryagin, *Ordinary Differential Equations* (Reading, Mass.: Addison-Wesley, 1962), especially pp. 103–26.

CHAPTER 10

The effect of real wealth balances on consumption demand was examined by, and has since been named for, A. C. Pigou, "The Classical Stationary State," *Economic Journal* (December 1943, pp. 343–51). G. Ackley pursued the issue in "The Wealth-Saving Relationship," *Journal of Political Economy* (April 1951, pp. 154–61), and discusses it at some length in his textbook, *Macroeconomic Theory* (New York: Macmillan, 1961, in particular pp. 269–73, and 555–61). The theoretical implications of explicitly taking into account this real wealth (or real balances) effect in a macroeconomic model are, of course, explored by Don Patinkin in *Money, Interest, and Prices* (New York: Harper & Row, 1965). In addition, B. P. Pesek and T. R. Saving consider the issue in *Money, Wealth and Economic Theory* (New York: Macmillan, 1967). For a theoretical discussion that includes a consideration of alternative price expectation hypotheses, the reader is referred to J. H. Power, "Price Expectations, Money Illusion and the Real Balance Effect," *Journal of Political Economy* (April 1959, pp. 131–43). A more empirical analysis of the importance of such a wealth effect appears in T. Mayer, "The Empirical Significance of the Real Balance Effect," *Quarterly Journal of Economics* (May 1959, pp. 275–91), and A. K. Ando and F. Modigliani, "The Life Cycle Hypothesis of Saving: Aggregate Implications and Tests," *American Economic Review* (March 1963, pp. 55–84).

CHAPTER 11

The question as to whether or not the national debt does constitute a burden has been much debated in the literature. James Meade has published several times on the subject: "Is the National Debt a Burden?"

Oxford Economic Papers (June 1958, pp. 163–83), "Correction," *Oxford Economic Papers* (February 1959, pp. 109–10), and "The Public Debt Reconsidered: A Reply," *Review of Economics and Statistics* (August 1960, pp. 325–26). F. Modigliani discussed the question in "Long-Run Implications of Alternative Fiscal Policies and the Burden of the National Debt," *Economic Journal* (December 1961, pp. 730–55). P. Diamond examined the issue in the context of a growth model in "National Debt in a Neoclassical Growth Model," *American Economic Review* (December 1965, pp. 1126–35). The reader might also consult James Tobin, "An Essay on Principles of Debt Management," in *Fiscal and Debt Management Policies* (Supporting Papers for the Commission on Money and Credit, Englewood Cliffs, N.J.: Prentice-Hall, 1963). The Meade and Modigliani articles, among several dealing with this topic, can be found in *Public Debt and Future Generations*, J. M. Ferguson, ed. (Chapel Hill: University of North Carolina Press, 1964), as well as other articles we have cited on money and growth.

CHAPTERS 12 AND 13

Our concern in the model was not principally with the theory of the causes of inflation (on which there is an extensive literature) but rather with the effects of and differences between anticipated and unanticipated inflation. An outstanding paper testing empirically the extent to which the public comes to anticipate inflation correctly is P. Cagan, "The Monetary Dynamics of Hyperinflation," in *Studies in the Quantity Theory of Money*, M. Friedman, ed. (Chicago: University of Chicago Press, 1956).

Models that examine the effects on the real sector of the economy include James Tobin, "Money and Economic Growth," *Econometrica* (October 1965, pp. 671–84); H. G. Johnson, "The Neo-Classical One-Sector Growth Model: A Geometrical Exposition and Extension to a Monetary Economy," *Economica* (August 1966, pp. 265–87); Miguel Sidrauski, "Inflation and Economic Growth," *Journal of Political Economy* (December 1967, pp. 796–810); R. Mundell, "Inflation and Real Interest," *Journal of Political Economy* (June 1963, pp. 280–83), and "Growth, Stability, and Inflationary Finance," *Journal of Political Economy* (April 1965, pp. 97–109); C. Kennedy, "Inflation and the Bond Rate," *Oxford Economic Papers* (October 1960, pp. 269–73); and D. Levhari and Don Patinkin, "The Role of Money in a Simple Growth Model," (*American Economic Review* (September 1968, pp. 713–53).

CHAPTER 14

For papers that deal with the possibility of capital gains on the capital stock in a manner similar to ours, the reader is referred to K. Shell, M. Sidrauski, and J. E. Stiglitz, "Capital Gains, Income, and Saving," *Review of Economic Studies* (January 1969, pp. 15–26), and D. Foley and M. Sidrauski, "Portfolio Choice, Investment, and Growth," *American Economic Review* (March 1970, pp. 44–63). On the related question of stability in dynamic models in which investment is partly determined by the possibility of such capital gains, the reader is referred to K. Shell and J. E. Stiglitz, "The Allocation of Investment in a Dynamic Economy," *Quarterly Journal of Economics* (November 1967, pp. 592–609), and F. Hahn, "Equilibrium Dynamics with Heterogeneous Capital Goods," *Quarterly Journal of Economics* (November 1966, pp. 633–46).

CHAPTER 15

There is an extensive literature of optimal growth models, and we shall not attempt to cite them all. Probably the first of such models is F. Ramsey, "A Mathematical Theory of Saving," *Economic Journal* (December 1928, pp. 543–59). Our analysis of optimal growth in a two-sector model depends heavily on David Cass (unpublished thesis), as in D. Foley, K. Shell, and M. Sidrauski, "Optimal Fiscal and Monetary Policy and Economic Growth," *Journal of Political Economy* (August 1969), and H. Uzawa, "Optimal Growth in a Two-Sector Model of Capital Accumulation," *Review of Economic Studies* (January 1964, pp. 1–24). Koopmans compares several alternative optimal models in "Objectives, Constraints, and Outcomes in Optimal Growth Models," *Econometrica* (January 1967, pp. 1–15). A collection of several different optimal models can also be found in *Essays on the Theory of Optimal Economic Growth*, K. Shell, ed. (Cambridge: M.I.T. Press, 1967). Explicit consideration of alternative government policies in an optimal model can be found in D. Foley, K. Shell, and M. Sidrauski "Optimal Fiscal and Monetary Policy and Economic Growth" (cited above), on which much of this chapter is based.

CHAPTER 16

An excellent presentation of a dynamic two-sector model in which trade is permitted is H. Oniki and H. Uzawa, "Patterns of Trade and Investment in a Dynamic Model of International Trade," *Review of Economic Studies* (January 1965, pp. 15–38). R. Mundell considers the problem of alternative stabilization policies as well as examines the further question of the choice between fixed and flexible exchange rates in several articles, including: "Capital Mobility and Stabilization Policies under Fixed and Flexible Exchange Rates," *Canadian Journal of Economics* (November 1963, pp. 475–85), "The Proper Use of Monetary and Fiscal Policy for International External Stability," *International Monetary Fund Staff Papers* (1962), and "The Monetary Dynamics of International Adjustment Under Fixed and Flexible Exchange Rates," *Quarterly Journal of Economics* (May 1960, pp. 227–57).

Index

E

F

G

H

I

J

K

L

R

S

W